D0908892

WITHDRAWN

TWAYNE'S WORLD AUTHORS SERIES
A Survey of the World's Literature

GERMANY

Ulrich Weisstein, Indiana University

EDITOR

Clemens Brentano

TWAS 615

Courtesy Abbey St. Boniface, Munich, Germany

Clemens Brentano

CLEMENS BRENTANO

By JOHN F. FETZER
University of California, Davis

TWAYNE PUBLISHERS
A DIVISION OF G. K. HALL & CO., BOSTON

Published in 1981 by Twayne Publishers,
A Division of G. K. Hall & Co.
All Rights Reserved

Printed on permanent/durable acid-free paper and bound
in the United States of America

First Printing

Library of Congress Cataloging in Publication Data

Fetzer, John F.
Clemens Brentano.

(Twayne's world authors series ; TWAS 615.
Germany)
Bibliography: p. 169
Includes index.
1. Brentano, Clemens, 1778–1842—
Criticism and
interpretation.   I. Title.   II. Series: Twayne's
world authors series ; 615.   III. Series: Twayne's
world authors series ; 615. Germany.
PT1825.Z5F39   838'.609   81–2314
ISBN 0-8057-6457-7   AACR2

For my mother,
  after all these years,
  after all she's done . . .

Contents

About the Author

John Francis Fetzer was born in New York City and received his higher education at New York University (B.A., 1953) and Columbia University (M.A., 1957). During the period between these degrees he attended the University of Munich as a Fulbright student and served in the United States Army. Following military duty he studied for the doctorate in German language and literature at the University of California, Berkeley, receiving the Ph.D. in 1965. Dr. Fetzer is now Professor of German at the University of California, Davis, where he has taught since 1965, following three years of teaching at Northwestern University. He has also been Visiting Professor of German at Dartmouth (1976).

His publications include articles on Goethe, E. T. A. Hoffmann, Friedrich Hebbel, Thomas Mann, Heinrich Böll, German exile writers, two annual bibliographies, and a book entitled *Romantic Orpheus: Profiles of Clemens Brentano* (1974). For the academic year 1980–1981 he was awarded a Guggenheim Fellowship in order to write a monograph *On the Threshold of German Romanticism*.

Preface

The aim of this study of Clemens Brentano (1778–1842) is twofold. On the one hand, the book seeks to introduce the English-speaking reader, who may not be familiar with the course which German literature has taken, to a romantic writer of considerable skill and charm whose works are both significant and problematic. On the other hand, it also attempts to offer those familiar with German literary history a thumbnail sketch and a critical survey of Brentano's career and creative writings from a perspective which will also throw light on the romantic age (the three decades from approximately 1797 to 1827) as a whole.

Except for the introductory chapter, which contains basically biographical data and a working definition of romanticism that is to be applied to the texts discussed, chapters 2 through 4 have a format which is relatively consistent: after a few summarizing remarks on Brentano's contributions to the literary genre under examination (the lyric, prose narrative, and plays respectively), key examples from each category are examined. Aside from the lyric poetry, the analysis of each individual work has four components: (1) a close look at the principal elements comprising the title of the work under consideration; (2) a content summary; (3) a survey of the critical reception accorded the work and/or the interpretive approaches previously applied to it; and (4) a commentary on the work based on the extent to which it conforms to Brentano's own concept of romanticism.

Whereas some might consider it pedestrian to recapitulate the "plot" or to reproduce the "story line" of a work of literature (and this, indeed, can be a trifling and inconsequential activity), there are also valid reasons for incorporating such summaries here. Brentano's plot structure is seldom linear or straightforward, but rather embellished with myriad details and seemingly irrelevant incidents; consequently, a synopsis of the major events which focuses on significant happenings without maximizing inherent distortions or minimizing subtle nuances of portrayal is a desideratum. In addition, the points stressed in reporting "what happens" or in showing how things are reported may often anticipate the direction which later interpretive analyses will take, so that in accordance with the above scheme, sections 3 and 4 will be prepared for in advance: they merely reap the harvest which had been sown earlier.

The specific aim of section 3 is to inform the nonspecialist of the extant interpretations of the work under consideration. Too often, scholars, after reading and digesting what their predecessors have said, recapitulate in their own words—with no intention of plagiarizing—concepts and conclusions which others have already formulated. Certainly, this might also be the case here; but in order to hold such inadvertent borrowings to a minimum, the results of earlier scholarship will be specifically acknowledged, then followed by what purport to be my own observations based on Brentano's theoretical concept of the nature of romanticism and its application as manifested in fictional contexts.

One of the world's leading authorities on Brentano, Wolfgang Frühwald, has cautioned us against any attempt to present an overall portrayal of the life and works of this poet in view of the still unclear philological situation.[1] Since the historical-critical edition is only now in the process of appearing, Fuühwald calls instead for individual studies concentrating on specific topics or on clearly defined problem areas. Surveying the present monograph in retrospect, I feel that perhaps Frühwald's advice should have been heeded more seriously, since many questions left in abeyance may be answered definitively once the Frankfurt edition with its critical apparatus and scholarly commentary becomes available. But since, at present, only a few of the planned almost forty volumes have been published, at least a decade might elapse before such an undertaking could make any headway, and the vast amount of material contained in this monumental edition would, in many cases, not be suitable for such an introductory study as this.[2] Consequently, the readily available, four-volume interim edition in the Hanser series was used as the basic text for all of Brentano's poetic works (unless otherwise indicated in the footnotes) with the reference to pages preceded by the volume number and the letter W.[3]

Translation into English proved to be a particularly difficult problem, with regard to quotations from prose or poetry and even the titles of individual works. I am especially indebted to Mr. Angel Flores for permission to quote in full the English versions of eight Brentano poems from *An Anthology of German Poetry from Hölderlin to Rilke in English Translation* and to Penguin Books Ltd. for allowing me to print the prose rendering of another lyric from *The*

Preface

Penguin Book of German Verse. Except for those rare instances where a published translation was available, the renderings into English are my own. For the convenience of the reader, the chronology contains both the original German title as well as its English counterpart for all works by Brentano treated in this study

Finally, acknowledgments of gratitude are due the University of California, Davis, for its patient support over the past several years through research grants, to the Department of German of that institution for many hours of typing assistance and Xeroxing, and to my colleagues, Clifford Bernd and Roland Hoermann, for their sage advice. To my undaunted typists a special word of appreciation for their equanimity and endurance when I handed them a battle-scarred manuscript full of illegible wiggles, mysterious arrows, hen-scratchings, and other cryptic symbols, only to find on my desk several hours later a clean copy of the text.

JOHN F. FETZER

University of California, Davis

Chronology

satire *Der Philister vor, in und nach der Geschichte (The Philistine in Pre-, Present-, and Post-History)*. Works on the unfinished novel *Der schiffbrüchige Galeerensklave vom Toten Meer (The Shipwrecked Galley Slave from the Dead Sea)*. Travels to Bohemia. Arnim marries Bettina Brentano. Completes *Aloys und Imelde (Aloys and Imelde)*, a drama.

1813   Victories against Napoleon give rise to *Viktoria und ihre Geschwister mit fliegenden Fahnen und brennender Lunte (Victoria and Her Siblings with Flying Colors and Burning Fuse)*.

1814   Failure of the revised *Ponce* (as *Valeria or Paternal Cunning*) at the Burgtheater in Vienna. Writes theatrical reviews for *Der dramaturgische Beobachter (The Dramaturgical Observer)* in Vienna. *Die Gründung Prags (The Founding of Prague)*.

1815   *Die Schachtel mit der Friedenspuppe (The Box Containing the Doll of Peace)*.

1816   First encounter with Luise Hensel; Brentano's initial proposal of marriage is rejected.

1817   Brentano's general confession marks his conversion to (or reversion back to) Catholicism. Pays his first visit to Anna Katharina Emmerick in Dülmen. *Die Geschichte vom braven Kasperl und dem schönen Annerl (The Story of Honest Casper and Fair Annie)* and *Die mehreren Wehmüller und ungarischen Nationalgesichter (The Numerous Wehmüllers and Hungarian National Countenances)*.

1818   *Aus der Chronika eines fahrenden Schülers (Excerpts from the Chronicle of a Traveling Student)*. Begins his six-year vigil in Dülmen.

1819   Prepares his entire library for auction—except for the theological works.

1824   Death of Anna Katharina Emmerick; the exhumation of her body.

1825   In the service of "Catholic propaganda" Brentano visits Joseph Görres in Strassburg. Anonymous contributions to the journal *Der Katholik (The Catholic)*.

1826   Interest in the work of the Sisters of Mercy in Coblence and elsewhere leads to *Die Barmherzigen Schwestern in Bezug auf Armen und Krankenpflege (The Sisters of Mercy with Regard to Nursing of the Sick and Tending of the Poor)* in 1831.

1833   *Das bittere Leiden unsers Herrn Jesu Christi (The Bitter Suffering of Our Lord Jesus Christ)*; short biography of Anna K.

Emmerick entitled *Lebensabriß dieser Begnadigten (Biographical Outline of This Blessed Woman)*. Brentano moves to Munich, the "headquarters of Catholic propaganda," where he meets and falls in love with Emilie Linder.

1834   Proposal to and rejection by Emilie Linder.

1835   Begins to revise his fairy tales (most of which had been written two decades before).

1837   *Gockel, Hinkel und Gackeleia (Gockel, Hinkel and Gackeleia)*, supplemented by the *Blätter aus dem Tagebuch der Ahnfrau (Pages from the Diary of the Ancestress)*. The *Rheinmärchen (Fairy Tales of the Rhein)* together with other revised tales are published in 1846–1847 by Guido Görres as *Die Märchen Clemens Brentanos (The Fairy Tales of Clemens Brentano)*.

1838   Religious legends in poetic form conceived. Renews contact with Luise Hensel.

1840   Publication of *Leben der heiligen Jungfrau Maria (Life of the Holy Virgin Mary)* commences.

1842   Brentano's brother, Christian, takes him from Munich to Aschaffenburg near Frankfurt where he dies on 28 July 1842.

1844   Appearance of Bettina's carefully edited correspondence with her brother under the title *Clemens Brentano's Frühlingskranz aus Jugendbriefen ihm geflochten (Clemens Brentano's Spring Wreath, Woven for Him from the Letters of His Youth)*.

1852   *Life of the Holy Virgin Mary*, edited and adapted from Brentano's posthumous papers by the abbot and later bishop, Daniel Haneberg, together with Christian and Emilie Brentano.

1852–   Publication of Brentano's *Gesammelte Schriften (Collected
1855   Works)* in seven volumes with two additional volumes of letters, edited by Christian Brentano in collaboration with Emilie Brentano and Joseph Merkel.

1857   Father Schmoeger receives Brentano's Emmerick papers for the purpose of editing them.

1858–   Schmoeger's edition of *Das Leben Jesu (The Life of Jesus)* in
1860   three volumes (based on Brentano's Emmerick notes).

1877–   For the centennial of Brentano's birth, the Jesuit fathers
1878   Johannes B. Diel and Wilhelm Kreiten complete the first major study of his life and works.

CHAPTER 1

Prelude

I *The Biographical Background*

WHEN Clemens Maria Wenzeslaus Brentano was born in Ehrenbreitstein on 9 September 1778, the literary scene in Germany was dominated by a generation of recalcitrant, young writers to whom posterity has granted the epithet "Storm and Stress." Goethe had portrayed the impetuous, angry figures of Götz von Berlichingen, Prometheus, and Werther, while Schiller was waiting in the wings with Karl Moor and *The Robbers*. The highly charged atmosphere of the times proved to be prophetic of the "storms" which Brentano would weather on the treacherous waters of the sea of life (one of his favorite metaphors)[1] and of the "stresses" he was to endure in both the public and private sectors.

The hereditary constellation of his parents was laden with a chemistry of temperament and talent destined for an uneasy coexistence. His father, Peter Anton Brentano, the descendant of an Italian family whose lineage could be traced back to Lombardian nobility of the thirteenth century, was a wholesale merchant in Frankfurt on the Main, a successful businessman with an authoritarian and utilitarian outlook on life. On the other hand, Brentano's mother, née Maximiliane von La Roche, the beautiful, dark-eyed daughter of the eighteenth-century novelist, Sophie von La Roche, was a woman of aesthetic and emotional sensibility who had attracted Goethe's attention and affection when he was on the "rebound" and still reeling from his short-lived romance with Charlotte Buff in Wetzlar. Even though recent research has sought to demonstrate that the relationship between Brentano's parents may not have been as strained or as volatile as their son believed it to be or as he depicted it vicariously in such autobiographically tinged works as the early novel *Godwi* (1801), the fact remains that Brentano saw it in this light and that this perspective lingered throughout his life and permeated his writing.[2]

It has been suggested, furthermore, that Brentano's perpetual campaign against the "philistine" mentality—against those of predominantly pedestrian outlook and prosaic concerns, insensitive to art and oblivious to any tender human emotions—was actually a struggle against his father image.[3] By the same token, the thesis has also been propounded that Brentano's unending quest for love, for female companionship, and for the perfect soul mate represents a kind of sublimated desire to fill the gap left in his life by the death of his mother in 1793 at the early age of thirty-seven.[4] Not only did Brentano have to reconcile himself to this tragic loss when he was just fifteen years old, but the subsequent death of his father in 1797 was also a traumatic shock, since it made clear to this young man of not yet twenty that he and his siblings—of which there were many—had to venture out on to that uncharted "sea of life" on their own, without parental guidance.

Just as Brentano's early youth, most of which was spent in the family home in Frankfurt, is marred by the conflict which he detected between his father and mother, so, too, his subsequent upbringing and education were replete with misguided experiments and nerve-wracking blunders that left indelible traces on his later life.[5] The first unfortunate step in the above direction was taken in 1784 when Clemens and his sister, Sophie, were sent to the home of their maternal aunt, Luise von Möhn, in Coblence. The two years spent here were characterized by such bizarre events as the daily "cold water cure," which entailed an ice-cold shower each morning that was calculated to elicit from the children the maximum productivity from the early hours. After having attended a Jesuit school in Coblence, Brentano was transferred to Johann Jakob Winterwerber's "Palatine Public Institution for Pupils of the Male Sex and of All Three Christian Faiths" in Mannheim. The stilted title of this school reflects the kind of regimentation to which the students were subjected. In retrospect, Brentano was to poke fun at both of these early, unhappy childhood experiences, but his exposure to a rigid, senseless routine and to an unbending discipline was to prove psychologically damaging at this stage of his development.

One respite from such torment were the periodic visits to Frankfurt, the reunion with his mother, the opportunity to meet his siblings both old and new, and to establish once again contact with the family accountant, a certain Mr. Schwab (an idiosyncratic character who had always filled the mind of the boy with strange and sometimes wonderful tales). At home Brentano could also escape to the attic of the family house where he had established a kind of private refuge in a large sugar barrel. Here he would while away the hours reading the works of Gozzi or dreaming of the never-never land of Vadutz, a realm which he believed to be an invention of his own fantasy until he was unceremoniously informed by Mr. Schwab that it was a geographical reality, the capital of Liechtenstein. The sudden demise of Vadutz was only the first of many a paradise lost by Brentano in his quest to discover some surrogate happiness for the joy which the real world denied him.

The years from 1794 to 1798 were wasted on a number of abortive university and on-the-job work experiences. After struggling with the study of mining and mineralogy at the University of Bonn in 1794, Brentano was summoned home to the office of his father in Frankfurt, where his unruly antics behind, over, and under the sales counter became legend. Clemens's antimercantile pranks so exasperated Peter Anton, that he banished his son to Langensalza in Thuringia to the firm of an acquaintance. There followed the notorious days during which Brentano preferred to shock the clientele by the outrageous colors of his outlandish clothes (parrot-green coat, scarlet-red vest, peach-blossom pants, etc.) rather than ply a trade. After another short-lived attempt at mastering public finance and administration at the University of Halle in 1797, Brentano matriculated at Jena following the death of his father, ostensibly for the purpose of studying medicine. Jena marks the watershed in his development, for rather than completing an apprenticeship to any profession, he was now in a position to begin an apprenticeship to life. In Jena (1798–1800) he not only came into contact with the leading romantic writers in the social circles surrounding Friedrich Schlegel and Ludwig Tieck, but he also met the first of the three women who were to become determining forces in his career and creative output: the sometime poetess Sophie Mereau, who, at this moment, was still the wife of a professor of law at the university.

Brentano's relationship with Sophie Mereau (1798 until her death in 1806) is as complex as were his subsequent erotic ties to Luise Hensel (1816–1824) and his liaison with Emilie Linder (1834–1842). To be sure, this triadic nucleus of major romances was surrounded by a host of lesser affairs, some of which left significant traces on his work, not to mention scars on his life. Aside from early infatuations, such as his attraction to Minna Reichenbach (1799–1800) during a period when he became estranged from Sophie or his passing interest in those women he encountered on a Rhine journey of 1802 (Benedikte

Korbach) or in the Lahn Valley (Hannchen Kraus), the most fatal
move he made was his precipitous marriage, in the wake of Sophie's
sudden passing, to the seventeen-year-old Auguste Bußmann (1807),
an emotionally unstable and immature girl. Their life together was
filled with constant bickering, histrionics on both sides, and culmi-
nated in a bitter divorce action in 1812 (Auguste committed suicide in
1832). Finally, one might also mention Clemens's brief encounter
with the Prague actress Auguste Brede in 1811, since this had literary
consequences, as did his earlier acquaintance with another per-
former, Marianne Jung (subsequently Marianne von Willemer), and
his chance meeting late in life (1838) with Luise Hensel at a time when
such reminders of the past could at best open wounds which the
intervening years had mercifully but unsuccessfully sought to heal.

Sophie Mereau and Brentano were married in 1803 following
several stormy years of an on-again, off-again romance (she received
her divorce from Professor Mereau in 1801) and many protests on the
part of his friends and family. One cannot claim that their conjugal life
(1803–1806) proved any less hectic than the period of courtship which
preceded it. Complaining of his "domestic death" when forced to
remain at home,[6] Brentano took frequent trips in order to escape
from this prison, only to find that he was a prisoner of love after all;
when separated from Sophie, his desire to be with her exceeded all
his aversion to the fetters of marriage. Undoubtedly a great blow to
their union was the fate of their three children, all of whom either
lived a few short weeks or were stillborn. Sophie's own death at the
birth of their third child signaled not only the closing chapter to this
relationship, but also the beginning of a quest for another companion
who could help him anchor his existence. He did not want to be cast
adrift on those treacherous "waters" which he knew only too well and
feared only too much. His rash decision to marry Auguste, the siren
and Circe,[7] must be regarded in this light.

By the time of his marriage to Sophie in 1803, Brentano had already
launched himself on a career as a writer of considerable repute with
the biting satire *Gustav Wasa* (1800), a novel *Godwi or The Stone
Statue of the Mother* (1801), a comedy *Ponce de Leon* (1801), as well as
a number of poems, many of which are of incomparable lyric beauty
and striking musicality.[8] During the period following the intrusion of
Clemens or "Demens" into the literary cliques of Jena,[9] he expanded
his circle of friends as well as his intellectual horizon. His acquaintance with the scholarly jurist Friedrich Karl von Savigny (who later
was to marry Brentano's sister, Kunigunde), dating from 1799,

brought him into contact with a unique individual who, in spite of a natural affinity for order, legal restrictions, and a certain regimentation, still did not fall prey to the pitfalls of philistinism. A second friendship from this early period (and one which was to have a major influence on the course of Brentano's life) stems from his meeting with Ludwig Achim von Arnim in 1801. A memorable boat ride down the Rhine with the newfound friend in 1802 led to a burst of enthusiasm for folksongs, and following Arnim's cavalier's tour of the Continent, the two collaborated on the first volume of the collection entitled *The Youth's Magic Horn* (or cornucopia) which appeared in 1805. This joint effort was well received by reviewers such as Goethe (to whom it was dedicated), even though opponents were quick to criticize the philologically suspect methods employed by the "editors" in recording poems from oral sources or from rare and inaccessible documents.[10] A third friendship which Brentano struck up at this time was with Joseph Görres, a man of encyclopedic learning who ultimately became a professor at several universities and a scholar of note. One immediate literary result of this relationship was an antiphilistine satire of 1807 with the baroque title: *Either the Strange Story of BOGS the Watchmaker (How He, Although Having Long Ago Departed from Human Existence, Still Hopes to be Accepted into the Civic Gun Club after Considerable Musical Suffering at Sea and on Land) or The Concert Review which, as a Supplement, Overflows the Banks of the Baden Weekly.* In the following year Brentano again collaborated with Arnim in founding the *Journal for Hermits,* a publication of short duration which had the goal of presenting the romantic perspective through contributions by leading writers of that persuasion (to counter the attacks of the antiromantic faction which had clustered around the most avid and adamant opponent of this credo, Johann Heinrich Voß).[11] But even though by the end of 1808 two additional volumes of *The Youth's Magic Horn* had appeared, the collapse of the *Journal for Hermits* marked a kind of turning point in the lives of the group of romantics which had gathered in Heidelberg. In the same year Brentano left that city for Landshut in Bavaria (where Savigny, now his brother-in-law, had accepted a teaching position at the university), Görres moved to Coblence, and Arnim set out for Berlin.

Much of the year which Brentano spent in Bavaria (1808–1809) was devoted to a kind of hide-and-seek (or cat-and-mouse) game with his second wife, since he had reached the point where he could not tolerate this "belle dame sans merci" and her temper tantrums.

When the home of friends no longer offered safe refuge, he undertook late in 1809 a trip to Berlin, where the happy prospect of seeing Arnim again bolstered his spirits. On the way Brentano paid a courtesy call on Goethe in Jena and also visited other notables, including the philosopher Hegel in Nuremberg. Berlin at this particular moment was the hub of much excitement and activity. The university was founded there in 1810, and Brentano received a commission to write a poetic cantata for its dedication.

Several months after his arrival in this Prussian territory, Brentano composed his famous "confessional" letter to the artist Philipp Otto Runge, in which he made some perceptive observations concerning his own mode of creativity as well as Runge's type of artistry. Brentano's purpose in writing was to enlist the talents of the painter for a joint enterprise—the poetic-pictorial representation of a lyrically conceived epic entitled *The Romances of the Rosary*. Brentano had been toying with this project on and off since 1803, and had he succeeded in gaining a commitment from Runge, it is possible that the work would have progressed well beyond the fragmentary form in which it has come down to us.[12] Runge's untimely death in 1810, however, put an abrupt end to this grandiose scheme; and Brentano never really regained his enthusiasm for the romances, only finding time in his later years to condemn them as the wanton sins of an unchristian youth.[13]

While still in Berlin Brentano had the opportunity to join forces with a writer of note, Heinrich von Kleist, on the latter's journalistic experiment the *Berlin Evening News*—another of those undertakings which had more promise than patronage. The important fact to bear in mind, however, is Brentano's obvious need for the support of others, whether this be in the form of female affection (from his mother on down), artistic collaboration (Arnim, Görres, Runge, etc.), or simply friend-to-friend cooperation. The latter may have induced him to become a member of the patriotic and chauvinistic group known as the "Christian-German Table Society," an organization in Berlin which also included such dignitaries as Fichte, Kleist, Savigny, the composer Karl Friedrich Zelter, the architect Karl Friedrich Schinkel, and the writer of political-sociological tracts, Adam Müller. At one of the first meetings of this club in 1811, Brentano read aloud his trenchant satire *The Philistine in Pre-, Present-, and Post-History,* a work which well suited the posture of the members in both their antipedantic and anti-Semitic attitude.[14]

The year 1811 held in store for Brentano other events which were to exert a profound influence on his later life. The marriage of his "brother in song" and close friend, Arnim, to the mercurial and quixotic Bettina Brentano may have indeed linked the aristocratic Prussian more intimately to the clan, but it gave rise, in the case of Clemens, to a sense of estrangement since the couple now had their own life to lead, a life which did not necessarily include him. Therefore he welcomed the chance to travel to Bohemia to help administer an estate which his family had purchased there and which Christian, Brentano's younger brother, was struggling to manage. Excursions to Prague brought him into the orbit of the actress Auguste Brede, the result of this being a love for her which was intense but of short duration. At this time Brentano also began a flurry of creative work on a larger scale after several relatively lean years.

The Brede affair found its literary ramifications in a strange novel fragment *The Shipwrecked Galley Slave from the Dead Sea*, a puzzling work, yet one of great potential. However, it was not so much prose fiction which was to occupy Brentano's attention for the next few years, but rather the stage. As early as 1811 he had begun work on *Aloys and Imelde,* a Romeo-and-Juliet-like play about star-crossed lovers in which malicious chance and coincidence, combined with a particular weapon fatal to several generations, comprise the major ingredients. This so-called "fate tragedy" experienced a unique fate in its own right: Brentano had entrusted the manuscript to Karl August Varnhagen von Ense, a literary opportunist, who confiscated it because his future bride, the Jewess Rahel Levin, took umbrage at some of the anti-Semitic comments ascribed to the "Christian-German Table Society." Due to Varnhagen's stubborn refusal to give back this document, Brentano began a second version of the play, this time in blank verse instead of prose, and he incorporated unflattering traits of both Varnhagen and Rahel into the fictional characters. The effects of the Bohemian atmosphere—the landscape as well as the customs of the land—on Brentano can be seen most directly in his ponderous historico-mythological drama *The Founding of Prague* (1813–1814), the first part of a massive trilogy planned by the poet to trace the roots and the rise to prominence of the Czech people.

A sojourn in Vienna in 1813 led to the revival and revision of his earlier comedy *Ponce de Leon* under the new title: *Valeria or Paternal Cunning.* But even though Brentano had the pleasure of seeing this piece performed at the prestigious Burgtheater, he also had to en-

dure the pain of its resounding failure. Further theatrical dissapoint-
ments were in store for him with the stage spectacle *Victoria and Her
Siblings with Flying Colors and Burning Fuse*. Caught up in the
nationalistic spirit of the Wars of Liberation against the forces of
Napoleon (1813–1815), Brentano had written this cumbersome piece
of patriotic propaganda to celebrate the imminent victory of the allies
over the French invader. But such a work was still too volatile for
actual performance, and thus it was forbidden by the censor and only
became known following the hostilities (1816). In spite of such adver-
sities, Brentano managed to keep his finger in the theatrical pie by
writing drama reviews for a Viennese journal, the *Dramaturgical
Observer*, in 1814 (in addition to his critiques of stage works, he also
contributed commentary on the musical scene). A strange paradox
manifests itself in conjunction with Brentano's preoccupation with
the theater as both creative writer and critic: whereas in the first
capacity he betrays all the weakness of a poet who persists in dabbling
in a genre to which his temperament and talents are entirely unsuited, in the second category he reveals keen theoretical awareness
of what constitutes good theater.

Brentano must have been a disheartened writer when he left
Vienna late in 1814 and headed for Berlin (again the only bright spot
on the horizon being a reunion with Arnim, both at the latter's estate
in Wiepersdorf and in the Prussian metropolis itself). Already at this
time—and perhaps as an aftermath of his recent dramatic failures—
Brentano had begun to reveal in his correspondence traces of that
dual artistic crisis which was to characterize his later life: a loss of
poetic inspiration and a lack of faith in the validity of literature or its
medium, language, to convey anything of essential value. Whereas
scattered evidence of this growing skepticism may be found in his
early letters and literary efforts, the degree of despair and doubt
became proportionately (both quantitatively and qualitatively)
greater with his increasing age, and each successive year seemed to
bring further affirmations of the frightening hypothesis that the path
of art-for-art's sake must, of necessity, lead down a blind alley. But as
is so often the case in Brentano's career, a change of scene resulted in
a change of heart. During his second stay in Berlin (1814–1817), for
instance, he not only turned to a new circle of friends, but he also
returned to an old medium—prose fiction—with fresh zeal, produc-
ing both original stories (*The Box Containing the Doll of Peace*, 1815;
The Numerous Wehmüllers or Hungarian National Countenances,
1817; *The Story of Honest Casper and Fair Annie*, 1817) and revising

for publication a work which he had begun in 1802, *The Chronicle of the Traveling Student*, and which now appeared in fragmentary form as *Excerpts from the Chronicle of a Traveling Student* (1818).

These Berlin years were significant in Brentano's life also for religious and emotional reasons. Having been alerted by the reports of a friend to the revivalist movement in Bavaria, Brentano took an interest in this phenomenon, and when he and several others formed an evening discussion group for political and literary topics—the official title was the "Maikäferei" which, although derived from the name of the innkeeper Mai, can be translated as "Ruminations" or "Ponderings"—the subject of religious revival in North Germany frequently appeared on the agenda. Already in 1816 Brentano had heard the initial reports about the Augustinian nun of Dülmen, Anna Katharina Emmerick,[15] whose body reputedly bore traces of the stigmata of the Crucifixion. This supernatural event, in conjunction with Brentano's steadily increasing religious concerns and convictions, led in the next years to two decisions giving scope and character to the remainder of his life: his own universal confession of faith (1817) which officially brought him back into the fold of the Catholic Church, and his resolve (1818) to remain at the bedside of the stigmatized nun, recording as a faithful amanuensis, her visions and her ordeal. This difficult task occupied him for almost six years until Anna Katharina's death in 1824, and the material he collected supplied him with enough raw data to challenge his writing talents for the remainder of his days. Running contrapuntally with this religious happening was an emotional experience, the second of the three major romances in Brentano's life, the object of his affections being this time the poetess Luise Hensel.

Brentano's first contact with Luise was at a Berlin soirée in 1816, and this spawned many subsequent meetings and poems to her. Toward the end of 1816 she refused his initial offer of marriage. Their entire relationship is so closely linked with the religious sphere and the events surrounding Anna Katharina, that it is only in recent times that scholars have been able to piece together satisfactorily the pertinent details.[16] For instance, the extent of Luise's role in influencing Bretano to return to Catholicism has been hotly disputed, as has his part in her conversion of 1818. On the aesthetic plane, the authorship of several poems attributed to her has also been ascribed to Brentano, and he seems to have borrowed liberally from her lyrics, perhaps unknowingly at times, since he regarded much of the phraseology as their common property.[17] Together they prepared in 1817 a new

edition of *Trutznachtigall,* the work of the seventeenth-century
Jesuit poet, Friedrich von Spee, and Luise spent a considerable
amount of time with Anna Katharina in Westphalia. But when Luise
rejected Brentano's proposal of marriage for the second time in early
1819, he seems to have resigned himself to the inevitable, and for the
next few years he worked with full vigor as the self-appointed
secretary-scribe of the stigmatic, recording her visions in order to
transmit to posterity the miracle he was privileged to witness.

But even this was not to be an easy task for Brentano, since both the
ecclesiastical and secular authorities began to look askance at the
incidents surrounding Anna Katharina's stigmata, and consequently
an investigative commission was established by the Prussian gov-
ernment (under whose jurisdiction the part of Westphalia in which
Dülmen was located, fell). Although Brentano, somewhat quixoti-
cally perhaps, volunteered to serve as an adviser to this group, his
offer was not accepted—in fact, he was specifically excluded from the
proceedings. Nevertheless, he dutifully prepared a report of this
procedure which documents for posterity his version of the entire
process.[18] While still wrangling with the Emmerick commission,
Brentano was also preparing for auction his collection of art works as
well as his immense library holdings (which ostensibly included
manuscripts and incunabula).[19] He retained, however, his books on
theological subjects. This deliberate de-secularization of his personal
library, coupled with his universal confession and the rejection by
Luise Hensel, were factors which gave direction to his activities
during the next decades.

As early as 1820 Brentano had begun to assemble Anna Katharina's
visionary pronouncements dealing with the life of Christ. The following list represents those works on the subject which were either
published by Brentano himself, prepared by him for publication, or
reconstructed and edited from his notes by authorized persons: (1)
The Bitter Suffering of Our Lord Jesus Christ (1833); (2) *The Life of
the Holy Virgin Mary* (1852); (3) *The Life of Jesus* (1858). Recent
research has put forth the hypothesis that Brentano actually intended
to write a trilogy dealing with Jesus' birth and youth, his years of
apprenticeship and teaching, and his passion and crucifixion.[20] This
"task of a lifetime" as Brentano called it, a monumental historical-
symbolical biography of Christ which he believed he had heard from
the lips of the divinely inspired nun of Dülmen, would have formed
an effective counterpart to the secularized and de-mythologized
version by David Friedrich Strauß, *Das Leben Jesu* (1835), had

Clemens been less scrupulous in his efforts to delete any possible "poetic" elements which might have intruded into the account via his creative fantasy.[21]

In addition to the above Emmerick material, Brentano also compiled a treatise on the nun's intuitive knowledge of sacred relics and a sketch of her life—*Biographical Outline of This Blessed Woman*—which he appended to the *Bitter Suffering* of 1833. Ever since the publication of the latter work, a heated controversy has raged among Catholic clergy and lay scholars concerning certain points: the extent to which this actually represents the unadulterated report of the nun, the manner in which Brentano may have induced or even extorted visions from her by readings from religious literature, or the degree to which his irrepressible imagination and poetic flair may have colored what were purported to be divinely inspired insights. For over a century vast amounts of Brentano's unpublished papers lay under lock and key in the archives of various religious orders in Rome or in other church libraries, and these circumstances made an accurate assessment impossible. However, in the past decades scholars have gained access to this material, so that today we are beginning to form some idea of the ultimate—and perhaps ulterior—aim of this writer who, in his desire to serve as the faithful scribe for the stigmatic, still found it impossible to deny at all times the innate poet in him.[22]

After spending the better part of six years in Dülmen, Brentano felt himself no longer bound to that city following the death of the nun in 1824 and the exhumation of her body. During the next decade he functioned as a dedicated proselytizer for the Catholic Church, so that Heine could characterize him somewhat maliciously, in his not unbiased study entitled *The Romantic School* (1834), as "a corresponding member of Catholic propaganda."[23] Even Brentano's itinerary after his departure from Dülmen reveals a marked religious orientation. A trip to the Alsatian region, for instance, brought him into contact again with another staunch friend of the faith, Görres, and in Strassburg the two conceived a joint enterprise involving the propagation and dissemination of strongly Catholic literary texts. During the 1820s Brentano contributed anonymous articles to the journal *Der Katholik (The Catholic)* and subsequently to the religiously oriented *Historisch-Kritische Blätter*.

In the course of his travels Brentano came to know and appreciate the work of the Sisters of Mercy, an order whose hospitals he toured in Paris and elsewhere with his newly found friend, Hermann Joseph

Dietz, an alderman of Coblence and founder of a hospital in that city, at which the Sisters performed their charitable work. By 1830 Brentano had completed a brief history of this order, which appeared in 1831 with a title and description indicating both its content and aim: *The Sisters of Mercy with Regard to Their Nursing of the Sick and Their Tending of the Poor* (Together with a Report on the Civic Hospital in Coblence and Explanatory Supplements. For the Benefit of the Charity School of the Coblence Women's Guild). As part of a projected library of popular reading material for Catholic audiences, Brentano contributed a new edition of the *Güldenes Tugendbuch* (Golden Book of Virtue) by Friedrich von Spee, writing the foreword and reworking some of the lyrics. In the same vein he provided a preface to *Die Parabeln des Vaters Bonaventura* (*The Parables of Father Bonaventura Giroudeau*) which bore the subtitle: *An Excellent Little Manual for Spiritual Guides* (Seelensorger), *Teachers, and Parents for the Purpose of Illustrating Christian Truth and Morality.*

The final stage of Brentano's odyssey of faith was reached in 1833 when he moved to Munich, the "headquarters of Catholic propaganda" and that same Bavarian capital where he had previously spent some hectic months eluding Auguste Bußmann. He was to spend his declining years here, editing the Emmerick papers, entering into discussions with the intellectual coteries of Görres and the Nazarene painters,[24] and engaging in his last great love affair with the Swiss paintress Emilie Linder. This relationship elicited the final flowering of his poetic muse, in spite of his previous injunctions against the art of poetry and the impropriety of literature in general.[25]

For over a century the mystique persisted that Brentano's correspondence with Emilie Linder had been lost, that their relationship could at best be pieced together via hearsay, secondhand reports, and the few extant letter fragments published in truncated form with all names deleted in the *Collected Works* of 1855. However, a happy stroke of fortune led the German scholar Wolfgang Frühwald to the archives of the cloister of Gars on the Inn River in Bavaria, and here he discovered virtually intact the extensive exchange of letters from the years 1834 to 1841. What emerges from this evidence is another of those erotic tragedies—or perhaps the term tragicomedy would be more appropriate—in Brentano's life. An initial encounter followed by headlong wooing, headstrong rejection on the part of the woman (1834), reluctant acceptance of the situation by the poet, and eventual reconciliation with the hard facts of reality.

One interesting aspect of the love poems written for Emilie is the discovery that many of them are actually reworkings of lyrics originally destined for Luise Hensel.[26] The practice of constantly revising and refining previously written material in new contexts is a trait to be found in Brentano's entire œuvre. "Contrafacture" (a neologism derived from the German *Kontrafaktur*), a quasi-musical technique whereby secular tunes are converted into religious melodies (or vice versa), is a consistent facet of his creative process. Some of his poems exist in a number of versions with slightly altered emphasis or change in tone reflecting, so to speak, a change of mood or a different recipient. One of the best examples of this practice, for instance, is the poem "Der Jäger an den Hirten" ("The Hunter to the Shepherd," 1803), originally secular in tone but later recast with religious overtones so that in 1817 a work with a marked shift in emphasis results.[27] The Linder adaptations of Hensel poems include such lyrics as: "Die Abendwinde wehen" ("The evening breezes blow," W, 1:567–69) and "Einsam will ich untergehen" ("Alone I wish to die," W, 1:596–600).

Brentano's creative renaissance in consequence of the Linder experience was not only marked by contrafacture, but it was also characterized by counterpoint. Aside from deploying his earlier, personalized love lyrics for Luise Hensel in new emotional contexts, he strove—contrapuntally, as it were—to depersonalize the visions transmitted to him via the stigmatic nun, to minimize the intrusion of his own subjective fantasy into the presentation, a task at which, according to the consensus of scholars today, he failed.[28] Another phase of his revisionary activity during the 1830s entailed changes in several of the fairy tales he had written at an earlier date. There are, in essence, three groups of these stories, the majority of which were conceived between 1805 and 1816: (1) *Tales of the Rhine;* (2) the minor (or "little") Italian tales; (3) the major (or "large") Italian tales. The first group were essentially Brentano's own creations, but permeated with motifs from local sagas, legend, and folklore; the second and third groups were based to a large extent on material from *Lo cunto deli cunti* or the *Pentamerone* by the seventeenth-century Italian poet Giambattista Basile. Although Brentano apparently never intended to publish his fairy tales, some did creep into print without his knowledge or consent. In 1826, for instance, his friend, Johann F. Böhmer, to whom he had entrusted the manuscript of the Rhine tales, published excerpts from this collection anonymously in the journal *Iris*, much to the dismay of Brentano, who, when he learned of this action, implored Böhmer to refrain from such unauthorized acts in the future.

Of the three tales which compromise the "major" Italian group, *Fanferlieschen Schönefüßchen*, which had originated between 1805 and 1811, was revised in 1817, and then extensively reworked from

1836 to 1838. The most sweeping changes, however, were under-taken in the case of *Gockel and Hinkel* which, although written most likely in 1815–1816, was expanded after 1835 not only internally but also externally—being preceded by a "Heartfelt Dedication" in which the author, in highly encoded and cryptic allusions, pays homage to several key women in his life, and followed by the *Diary of the Ancestress* in which biographical data are fused with fictional and legendary material.[29] Whereas *Gockel, Hinkel and Gackeleia* did appear in print in 1838 with a set of lithographic illustrations ostensi-bly based on sketches by the author himself, the entire corpus of the earlier fairy tales was only to be published after his death. In 1846–1847, Guido Görres, the son of Brentano's lifelong friend, edited and published two volumes entitled simply *The Fairy Tales of Clemens Brentano* with the following explanatory note: "For the Benefit of the Poor in Accordance with the Last Wishes of the Author." In this instance, the two strands of creativity in Brentano's last years—contrafacture and counterpoint—became interwoven posthumously: the fairy tales from previous years were imbued with new dimensions of meaning in keeping with the religious orientation of his later life, and the profits from the entire enterprise were channeled into the cause of "caritas," the same goal toward which his religiously edifying writings had been directed. Aside from the Emmerick papers, one might also mention in this regard a large number of versified saints' legends and martyrs' lives such as those of Solinus and Marina.

Despite the revitalization of his creative powers during the period from 1833 to 1842; and in spite of a fairly stable contingent of friends both old (Görres) and new (the artist Eduard von Steinle), Brentano spent his declining years under the shadow of illness and alienation, aloof from a pragmatically oriented world which he no longer under-stood and which, for an even longer time, had not understood him. Aspects of this "loss of resonance" as it has been dubbed,[30] can be detected in his renewed contact with Bettina following the death of Arnim in 1831. After Arnim's passing Bettina likewise seems to have revived her fallow literary talents with full elan, and the first fruits of this are found in her controversial book *Goethes Briefwechsel mit eine Kinde (Goethe's Correspondence with a Child*, 1835)—the child in question being Bettina herself, and the account, a curious amalgam of fact and fiction. Brentano, who at this time was striving to temper the expression of personal feelings and allusions in literary works (so that much of his late writing has to be read like a detective story), was taken aback by Betttina's blunt revelations of private matters and admonished her in passages such as the following: "it angers me that you dare to blurt out the whole secret," "truly you have sealed up for him [Goethe] with yourself a monument, what need does he have for one of marble?" and finally: "I know all the torment of having to create for oneself an idol and to lovingly animate and worship it with all the force of one's soul and that of nature, in spite of the innermost warning that this is madness."[31]

One can only speculate what Clemens's reaction might have been to another of Bettina's pseudo-autobiographical concoctions, the edition of her correspondence with him from the turn of the century under the title *Clemens Brentano's Spring Wreath Woven for Him from the Letters of His Youth.* Brentano did not live to see the publication in 1844 of this fanciful opus, since he succumbed in 1842 to the maladies which had plagued him for over a decade—a combination of dropsy (or edema) and heart trouble. There is, to be sure, a certain touch of irony in the fact that Brentano's ultimate demise should be connected in some way with an edematose (the swelling of body organs due to an accumulation of fluids in the tissue) condition, since those "waters of life" onto which he ventured with great trepidation came back to haunt him in the form of a disease the very name of which, at least in German, calls to mind this hazard: *Wassersucht.*

There is, furthermore, an air of anachronism surrounding Bettina's *Spring Wreath,* a work which harks back to the heyday of romanticism, since by the mid-1840s the romantic spirit had eroded almost completely, becoming either the butt of parodistic barbs or the province of the epigone. The pragmatic world view which had supplanted the romantic vision was one which Brentano subsumed under the concept of "philistinism," even though he suspected, deep down, that because the materialistic temperament was made of sterner, more resilient stuff, it would outlive the fragile soap-bubble dreams of romanticism. Thus Bettina's book, instead of "squaring the circle" as it were, and raising the romantic credo to its highest potential, touched on the "square root" of romanticism's problem, that of a moribund movement leading an artificially prolonged existence in a hostile environment. What the exact nature of that romantic syndrome had been for Brentano, however, and how it had manifested itself in his writing will serve as the focal point for the next section of this study.

II *The Romantic Foreground*

When the nineteen-year-old Clemens Brentano arrived in Jena in 1798, this city had already become established as the hotbed of incipient romanticism, and the young firebrand was prepared to contribute a lion's share to the new style of living and writing. The exact nature of "romanticism" as a movement in literature or as a mode of life defies procrustean definition, and the precise meaning of the term is still a matter of scholarly dispute, as can be deduced from the plethora of critical studies devoted to the problem.[32] Rather than summarize the results of these myriad investigations and perpetuate the ambiguity stemming from the often contradictory information contained in them or from the confusing impression that emerges due to Europe's many "romanticisms," the discussion here will be confined to Brentano's own pronouncements on the subject. Even though he is generally acknowledged to have been no friend of theory for the sake of theory, Brentano did expound perceptively—albeit in the fictional context of his first major work, the novel *Godwi or The Stone Statue of the Mother* (1801)—on the romantic world view and by indirection, on the application of this principle to the arts. The measure to which he adhered to or deviated from the romantic norms which he himself postulated might provide a yardstick by which to measure the various phases of romanticism in Germany, since the chronology of Brentano's youth, manhood, and old age coincides almost perfectly with the flowering, maturity, and decay of the movement as a whole.[33]

In volume 2 of the novel there appears a dialogue on the nature of romanticism between Godwi, the titular hero of the piece, Maria, the author-editor of volume 1, and Haber, a translator of Tasso and a pseudo-intellectual. The latter serves as a humorous foil to the repartee and brilliant aperçus of the other participants. Maria begins the analysis by presenting in general terms what might be described as the romantic point of view: "Alles, was zwischen unserm Auge und einem entfernten zu Sehenden als Mittler steht, uns den entfernten Gegenstand nähert, ihm aber zugleich etwas von dem Seinigen mitgiebt, ist romantisch" (*W,* 2:258)[34] ("Everything which stands between our eye and a distant visible object as an intermediary, and which brings us closer to the distant object, but which also simultaneously contributes something of its own, is romantic").[35] This rather abstract principle elicits a reaction of noncomprehension from the dull-witted and pedestrian Haber, so Godwi clarifies the concept by putting it into more tangible terms: "Das Romantische ist also ein Perspektiv oder vielmehr die Farbe des Glases und die Bestimmung des Gegenstandes durch die Form des Glases" *W,* 2:258–59) ("The romantic is then a field-glass, or rather the colour of the glass, and the definition of the object by means of the form of the glass").[36] Immediately Haber counters with an objection, declaring that romanticism so delineated must imply formlessness, a remark which induces Maria to elucidate what is meant by romantic form.

Again Maria begins abstractly and even paradoxically, explaining that an entity devoid of the accoutrements of form may, in the final analysis, actually possess more form than the consciously formed object—an assertion which is then recapitulated aphoristically: "Form is the proper delineation of what the mind conceives." Any artistic form which fails to meet these criteria suffers either from an excess or a dearth of formal attributes, and thus it can be classified as a nonform. Such subtleties have by now boggled Haber's mind completely; so the other speakers resort to references to translation, the area of expertise in which Haber reputedly is most proficient, and reiterate their positions on the romantic mode of perception in this related idiom. Maria comments:

nach meiner Meinung ist jedes reine, schöne Kunstwerk, das seinen Gegenstand bloß darstellt, leichter zu übersetzen als ein romantisches, welches seinen Gegenstand nicht allein bezeichnet, sondern seiner Bezeichnung selbst noch ein Kolorit giebt, denn dem Übersetzer des Romantischen wird die Gestalt der Darstellung selbst ein Kunstwerk, das er übersetzen soll. . . . die romantischen Dichter haben mehr als bloße Darstellung, sie haben sich selbst noch stark. (W, 2:260)

In my opinion, every pure and beautiful work of art which presents its object *per se* is easier to translate than a Romantic work of art which not only depicts its object but also imparts to the depiction a certain coloring, since, for the translator of the Romantic persuasion, the form of the presentation is itself a work of art which he must also translate. . . . the Romantic poets have more than mere depiction to be concerned about, they also have themselves to a great degree.

Maria rounds off his definition with the sententious remark: "Das Romantische selbst ist eine Übersetzung" (W, 2:262) ("The Romantic element is itself a translation"). Again, as if to illustrate this statement on a more concrete plane, Godwi and Maria point out how the sunlight shining, at that very moment, through an emerald-tinted glass basin, bathes the room in a verdant hue; the romantic atmosphere is attributable to the fact that the green glass becomes the medium for the transmission of the sun's rays. We perceive the objects in the area mediated through an intervening "third party," and this becomes an integral and indispensable part of our perception. Later we learn parenthetically that the basin itself is the handiwork of a fifteenth-century craftsman from Strassburg, an artisan who, even at this early date, exhibited a "phantastischen romantischen Stil" *(W,* 2:265) ("fanciful, romantic style").

One might pause at this point to mention in passing some related remarks of Brentano's contemporaries on what constitutes romanticism. There is, for example, the fragment of Novalis (Friedrich von Hardenberg) concerning the romanticization of the world through a qualitative exponential heightening of the real, a magico-mystical process of the mind whereby the commonplace and the uncommon, the known and the unknown, the ordinary and the extraordinary, the finite and the infinite are brought into a dialectical and mutually enriching correlation with one another.[37] Then there is Friedrich Schlegel's oft-quoted aphorism 116 from the collection published in the *Athenäum,* describing the progressive, and consequently tenuous and provisional, aspect of romantic poetry which, hovering precariously between the "dem Dargestellten und dem Darstellenden, frei von allem realen und idealen Interesse auf den Flügeln der poetischen Reflexion . . . diese Reflexion immer wieder potenzieren und wie in einer endlosen Reihe von Spiegeln vervielfachen"[38] ("portrayed and the portrayer, free of all real and ideal self-interest, on the wings of poetic reflection, . . . can raise that reflection again and again to a higher power, can multiply it in an endless succession of mirrors").[39]

In spite of individual variation of expression from one writer to the next, a feature explicit in Brentano and implicit in both of the above statements is that the romantic quality involves the mode of mediation between two entities, the transmission or "translation" from one to the other via a receptive third force which, in turn, imbues the thing so transmitted with a component previously not manifest. What makes the presentation romantic seems to be the fact that what is represented through the medium of art, for instance, is neither the unadulterated "thing-in-itself" (the use of this familiar epistemological concept is not entirely amiss, given the links of many romantic writers to Kantian thought and its Fichtean modifications), but rather the "thing" as it is prismatically filtered through the unique apparatus of apprehension in the mind's eye of the artist. What results, therefore, is an artifact that transcends the objective "given" by the infusion of a subjective addendum. Godwi, in explaining the ingredients which comprise his way of seeing the world, fuses Novalis's theory of romanticizing with Schlegel's thesis of romantic progression, when he declares: "Es ist wunderbar, . . . daß ich nie eine Sache an sich selbst betrachte, sondern immer im Bezuge auf etwas Unbekanntes,

Ewiges; . . . und so komme ich dann nimmer zur Ruhe, weil mit jedem Schritte, den ich vorwärtstue, der Endpunkt der Perspektive einen Schritt vorwärtstut" *(W,* 2:148–49) ("It is amazing . . . that I never regard a thing for itself, but always in relation to something unknown, something eternal . . . and thus I never come to rest, because with every step which I take forward, the focal point of my perspective likewise takes a step forward").

The romantic work as a "trans-lation" (from the Latin, *translatus*—carried across) serves as a bridge on which the traffic from two diverse realms (the object portrayed and the apprehending subject) intersect and intermingle for a *brief* moment—and the romantic spirit does indeed express itself best in works of smaller scope and short duration—becoming a third force which then synthesizes the components in such a manner that they mutually illuminate each other. A triadic quality emerges from all the above elucidations, beginning with Brentano's view of a mediating force between our eye and what we see in the distance to Novalis's mingling of the disparate spheres to form a unique amalgam and Schlegel's precarious hovering between the "portrayed and the portrayer." The frequently heard assertion that romantic art tends toward the symbolic can be reinforced in the light of the above, as well as in view of Brentano's later (1812) claim that the symbol

soll nur ein Wink sein, der sich zugleich wieder selbst deutet, es ist gewissermaßen eine vor unsern Augen vorgehende Metamorphose der Sache in ein Bild ihres Sinnes. Es liegt eine Bewegung, ein Werden in dem Symbol, kein Nachmachen, Vorstellenwollen, keine handelnde Abspiegelung, . . . so auch muß das Symbol ideal gewachsen sein und . . . nicht aber real zusammengeknüpft. (W, 2:1051–52)

should only be a hint, which coincidentally reinterprets itself; it is to a certain extent a metamorphosis, taking place before our eyes, of matter into an image of its meaning. Within the symbol there is movement, transformation, no mimicry, no intent to portray, no active mirroring . . . also the symbol must evolve from the ideal . . . but not be contrived from the real.

Both Brentano's delineation of romanticism and his definition of the symbol underscore a certain "threshold" condition, a no-man's (or everyman's) land between the frontiers of objective "reality" and subjective mediation of that reality, whereby neither the former nor the latter in isolation, but each in mutual refraction gives birth to an entity which subsumes both in a new and unique amalgam.

In the course of the following analyses of Brentano's accomplishments and shortcomings in individual genres, it will become increasingly apparent that during the latter phases of his life, he underwent a dual crisis in his attitude toward literature in general and his poetic métier in particular. Periodically he suffered a "loss of inspiration," during which time the validity of the individual verbal utterance became highly dubious to him. On such occasions, he sought an outlet in treating already extant works (editing folksongs or the writings of earlier poets) or in collaboration with some more stable contemporaries (Arnim, Görres). But he ultimately grew leery of the ability of language to articulate properly those emotions and situations which the *poeta vates* reputedly is empowered to express. This two-fold breakdown led to his search beyond the borders of art for a field of endeavor in which he could enlist his still salvageable talents to serve some suprapersonal cause. Anna Katharina Emmerick's visions and Brentano's self-appointed scribal duty seemed to provide the answer. His goal entailed the complete exclusion of the subjective component in order to function as a vehicle for a divinely ordained reality. Thus he writes to a friend in 1826:

Wer nur einen Moment des Lebens, nur das kleinste Fragment der Natur, ich will nicht sagen, versteht, nein, nur ruhig stehen läßt und vorübergehend anschaut, ohne daran zu zerren, zu modellieren, zu metamorphosieren: der findet eine so unendliche, tiefe, hohe und doch naive, einfältige Würde und Bedeutung in jeder Realität ohne übrige Deutung, daß für das Empfangen nur Dank und für das Besitzen nur Opfer übrig bleibt, um es zu würdigen. Aller übrige Umgang mit den Dingen, der sie dreht und wendet und färbt und schmückt und überdestilliert, was die Poesie besonders will, ist am Ende nur ein Götzendienst, der durch seine Spiritualität um so gefährlicher ist.[40]

Whoever allows one moment of life, the tiniest fragment of nature, to stand calmly on its own, or who simply regards it incidentally—I certainly do not imply that he understands it—without distorting, fashioning, or transforming it, that person finds such an infinite, deep. lofty and yet naive, simple dignity and significance in all reality without any further interpretation, that to appreciate this properly there remains only thanks for such receptivity, for such a possession, only sacrifice. Any other dealings with things which twist them, turn, color, adorn and over-distill them—something which poetry especially seeks to do—are, in the final analysis, only idolatry which, due to its spiritual nature, is all the more dangerous.

Such a stance seems to repudiate, once and for all, the romantic postulate of imparting "something of ourselves" to what we see.

However, it has been amply documented that Brentano was eminently unsuccessful in this venture of unbiased reporting, that he was not able to suppress the dictates of his unbridled fantasy even when this became his avowed aim. There is, consequently, a kind of romantic continuity to his total production, a persistence of certain practices and problems, resulting in the fact that even though the subject matter of his writing changed radically, that penchant announced at the outset of *Godwi*—to function as a mediating subject—remained intact. By investing, during the process of mediation, the thing mediated with a quality that threatens to become of greater moment than the entity which gave rise to the mediation or the formal means employed to transmit it, he affirmed a principle which lies at the root of his definition of romanticism: the medium is the message.

Even his famous and oft-quoted remark of 1842 that "wir hatten nichts genährt als die Phantasie, und sie hatte uns teils wieder aufgefressen"[41] ("we had nurtured nothing but fantasy, and it had, in turn, consumed us in part") should not be regarded so much as a confession of error as it is a concession to truth: the romanticist in Brentano, who heightened the commonplace by the dimension of imagination and elevated the realistic beyond its limits through the agency of the fantastic, never really deserted him. He remained to the end a romantic at heart, even though he was heartbroken to discover that the world of romanticism was collapsing around him like a house of cards.

CHAPTER 2

The Lyric Poet

I F Brentano is known at all to the average German reader, it is
perhaps as the author of a few fairy tales, of a familiar short story or
two, as the coeditor of *The Youth's Magic Horn*, but most likely as the
creator of some memorable lyric verses. For the European reading
public at large, on the other hand, the name Brentano may be
associated with a handful of poems, but not with much more. In
essence, then, Brentano's reputation rests on his poetry, and this is as
it should be, for he was and remains a master weaver of fascinating
lyric textures which haunt our hearts and minds because they articulate with relentless and seemingly effortless, but actually deceptively
artless, consistency , emotions and situations which are basic to the
all too human condition.[1] On various occasions, Brentano characterized himself or his fictional counterparts as a poem rather than a
poet, sometimes even as the object of a poem; and although he
declared his life to have been the "most wonderful poem" ever
written, he was convinced that it would find approval neither in his
own eyes, in those of mankind, nor in God's.[2]

I Lyric Poetry: Problems of Translation, Selection, and Transmission

There are several hurdles to be cleared by the critic when discuss-
ing lyric poetry. If the analysis is in the original language of the poem,
then the interpreter must be careful to distinguish between the use of
identical terms in lyric contexts and rational discourse, between the
poetic significance and the "commonplace" meaning of the same
word. This is a subtle distinction which is not easily attained or
maintained. If, on the other hand, the analysis of a poem is in a
language different from the original, then the perennial monster of
translation rears its ugly head. The felonious assault committed
against the integrity or unity of a poem by critical explanation or
rational exegesis is compounded by the acknowledged impossibility

of transmitting the essentials of the lyric mode and mood adequately through a different set of sound patterns and semantic referents.

Whereas translation of literary texts may be a stumbling block in prose fiction or expository writing, it becomes a virtual road block in the case of poetry, where so much depends on acoustical properties, subtle shading and nuances of meaning peculiar to one language but not necessarily a factor in another, syntactical juxtaposition and contextual structure as well as rhythm and rhyme. In Brentano's case there seems to be literally more truth than poetry to the familiar axiom that the greater the lyric poet, the more untranslatable his work will be; it is particularly difficult to render the essence of Brentano's verses through another linguistic medium without doing violence to those very qualities which made them great to begin with.[3]

A second difficulty—and to some extent an even more perplexing one—involves the question of selection, since this introductory study is not meant to be comprehensive but representative. Assuming that there were available in English translation more than the approximately twenty poems which have actually appeared,[4] then what criteria should one use to choose a limited number for closer scrutiny? One might, for instance, follow the practice introduced in the *Collected Works* and group the entire corpus of lyrics according to major rubrics (in this case, "secular" and "religious"), then further subdivide these larger categories into specific subjects (the former including occasional poems, love, pictures, fatherland, legends, songs, etc.)[5] and finally select a poem or two from each subdivision for discussion.[6] The most serious drawback here is the makeshift and catchall nature of the arbitrary pigeonholing according to thematic typology. An alternative approach would be to peruse the major anthologies of German verse, of the romantic period *or* of Brentano's lyrics in particular, to discover which of his poems have most frequently been included and then make a random sampling from these for interpretation.[7] A similar procedure might be applied to the various generic histories of the lyric, either for all of German literature,[8] for the romantic period,[9] or, more specifically, for specialized Brentano studies.[10]

A final criterion for selection from among Brentano's more than three hundred poems would be that of chronology, an extremely complex and yet crucial aspect of his productivity, since the lyrics have come to be regarded as "the most tangible continuum of this mangled œuvre and existence."[11] The difficulties here stem from the fact that the precise or sometimes approximate dating of certain poems is unreliable, even with the aid of modern technological devices (detectivelike methods based on quality and age of the paper, the ink, orthographical clues, etc.).[12] Such problems are due, in part, to the author's eccentric manner of composition as well as to the arbitrary editorial policies of his friends and relatives.[13] Internal evidence in poems (in the form of recurrent imagery, parallel phraseology, or similarity of motifs) likewise does not provide a fool-proof basis for chronology, since Brentano sometimes carried around previously articulated ideas and images in his mind for decades until a suitable stimulus triggered the new lyric statement. Nevertheless, in 1933 René Guignard published for Brentano's poems a chronology which, with some modifications due to subsequent manuscript discoveries, has proved to be a fairly reliable guide to the dating of individual works.[14]

Twentieth-century scholars have utilized the chronological approach to an understanding of Brentano's poetry in a variety of ways and with various degrees of success. Three basic critical trends can be distinguished in this regard: advocates of the early lyric as most incisive; proponents of the late poetry; and, most recently, the view that works from all stages in the author's career should be considered, since a number of thematic and technical constants in his total output can be isolated.

In one of the most penetrating analyses of lyric-poetic creativity, Emil Staiger sought to find the essence of Brentano's style by means of a detailed *explication de texte* of a single poem from the pre-1803 period.[15] In the wake of this pioneering study,[16] numerous other interpreters looked to the early lyrics as definitive for the poet's creative attitude and existential outlook.[17] The hegemony of the Staiger school, which dates from the late 1930s, was only seriously challenged in the early 1960s by Hans Magnus Enzensberger, himself a poet, who claimed that the "real" Brentano, the "radical artist" and creator of pure, hermetically sealed and self-contained lyrics, only emerged after 1817.[18] For several years Enzensberger's theory was greeted with open arms, and his critical stance adopted by students and scholars alike.[19]

The sobering counterweight to the short-lived Enzensberger euphoria, however, came from those charged with the responsibility for the editorial and philological policies of the projected historical-critical edition of Brentano's works.[20] Ever since the postwar period a fierce campaign has been waged to collect in one central location original manuscripts or, failing that, photocopies, of every scrap of

Brentaniana; and aside from some documents lost during the conflict, the quest has been successful.[21] The results of this positivistic renaissance in interaction with the Staiger-Enzensberger theories have been beneficial for Brentano scholarship in general and for the lyric poetry in particular.[22] For example, in his book *Homo poeta*, Bernhard Gajek (who is intimately involved with the forthcoming edition), attempts to modify some of the claims to priority for specific periods by demonstrating a "continuity of problem constellations" running through Brentano's entire life.[23] The poetic texts cited to undergird this hypothesis are previously neglected works of limited aesthetic appeal, but the evidence is solidly documented and derived from philologically sound criteria. The upshot of this scholarly analysis should be a revamping of the stereotyped concepts of Brentano as a poetic genius of either early *or* late vintage, of "secular" *or* "religious" verse, of light, occasional *or* profoundly experiential poems, of "naive" *or* "sentimental" stamp.[24] He emerges as a poet whose verse was permeated by certain ubiquitous and *basso ostinato* or *continuo* themes, by quasi-musical techniques which remain unchanged even though the upper voice may sing a different tune or dance to a different melody. This means that some of the chronological schemes for lyric productivity such as Guignard's rather standardized format (youth; years of turmoil; period of conversion; the final decades)[25] or other more elaborate and ingenious divisions such as those neatly worked out by Wolfgang Pfeiffer-Belli (poetic youth, 1778–1798; poetic spring, 1798–1802; poetic heights, 1802–1806; poetic confusion, 1806–1814; and poetic retreat, 1814–1842)[26] will have to be scrutinized in light of either more modern and subtle distinctions[27] or perhaps rejected in favor of no chronological lines of demarcation at all.[28]

The third and last impediment to a synoptic glance at Brentano's lyricism derives, like the problem of dating the poems, from the philological discoveries mentioned above. Brentano not only gave variations of the same poem to different friends at different times, but these acquaintances also made handwritten copies of their own; in certain cases, only the latter are now extant. In addition, there were also published versions of certain poems which differ in major or minor ways from any or all of the manuscript forms. As a result, some lyrics exist in a number of adaptations, and it may only be when all these have been collected and collated, that a more definitive—but not necessarily *the* definitive—version can be determined.

Two final complications: many of Brentano's most famous poems are known by titles given to them by the editors of the *Collected*

Works but not authorized by the poet himself. At times critics have
been misled in their interpretations by such editorial encroachments
on authorial prerogatives,[29] while in other instances these infringe-
ments have been relatively harmless.[30] On the other hand, editors
and critics alike have sometimes committed serious infractions in a
different direction: lyric poems occurring within the context of a
prose work or a play (the two genres which, in addition to the letters,
provided suitable "housing" for these verses) are torn out of this
environment and interpreted as independent creations rather than
with reference to the original surroundings. This has led in some
cases to the existence of two independent versions of the same poem:
one as integrated into its fictional milieu and the other in isolation.
Some critics argue that this dual-track procedure is not legitimate,
since it postulates a *modus vivendi* for the poem which the author did
not necessarily intend; what we gain is a product of the critic's mind
rather than of the poet's pen.[31] This situation is not without a touch of
poetic justice, since Brentano himself "restored," in accordance with
his own aesthetic sensibilities and artistic preferences, many of the
poems which he and Arnim collected for *The Youth's Magic Horn*,
and this issue has stood at the center of a storm of controversy ever
since the appearance of the three-volume work.[32]

Bearing in mind the three main sources of difficulty in dealing with
lyric poetry (availability and quality of translations; criteria for establishing a representative cross-sampling; manuscript transmission and
editorial modifications), the following discussion will analyze nine
poems:[33] (1) "Sprich aus der Ferne" (1800) from *Godwi* I; (2) "Zu
Bacharach am Rheine" (1800) from *Godwi* II; (3) "Es sang vor langen
Jahren" from *Excerpts from the Chronicle of a Traveling Student*
(1818; written 1802); (4) "Hör,' es klagt die Flöte wieder" from *The
Merry Minstrels* (1802); (5) "singet leise, leise, leise" from the *Fairy
Tales of the Rhine* (1811); (6) "Nachklänge Beethovenscher Musik"
(1814); (7) "Frühlingsschrei eines Knechtes aus der Tiefe" (1816); (8)
"Ach alles geht vorbei" (1817); (9) "Was reif in diesen Zeilen steht"
from *Gockel, Hinkel and Gackeleia* (1838).

A glance at the dates of the respective poems reveals that they
extend from Brentano's earliest creative years to his last and thus may
be said to be representative, at least from the standpoint of chronology. The analyses will show that they are also characteristic of the
poet's overall production with regard to thematic substance and
prosodic technique. Even though the post-1817 period is limited to a

single poem, this is certainly not meant as an affront against those critics who consider that Brentano's truly original genius emerged late. This limitation is rather based on the fact that the art of translation has not yet caught up with the trends in criticism. The almost total absence of suitable—or better, *any*—professionally translated English versions of the late lyrics must necessarily lead to a correspondingly restricted treatment of this phase of Brentano's creativity. Yet one might also argue that the poem in question, which is usually given the unauthorized title "Prelude" in anthologies, contains, in germinal and seminal form, thematic configurations and technical structures which extend across the entire spectrum of the poet's career and support the above-mentioned argument for a "continuity of problem-constellations" in spite of shifting focus.

Since one aim of the present study is to isolate elements of the romantic perspective, an attempt was made to present an assortment which shares aspects of a common mode of perception. As will be stressed during the individual analyses, there is indeed such a unifying bond in this group, for each poem, in its own fashion, underscores the presence or absence of ties to some other force in the universe, be it cosmic or erotic, transcendental or terrestrial. There is a kind of kaleidoscopic quality in this cluster of nine poems; the design which we perceive when we first look into the kaleidoscope is analogous to, but not identical with, our final impression, with all manner of gradations and configural combinations in the poems which intervene. Each "turn" of the kaleidoscopic lens alters the pattern of the component elements slightly, but their fundamental constellation remains intact.

But whereas the two poems forming the outermost chronological extremes of the group (1 and 9) stress ideal congruence, the coexistence and coincidence of two worlds, and the middle three (4–6) indicate access routes leading to such rapport, the remaining lyrics all treat separation, disparity, and conflict. The frame poems thus function like two eyes focusing on a single object, transmitting to the brain an image with full depth perception. The three middle poems hint at various possibilities of synthesis, using all sensuous media at our disposal. Optical, aural, and tactile functions are called into play and interplay, and, if necessary, Brentano would have drawn upon our olfactory and gustatory senses as well. However, the remaining four poems (2, 3; 7, 8) are akin to a photographic double exposure or to the slightly askew superimposition of one photographic image on another, whereby the discrepancies and distinctions stand out instead of the intended identity. In the process, they deploy the principal symbolic concepts in the poet's repertoire with which he depicted the plight of man in a universal or personal world "out of joint" (Paradise Lost, melancholy, the mirror) together with those images which suggested reintegration (the child). Consequently, a study of these nine poems should yield insights into Brentano's idealized vision as well as into the conditions which distorted or destroyed this view.

II *Analyses of Nine Brentano Poems (1800–1838)*

(1)

Sprich aus der Ferne
Heimliche Welt,
Die sich so gerne
Zu mir gesellt.

Wenn das Abendrot niedergesunken,
Keine freudige Farbe mehr spricht,
Und die Kränze stilleuchtender
    Funken
Die Nacht um die schattigte Stirne
    flicht:

Wehet der Sterne
Heiliger Sinn
Leis durch die Ferne
Bis zu mir hin.

Wenn des Mondes still lindernde
    Tränen
Lösen der Nächte verborgenes
    Weh;
Dann wehet Friede. In goldenen
    Kähnen
Schiffen die Geister im himmlischen
    See.

Glänzender Lieder
Klingender Lauf
Ringelt sich nieder,
Wallet hinauf.

Wenn der Mitternacht heiliges
  Grauen
Bang durch die dunklen Wälder
  hinschleicht,
Und die Büsche gar wundersam
  schauen,
Alles sich finster tiefsinnig
  bezeugt:

Wandelt im Dunkeln
Freundliches Spiel,
Still Lichter funkeln
Schimmerndes Ziel.

Alles ist freundlich wohlwollend
  verbunden,
Bietet sich tröstend und traurend
  die Hand,
Sind durch die Nächte die Lichter
  gewunden,
Alles ist ewig im Innern verwandt.

Sprich aus der Ferne
Heimliche Welt,
Die sich so gerne
Zu mir gesellt.

(W, 1.66 66)

(Speak from the distance, / World-mystery / That gladly welcomes / Friendship with me! / When the red of the evening has sunken, / And no color
speaks joyfully now, / And the garlands of quiet gleaming sparkles / Night
binds round her shadowing brow / Wafts holy meaning / Of heavenly star / To
me in the distance, / Waiting afar. / When the tears of the moon softly
soothing / Release the nights' deep hidden pain, / Peace breathes anew. And
on little barks golden / Sail spirits along on the heavenly main. / Radiant
ballad's / Resonant flow / Undulates upward, / Circles below. / When the
midnight's awe-filled apprehension / Glides through forest in darkness and
fear, / And each bush shows extraordinary tension, / All things profound,
melancholic appear. / Flits in the darkling / Friendliest play, / Tranquil lights
sparkling / Bright goal display. / Kindly and friendly is each bound with
other, / Trustfully, comforting, offers the hand, / Lights have entwined
through the dark nights together, / All things forever are inwardly bound./
Speak from the distance / World-mystery / That gladly welcomes / Friendship with me!)   (Trans. Mabel Cotterell)[34]

One might call these verses a metaphysical love poem in which the speaker invokes a second, secret world with which mankind can establish a mystical union, thereby enriching or "raising to a higher power" the sphere of empirical reality. The poem from *Godwi* is attributed to Otilie, the naively childlike girl whose harmonious personality represents to the protagonist the apex of human (as well as female) potential. The night has a special radiance, a unique tonal quality which, when apprehended by those whose senses have not been dulled by humdrum routine, enriches human existence by new dimensions of experience. Day's dissecting light cedes precedence to the glow of darkness, a fuller spectrum of sights and sounds allays any fears one might have when crossing the magical threshold of midnight. In the penultimate stanza the *unio mystica* is celebrated not in images or metaphors of synesthesia, but rather as factual statement. Otilie then "squares the circle," as it were, sealing off the self-contained universe in circular fashion through repetition of the opening quatrain. But these verses have assumed new meaning in the process, for the union or re-union of world and world-mystery has become in the course of the poem a *fait accompli*.

The quiet confidence which manifests itself here is indicative of the positive and self-assured stance shared by many of the young romantics due to their optimistic faith in the transforming powers of poetry and in the poet's ability to create a new reality.[35] This was youth at its untested best; dichotomies and antinomies are overcome, subjective and objective distinctions blur as the speaker articulates the vision of an all-embracing unity in precise symbols of imprecise significance.[36]

It has been shown that throughout Brentano's career, there exists a kind of alternating rhythm between such periods of self-assurance (*Selbstsein*) followed by those of radical dependence on others (*Du-Bindung*) in order for him to survive, not to mention thrive, as both person and poet.[37] Elements of the second phase in this rhythmic pattern manifest themselves in another *Godwi* poem, the balladlike lines ascribed to a figure diametrically opposed in temperament to Otilie and the latter's exemplary deportment: the prostitute Violetta. This young woman, compelled by her mother to lead a wanton existence, loses any residue of the self-esteem manifested by Otilie. One poignant example of Violetta's plight is the *ménage à trois* scene in which she sings the song of the Lore Lay to her mother and the latter's lover, Godwi, the man whom Violetta also loves and who ultimately spurns her:

(2)

Zu Bacharach am Rheine
Wohnt eine Zauberin,
Sie war so schön und feine
Und riß viel Herzen hin.

Und brachte viel zu schanden
Der Männer rings umher,
Aus ihren Liebesbanden
War keine Rettung mehr.

Der Bischof ließ sie laden
Vor geistliche Gewalt—
Und mußte sie begnaden,
So schön war ihr' Gestalt.

Er sprach zu ihr gerühret:
"Du arme Lore Lay!
Wer hat dich denn verführet
Zu böser Zauberei?"

"Herr Bischof laßt mich sterben,
Ich bin des Lebens müd,
Weil jeder muß verderben,
Der meine Augen sieht.

Die Augen sind zwei Flammen,
Mein Arm ein Zauberstab
O legt mich in die Flammen!
O brechet mir den Stab!"

"Ich kann dich nicht verdammen,
Bis du mir erst bekennt,
Warum in diesen Flammen
Mein eigen Herz schon brennt.

Den Stab kann ich nicht brechen,
Du schöne Lore Lay!
Ich müßte dann zerbrechen
Mein eigen Herz entzwei."

"Herr Bischof mit mir Armen
Treibt nicht so bösen Spott,

Und bittet um Erbarmen,
Für mich den lieben Gott.

Ich darf nicht länger leben,
Ich liebe keinen mehr—
Den Tod sollt Ihr mir geben,
Drum kam ich zu Euch her.—

Mein Schatz hat mich betrogen,
Hat sich von mir gewandt,
Ist fort von hier gezogen,
Fort in ein fremdes Land.

Die Augen sanft und wilde,
Die Wangen rot und weiß,
Die Worte still und milde
Das ist mein Zauberkreis.

Ich selbst muß drin verderben,
Das Herz tut mir so weh,
Vor Schmerzen möcht' ich sterben,
Wenn ich mein Bildnis seh'.

Drum laßt mein Recht mich finden,
Mich sterben, wie ein Christ,
Denn alles muß verschwinden,
Weil er nicht bei mir ist."

Drei Ritter läßt er holen:
"Bringt sie ins Kloster hin,
Geh Lore! — Gott befohlen
Sei dein berückter Sinn.

Du sollst ein Nönnchen werden,
Ein Nönnchen schwarz und weiß,
Bereite dich auf Erden
Zu deines Todes Reis'."

Zum Kloster sie nun ritten,
Die Ritter alle drei,
Und traurig in der Mitten
Die schöne Lore Lay.

"O Ritter laßt mich gehen,
Auf diesen Felsen groß,
Ich will noch einmal sehen
Nach meines Lieben Schloß.

Ich will noch einmal sehen
Wohl in den tiefen Rhein,
Und dann ins Kloster gehen
Und Gottes Jungfrau sein."

Der Felsen ist so jähe,
So steil ist seine Wand,
Doch klimmt sie in die Höhe,
Bis daß sie oben stand.

Es binden die drei Ritter,
Die Rosse unten an,
Und klettern immer weiter,
Zum Felsen auch hinan.

Die Jungfrau sprach: "da gehet
Ein Schifflein auf dem Rhein,
Der in dem Schifflein stehet,
Der soll mein Liebster sein.

Mein Herz wird mir so munter,
Er muß mein Liebster sein! —"
Da lehnt sie sich hinunter
Und stürzet in den Rhein.

Die Ritter mußten sterben,
Sie konnten nicht hinab,
Sie mußten all verderben,
Ohn' Priester und ohn' Grab

Wer hat dies Lied gesungen?
Ein Schiffer auf dem Rhein,
Und immer hat's geklungen
Von dem drei Ritterstein:

    Lore Lay
    Lore Lay
    Lore Lay

Als wären es meiner drei.

(W, 1:112–15)

(At Bacharach on Rhine-bank / A sorceress did dwell, / She was so fine and handsome / On all she cast her spell. / Full many a man around her / To grievous shame she brought; / No more could he be rescued / Who in her toils was caught. / The bishop sent to bid her / Before his court appear; / Yet must he grant her pardon / She was so passing fair. / He spoke to her with tremors, / "Thou poor young Lore Lay, / Who then has thus misled thee / To evil sorcery?" / "Lord Bishop, let me perish, / I'm weary now to live, / For all that look upon me / Alas, must come to grief. / Thy eyes like flames are burning / My arm's a magic staff, / O lay me in the burning, / O break for me my staff!" / "I cannot yet condemn thee / Till thou hast made me know / Why in thine eyes so burning, / My heart begins to glow? / The staff I cannot shatter, / Thou Lore Lay so fine, / For then I have to sever / In twain this heart of mine." / "Lord Bishop, to poor maiden / Show not such cruel scorn: / But beg that God have mercy / On maiden so forlorn. / I dare to live no longer; / I love none any more; / Death is what you must give me, / For that is why I'm here. / My lover hath betrayed me, / From me hath turned away, / Gone forth on distant journey / In foreign land doth stray. / Eyes that are wild and timid, / The red and white in cheeks, / Words sounding quiet and gentle, / My magic circle makes. / Me too it brings to ruin, / My heart is woe in me, / For sadness would I perish / When I my likeness see. / Then let my judgment find me, / As Christian let me die; / For everything is empty / Since he's no longer by." / He had three knights brought thither: / "To convent take her hence." / "Go Lore! In God's keeping / Be thy distracted sense! / Thou now shalt be a novice, / In black and white a nun; / On earth thou shalt prepare thee / For when life's days are done!" / To convent now they're riding, / All three the knights go by, / And sadly in the middle / The lovely Lore Lay. / "O knights, I pray you let me / Climb this great rocky hill, / Once more I'd see the castle, / Where my dear love did dwell. / Once more to look I'm longing / Into the deep Rhine flood, / Then will I to the convent / And virgin be of God." / So steep the rock was standing, / Precipitous its face, / Yet climbed she to the summit / And stood at topmost place. / Their steeds the three knights tethered / And made them fast beneath, / Then up above they clambered / And rocky summit reached. / Then said the maid: "There journeys / A little skip on Rhine / The one who stands on shipboard / Must be that love of mine! / It must be my beloved / So blithe my heart doth grow." / Then leaned she down and over / And plunged to depths below. / Nor could the knights from summit / Descend their lives to save, / Up there they all must perish, / With neither priest nor grave. / And who has sung this ditty? / A boatman on the Rhine, / And ever has the echo / Come from the Three-Knights-Stone: / Lore Lay! / Lore Lay! / Lore Lay! / As were the three my own.   (Trans. Mabel Cotterell)[38]

    The long poem might be divided into three sections: the introductory segment (stanzas 1–3) locates the action near the Rhine city with the vowel-rich, internally rhyming name of Bacharach, and sets the background for the saga by telling of the demonic and destructive force exerted by Lore Lay's[39] beauty on apparently all men with whom she comes into contact—including the bishop who summons her to appear before him. The second part (stanzas 4–13) consists of a dramatic dialogue typical of the ballad genre pitting Lore Lay's death wish against the reluctance of the cleric to grant this request because of his own growing infatuation. When she plays her trump card—the only man she ever loved is the only one ever to not love her—the bishop counters with a makeshift solution (a variation of Shakespeare's "get thee to a nunnery") which sidesteps the central issue. Consequently, as Lore Lay, in the third section (stanza 14 to the end) is led to the cloister by the three knights, a plan to escape this unwelcome resolution ferments in her mind. Her ascent to the precarious heights of the rock,[40] her teichoscopic account of the little skip in which she spies the man who must be her lover (a "must" of wishful thinking rather than necessity),[41] and her deliberately accidental plunge into the watery depths below follow in rapid succession and constitute the tragic conclusion to a life of tragedy.

Not only was Lore Lay unable to establish any lasting love relationship, but she eventually reached the point of self-alienation: her own beautiful mirror image became anathema to her.[42] Paradoxically, beauty which should uplift man and in some way make him receptive for—or stir reminiscences of—the realm of the absolute, instead wreaks havoc on both the personal and the societal levels. It incites spiritual disruption (the bishop's helpless confusion) and existential disorientation: the three knights are unable to return to normalcy after having been exposed to archetypical beauty, and we experience the self-annihilation of Lore Lay. Whereas her leap into the Rhine waters might hint at a return to the fundamental element (and for Wagnerites, at a possible restoration of equilibrium in the world) Brentano's ironically tinged close precludes any such harmonious resolution.

The identity of the boatman who sang the ditty and caused the proliferation of the unforgettable name of the heroine has led to much speculation.[43] However, in the final analysis this type of ironic byplay is more indicative of the social and personal upheavals caused in men's lives by the bearer of that musical name than it is of any sort of concord or potentially unifying force. Whereas the verb forms throughout the poem fix a time sequence either in the narrative past, the conversational perfect, or the dramatic present, the closing stanza, with its disruption of the standard metric format, also leaves the reader hovering in the limbo of the subjunctive,[44] a fittingly enigmatic ending to the sorceress's existential enigma.

(3)
Der Spinnerin Nachtlied

Es sang vor langen Jahren
Wohl auch die Nachtigall,

Das war wohl süßer Schall,
Da wir zusammen waren.

Ich sing' und kann nicht weinen,
Und spinne so allein
Den Faden klar und rein
So lang der Mond wird scheinen.

Als wir zusammen waren
Da sang die Nachtigall
Nun mahnet mich ihr Schall
Daß du von mir gefahren.

So oft der Mond mag scheinen,
Denk' ich wohl dein allein,
Mein Herz ist klar und rein,
Gott wolle uns vereinen.

Seit du von mir gefahren,
Singt stets die Nachtigall,
Ich denk' bei ihrem Schall,
Wie wir zusammen waren.

Gott wolle uns vereinen
Hier spinn' ich so allein,
Der Mond scheint klar und rein,
Ich sing' und möchte weinen.

                                                                   (W, 1:131)

The Spinner's Song

(In other time long gone / Here caroled the nightingale. / It told a sweeter
tale / When our two hearts were one. / I sing; I cannot weep; / I turn my
wheel, and there / The strand gleams pure and clear / While moonbeams
vigil keep. /When our two hearts were one, / Of joy sang the nightingale; /
Now all its changeful tale / Is but that thou art gone. / While moons wax
bright or wane / I think of thee, most dear, / My heart's truth pure and clear. /
God yield us joy again! / Since thou from me art gone, / The ceaseless
nightingale sings / And restless memories brings / Of how two hearts made
one. / God yield us joy! No sleep / Is mine; I spin while here / Moonlight
streams pure and clear. / I sing; I fain would weep.)
                                                    (Trans. Wyatt A. Surrey)[45]
    The perspective of dichotomous worlds which once were inti-
mately linked but now are irreconcilably estranged is reflected by the

dualistic structure of the poem as well as by its contrapuntal styles—folksonglike naiveté and conscious artistic craftsmanship.[46] The happy past, a lover's paradise now lost, is recalled in the odd-numbered stanzas and associated with the rhyme scheme built on the *a* vowel (*a/a/a/a*); the hapless present with its anguish (captured by the "ei" rhyme in words such as "weinen" and "allein") is set off against this memory.[47] This remembrance of things past, if allowed to recede into the limbo of forgetfulness, would be painful enough, but, because it is constantly recalled by the singing of the nightingale,[48] it robs the speaker, now a "spinster" in the literal as well as the figurative sense of the term, of any peace of mind in the present and does not augur well for the future. The poem is sung by the mother of Johannes, the wandering student of the *Chronicle*, as she sits alone in the moonlight, spinning on to while away the seemingly infinite, empty hours since the boy's father deserted her.[49] Gone is the calm, measured repose of an Otilie who could evoke and synthesize elements of cosmic mystery with empiric reality, but gone, too, is the fatal allure of a Lore Lay which drew all men, except the one who really counted, into her orbit. A faint glimmer of hope is stirred by the prayerful wish that "God might reunite us," but this appears more the act of quiet desperation by a person caught in a vicious circle than that of an individual moving toward a realistically attainable goal.[50] The only hope for those trapped in such a circularity is to create from this intolerable condition an aesthetic work of art, a compensatory surrogate, albeit deficient, for the paradise forfeited in reality.[51]

(4)

Fabiola

Hor', es klagt die Flöte wieder,
Und die kühlen Brunnen rauschen.

Piast

Golden wehn die Töne nieder,
Stille, stille, laß uns lauschen!

Fabiola

Holdes Bitten, mild Verlangen,
Wie es süß zum Herzen spricht!

Piast

Durch die Nacht, die mich umfangen,
Blickt zu mir der Töne Licht.

(W, 1:144–45)

(Harken how the flute complains, / And the fountains plash and glisten! /
Music drifts in golden rains; / Softly, softly let us listen! / Gentle-pleading,
mild desire / Sweetly tells the heart its plight! / Through the darkness, bright
as fire, / Gleams upon me—music's light.)   (Trans. Herman Salinger)[52]

   In contrast to the progression outlined in the first three poems from
an all-too perfectly synthesized union and unity to the loss of this
paradisal state through either the narcissistic self-destruction of the
Lore Lay's all-too perfect beauty or her—and the spinner's—inability
to establish or maintain a lasting relationship with another individual
(not to mention cosmic ties—"religio" in the sense of a renewed
bond), this poem takes the first step in retracing a path back to the
romantic ideal. Whether one interprets these few lines as a dramatic
stage dialogue between father and adopted daughter or as an independent poem liberated from the shackles of any "real" situation,[53]
one cannot help but perceive here a tentative return to Otilie's world
in which the border lines between external, objective reality and the
reality of internal subjectivity were obliterated, paving the way for a
receptivity of greater potential. Due to the cover of darkness, the
senses independent of the visual are first called into play (auditory,
tactile), only to interplay synesthetically with optical impressions as
the tones flitter down like gold and shine through the night. The
target is a sensual acuity which opens new access routes to a paradise
regained, a state of wholeness in which an aesthetic, unifying force
will overcome life's dichotomies. Or is this, one might wonder, only a
deceptive cadence, beautiful verbal music masking the ugly existential truth of isolation, just as in the play itself, the merry minstrels
with their boisterous tunes use the cover of darkness and timbres of
sweet tones to conceal the wretchedness of their lives?[54]

(5)

Lureley

Singet leise, leise, leise,
Singt ein flüsternd Wiegenlied,
Von dem Monde lernt die Weise,
Der so still am Himmel zieht.

Denn es schlummern in dem Rheine
Jetzt die lieben Kindlein klein,
Ameleya wacht alleine
Weinend in dem Mondenschein.

Singt ein Lied so süß gelinde,
Wie die Quellen auf den Kieseln,
Wie die Bienen um die Linde
Summen, murmeln, flüstern, rieseln.

(W, 1:247–48)

(Softly, softly, softly croon, / Croon a whispered lullaby, / Learn its cadence
from the moon, / Slow in heaven drifting by. . . . / Lisp a little lilting fable: /
Bees about the honeysuckle, / Silver springs upon the gravel / Mumble,
murmur, whisper, trickle.) (Trans. Herman Salinger)[55]

The world of the fairy tales of the Rhine in which this *sotto voce*
lullaby appears was one to which Brentano escaped in order to find
that great unifying design in life which eluded him in the empiric
sphere. The singer in the context of the story is a totally different
figure from the Lore Lay of the *Godwi* ballad, the two having hardly
even the name in common.[56] Lureley is the mother of the hero of the
cycle, Radlauf, and she is closely allied with the element of water (just
as his other female forebears were linked with the remaining three
elements or with the cosmic sphere of the moon). By finding her
sitting by his mill, Radlauf not only completes the cycle of his family
history, but also returns to the prime source of his life.

Lureley's mellifluous songs to her entourage make use of flowing
liquids (many *l* and *r* sounds), and the repetition of words and vowel
clusters lulls the senses of the listener into a state of blissful repose.
Echoes of the family ties to the celestial realm are contained in the
allusion to the moon and its melody (even though the lunar cadence
now seems silent, except for those attuned to the music of the
spheres). The second stanza in the original German has a strictly
narrative function in the fairy tale (even though the constellation
"Weinend in dem Mondenschein" ["weeping in the moonlight"] does
recall the situation of the spinner-spinster) and is invariably omitted
from anthologies (except for the *Werke* cited here which, in many
ways, anticipate the practices of the forthcoming critical edition). To
be sure, the second stanza does disrupt the transition from the first to
the third, both of which seek, ever so gently, to urge and persuade.
The last stanza brings the extraterrestrial reference of the first "down

to earth," so to speak, by comparing the dulcet tones of the lullaby to
sounds all of us can readily perceive. The last verse, simply a string of
four incantatory verbs with rich vowel clusters fading away in di-
minuendo fashion,[57] evokes the state of dreamlike slumber in which
one can indeed experience the "missing" links between the manifold
in which we live and the "secret world" lying beyond and behind the
pale of ordinary experience.

(6)

Gott, dein Himmel faßt mich in den
    Haaren,
Deine Erde zieht mich in die Hölle,
Gott, wie soll ich doch mein Herz
    bewahren,
Daß ich deine Schätze sicherstelle,
Also fleht der Sänger und es fließen
Seine Klagen hin wie Feuerbronnen,
Die mit weiten Meeren ihn umschließen;
Doch inmitten hat er Grund gewonnen,
Und er wächst zum rätselvollen Riesen.
Memnons Bild, des Aufgangs erste
    Sonnen,
Ihre Strahlen dir zur Stirne schießen,
Klänge, die die alte Nacht ersonnen
Tönest du, den jüngsten Tag zu grüßen:
Auserwählt sind wen'ge, doch berufen
Alle, die da hören, an die Stufen. —

                                                (W, 1:309)

(God, Thy heaven grasps me by the hair, / Thy earth drags me into hell; /
God, how shall I but preserve my heart, / That I might secure Thy treasures, / Thus implores the singer and his laments / Stream like fountains of
fire, / Surrounding him with distant seas; / Yet in the midst he's gained a
foothold, / And he grows, an enigmatic giant. / Memnon's statue, morning's
first suns / Shoot their beams at your forehead, / Tones, which midnight
conceived / You play to greet the dawning day: / Chosen are few, yet summoned / To the steps, all who hear. —)[58]

    At the outset, this poem, the second in a cycle called "Echoes of
Beethoven's Music,"[59] articulates in radical imagery a sense of alienation from the transcendental plane (in contrast to Otilie's affiliations
with it) as well as from the human sphere (found on the temporal level
in the spinner's song and on the existential in Lore Lay's demise). The

speaker seems torn from, and tossed between, the antithetical forces of both heaven and earth, so that those treasures which he, as one of the privileged few, guards in the innermost recesses of his being, are threatened with inundation by the very same creative waves of flame which gave rise to them (the dangers posed by the liquid element confirming Lore Lay's decision, but contradicting Lurelcy's lullaby). Yet exactly at the midpoint of the poem, after the first seven lines have recounted the turmoil in the soul of the singer-composer (that is, the creative artist),[60] there comes into view a beacon of hope in the form of solid ground, firm territory on which he, like Memnon's statue, can plant his feet. The reference is to the classical myth of Memnon, the son of Aurora (goddess of dawn) killed at Troy, whose statue, when struck by the first rays of the morning sun (his mother), emits musical tones. Having now recognized and reconciled himself with his mediating function between heaven and earth, the artist is no longer the storm-tossed victim of creative turmoil as at the outset, but rather the victor, a pillar of society with a mission: to greet the dawning day with those very songs conceived amid the agitation of the creative night (the German term *jüngster Tag* has eschatological overtones, since it also means Last Judgment). The religious aura evoked by references to God, heaven, hell, and, by inference, to Doomsday are reinforced in the closing couplet which develops the biblical concept: "many are called, but few are chosen." The chosen one here, the elite artist with a sacred "calling" from either a god or God (the fusion of classical myth and Christian "mythology" gives some of the familiar religious concepts a strange ambience), summons those less fortunate than he to witness the miracle of divinely inspired creation from the steps of the temple, from the threshold of that inner sanctum to which only he and those similarly favored by the deity, have access.

Frühlingsschrei eines Knechtes
au der Tiefe

Meister, ohne dein Erbarmen
Muß im Abgrund ich verzagen,
Willst du nicht mit starken Armen
Wieder mich zum Lichte tragen.

Jährlich greifet deine Güte,
In die Erde, in die Herzen,

Jährlich weckest du die Blüte,
Weckst in mir die alten Schmerzen.

Einmal nur zum Licht geboren,
Aber tausendmal gestorben,
Bin ich ohne dich verloren,
Ohne dich in mir verdorben.

Wenn sich so die Erde reget,
Wenn die Luft so sonnig wehet,
Dann wird auch die Flut beweget,
Die in Todesbanden stehet.

Und in meinem Herzen schauert
Ein betrübter bittrer Bronnen,
Wenn der Frühling draußen lauert,
Kömmt die Angstflut angeronnen.

Weh! durch gift'ge Erdenlagen,
Wie die Zeit sie angeschwemmet,
Habe ich den Schacht geschlagen,
Und er ist nur schwach verdämmet.

Wenn nun rings die Quellen schwellen,
Wenn der Grund gebärend ringet,
Brechen her die gift'gen Wellen,
Die kein Fluch, kein Witz mir zwinget.

Andern ruf' ich, schwimme, schwimme,
Mir kann solcher Ruf nicht taugen,
Denn in mir ja steigt die grimme
Sündflut, bricht aus meinen Augen.

Und dann scheinen bös Gezüchte
Mir die bunten Lämmer alle,
Die ich grüßte, süße Früchte,
Die mir reiften, bittre Galle.

Herr, erbarme du dich meiner,
Daß mein Herz neu blühend werde,
Mein erbarmte sich noch keiner
Von den Frühlingen der Erde.

Meister, wenn dir alle Hände
Nahn mit süßerfüllten Schalen,

Kann ich mit der bittern Spende
Meine Schuld dir nimmer zahlen.

Ach, wie ich auch tiefer wühle,
Wie ich schöpfe, wie ich weine,
Nimmer ich den Schwall erspüle
Zum Kristallgrund fest und reine.

Immer stürzen mir die Wände,
Jede Schicht hat mich belogen,
Und die arbeitblut'gen Hände
Brennen in den bittern Wogen.

Weh! der Raum wird immer enger,
Wilder, wüster stets die Wogen,
Herr, O Herr! ich treib's nicht länger,
Schlage deinen Regenbogen.

Herr, ich mahne dich, verschone,
Herr! ich hört' in jungen Tagen,
Wunderbare Rettung wohne
Ach, in deinem Blute, sagen.

Und so muß ich zu dir schreien,
Schreien aus der bittern Tiefe,
Könntest du auch nicht verzeihen,
Daß dein Knecht so kuhnlich riefe!

Daß des Lichtes Quelle wieder
Rein und heilig in mir flute,
Träufle einen Tropfen nieder,
Jesus, mir, von deinem Blute!

                                                    (W, 1:329–32)

(Master, may thy mercy hold me, / Else I bide in depths despairing, / Will
thy strong arms not enfold me / Once more into sunlight bearing. / Every
year thy loving bounty / Brings men's hearts and earth good morrow, / Every
year the flowers thou wakest, / Wak'st in me the ancient sorrow. / Born for
light alone intended, / I a thousand times must perish, / Lacking thee my way
has ended, / Lost unless thy goodness cherish. / When soft sun-filled airs
are wafting / And earth stirs in warm pulsation, / Then stir too those other
waters / Bound with death and tribulation. / And within my heart there
shower / Bitter founts, beclouded growing; / When without the springtime
hovers, / Comes the fear-flood to fresh flowing. / Woe! Through poison's
earthy layers, / As in time they've ever mounted, / The deep gorge I have

constructed / And but feeble 'tis accounted! / When the soil to birth is bringing, / When all round the springs are swelling, / Hither come the bitter breakers / Though no wit, no curse compelling. / "Swim, O swim," I call to others, / Though to me this call is fruitless, / For in me there mounts the Deluge / Fills my eyes, enraged and ruthless. / Evil breeds then come before me, / Seem as lambs in motley glitter, / Which I greeted, fruits of sweetness, / But which ripened, gall-like bitter. / Lord, bestow on me thy mercy, / And my heart-life newly fashion! / For of all the earthly springtimes / None has ever shown compassion. / Master, when they all draw near thee, / In their hands the sweet-filled vessels, / Ne'er with bitter gifts down-laden / Can my debt to thee be settled. / Ah, however deep I burrow, /   Scoop the waters, tears o'erflowing, / Never can I cleanse the torrent / Till pure crystal ground is showing! / Ever do the walls assail me, / Lies in every layer merging, / And my hands with labor bleeding / Burn within the bitter surging. / Woe! the space forever narrows, / Waves grow wilder still and rougher, / Lord, O Lord! my heart doth fail me— / Send thy rainbow with its succor. / Lord, I beg of thee to spare me! / In my youth, Lord, they were telling / That a wonderful salvation / In thy blood is ever dwelling. / And so cry I, thee beseeching / From bitter depths with clamoring fervent, / Even if thou ne'er couldst pardon / Such bold pleadings from thy servant. / That the source of light returneth / Pure and healing to restore me, / Jesus, let but one drop reach me / Of thy blood, I do implore thee!) (Trans. Mabel Cotterell)[61] ·

Hubris incurs nemesis, and the self-assured, almost arrogantly confident proclamation of artistic hegemony at the end of the Beethoven poem pales before the abject humility with which the servant now cries out from the depths to his distant master. This situation is certainly a "far cry"[62] from Otilie's injunction to the secret world to "Speak from the distance," and it is apparent that the rhythmic alteration in Brentano's life-cycle is headed for the downslope. The parallelism (and implied correlation) between the creative artist and the *creator spiritus* in the universe has reverted to a master-servant (virtually a master-slave) configuration. The servant-slave finds himself endangered, no longer able to bear that light which, in the case of the artist in the previous poem, was a source of aesthetic inspiration. But what are the dangers facing him? Rather than the internalized "fountains of fire" and the "flaming seas," it is, quite unexpectedly, the external thaw of springtime which threatens him. Instead of bringing the traditional rebirth and celebration to the season of the soul, springtime "lurks" ominously out there, unleashing torrents of fear against which the miner in his ill-equipped shaft would be powerless should the waters rise to flood stage.

The concept of the biblical Deluge is evoked (at which point the verse also overflows its limits and pours into the following line—

enjambement) just as the Beethoven poem made direct and oblique reference to religious topoi—but there the allusions seemed less deliberate.[63] Terms such as lambs, bitter gall, and the Deluge, have a frame of reference unmistakably biblical and Christian. Unlike the singer-poet of the Beethoven poems who discovered a firm "foothold" amid the inundation, this servant despairs of ever locating his "crystal [pure] ground." The droning repetition of the adjective "bitter," the image of singeing waves and of bloody hands, together with the use of alliterating consonant clusters at peak moments of anxiety ("Weh! der Raum *w*ird immer enger, Wilder, *w*üster stets die Wogen") almost engulf this despondent Noah for whom no Ark of the Covenant beckons, until the appearance of the one symbol which traditionally has marked God's reconciling grace toward man: a rainbow. Even here, however, Brentano is consistent in the ambivalence of his imagery, since the rainbow is, like the life-threatening spring flood, a product of water: rain drops reflecting and refracting the light. In contrast to the secure, earthbound solidity of Memnon's column from classical mythology, the Christian signs for salvation are much more intangible, fragile, and fleeting. They imply hope through faith, rather than confidence through knowledge. The indifferent Catholic apostate of 1800 daringly evoked a secret world beyond the real; the poet of 1816, groping ever closer to the church of his forefathers, is much less audacious. To the end he remains the servant crying out from the still bitter depths of his soul, pleading for the flow of divine light and for a few drops of Christ's redeeming blood, rather than for the eternal floods of springtime which had been so devastating because their intensity was matched by the uncontrollable flow of passion's blood in his own veins.

(8)

Schweig Herz! Kein Schrei!

Schweig Herz! kein Schrei!
Denn Alles geht vorbei!
Doch daß ich auferstand
Und wie ein Irrstern ewig sie
    umrunde,
Ein Geist, den sie gabannt,
Das hat Bestand!

Ja Alles geht vorbei,
Nur dieses Wunderband,

Aus meines Wesens tiefstem Grunde,
Zu ihrem Geist gespannt,
Das hat Bestand!

Ja Alles geht vorbei,
Doch ihrer Güte Pfand,
Jed' Wort aus ihrem lieben
    frommen Munde,
Folgt mir in's andre Land
Und hat Bestand!

Ja Alles geht vorbei!
Doch sie, die mich erkannt,
Den Harrenden, wildfremd an Ort
    und Stunde,
Ging nicht vorbei, sie stand,
Reicht mir die Hand!

Ja Alles geht vorbei!
Nur Eines ist kein Tand.
Die Pflicht, die mir aus seines Herzens Grunde
Das linde Kind gesandt,
Die hat Bestand!

Ja Alles geht vorbei!
Doch diese liebe Hand,
Die ich in tiefer, freudenheller
    Stunde
An meinem Herzen fand,
Die hat Bestand!

Ja Alles geht vorbei,
Nur dieser heiße Brand
In meiner Brust, die bittre süße
    Wunde
Die linde Hand verband,
Die hat Bestand![64]

(Peace, heart! no cry! / For everything goes by! / Yet that I rose again / And as
her planet e'er must circle round, / A spirit, whom she charmed, / That goes
not by! / Yes, everything goes by! / Only this wonder-band / From out my
being's deepest ground / To her own spirit spanned, / That goes not by! / Yes,
everything goes by! / Yet pledge from gracious hands, / Each innocent dear
word of hers / Follow to other lands / And go not by! / Yes, everything goes

by! / Yet she, who understood / The waiting one, with place and / hour unfound, / She went not by, she stood, / Gives me her hand! / Yes, everything goes by! / One thing alone is sure, / The promise which from out her heart's deep ground / The precious child did send, / That doth endure! / Yes, everything goes by! / Yet this beloved hand / Which I in deepest joy-illumined hour / Upon my heart did find, / That goes not by / Yes, everything goes by! / Only this fiery brand / Within my breast, the sweet and bitter wound / Bound there by gentle hand— / That goes not by!)

(Trans. Mabel Cotterell)[65]

This poem, written approximately one month before Brentano's official return to the church, is found in a letter to Luise Hensel which illustrates his practice of "re-stylizing love into religion,"[66] an existential trait which has its literary correlative in the contrafact.[67] Throughout this letter, Brentano wavers in his approach to Luise between tentative renunciation and active aggression. He vows never to harm her "inner or outer purity," and yet when he envisions her in the arms of a rival he can only assuage his heart by singing a "song of praise to the end of all things."[68] The same letter contains a second, more famous poem (labeled the "Cradlesong of a Lamenting Heart" by the editors of the *Collected Works*) which opens each of its six stanzas imploring: "O just be silent, heart!"[69] The companion poem "Peace, Heart! No cry!" has been accorded very little critical attention, perhaps because it stands in the shadow of its better known neighbor, and suffers by comparison.[70] Yet it has a unique profile all its own.

The poem is, in essence, a "statement of condition," as are many of Brentano's later lyrics, and it laments an unhappy plight in a set of highly artistic variations. The key here lies in the bittersweet ambivalence stemming from the ambiguous nature of the phrases: "Everything goes by" and "That endures" (or, as our translation reads: "That goes not by"). At first glance, something of duration, of lasting value would seem to be a positive attribute, especially in the case of Brentano who constantly sought refuge from the vicissitudes of life,[71] its unpredictable ebb and flow, and whose most characteristic style of living and writing have been described as *hingerissen* and *hinrei-ßend* ("overpowered" and "overpowering") respectively.[72] In this poem, too, the speaker equates his existence with a "shooting star" or comet (*Irrstern*), while referring to himself as an "utter stranger" (*wildfremd*), but one who had been offered a friendly hand by the unnamed woman. This offer of a helping hand, a gesture which seems to come directly from the heart, buoys his spirits and promises lasting affection as it "touches" his own heart. But it is at this point of intersection that the positive values we have been led to assign to the two concepts "Everything goes by" and "That goes not by" are suddenly reversed. The concluding stanza (not worthy of Heine's often jolting *pointes*) informs us that the hand of the gentle child which touched his heart also ignited a flame there, a wound which, although bandaged by that same kind hand, "goes not by." What does endure, what has permanence is the pain of rejection, the most cutting wound of all because no dressing can heal the spiritual damage it inflicts.

(9)

Was reif in diesen Zeilen steht,
Was lächelnd winkt und sinnend fleht,
Das soll kein Kind betrüben,
Die Einfalt hat es ausgesäet,
Die Schwermut hat hindurchgeweht,
Die Sehnsucht hat's getrieben;
Und ist das Feld einst abgemäht,
Die Armut durch die Stoppeln geht,
Sucht Ähren, die geblieben,
Sucht Lieb', die für sie untergeht,
Sucht Lieb', die mit ihr aufersteht,
Sucht Lieb', die sie kann lieben,
Und hat sie einsam und verschmäht
Die Nacht durch dankend in Gebet
Die Körner ausgerieben,
Liest sie, als früh der Hahn gekräht,
Was Lieb' erhielt, was Leid verweht,
Ans Feldkreuz angeschrieben,
O Stern und Blume, Geist und Kleid,
Lieb', Leid und Zeit und Ewigkeit!

(W, 1:619)

(What in these lines doth ripened stand, / Beckons with smiles, and thoughtful pleads, / Shall touch no child to grieve it. / Simplicity hath sown the seeds, / Sadness passed through it with its breath, / And longing has achieved it. / And is the harvest once cut down, / Poverty gleans the stubble, / Seeks ears that have been left unseen, / Seeks love that for her long went down, / Seeks love with her to rise again, / Seeks love that it may love her. / And has she, lonely and disdained, / Throughout the night with prayer and thanks / Rubbed the corn from its casing— / She reads, at cockcrow's break of day, / Words that hold love, blow grief away, / Upon the field cross written: / 'O star and blossom, spirit and garb, / Love, sorrow, time, eternity!'") (Trans. Mabel Cotterell)[73]

These twenty lines comprise what might be termed Brentano's version of "wisdom's final say" (der Weisheit letzter Schluß from Faust). The word "ripened" denotes a maturity which can look back at the sum and substance of life with both a serene smile and a pensive frown. The poet enumerates a number of concepts which form recurrent concerns of romantics in general: childlike simplicity,[74] a nagging melancholy due to unaccomplished aesthetic goals and unrequited affection,[75] the yearning for Paradise Lost (a realm which Brentano had circumscribed with such magic sounding names as Vaduz, Thule, and Alhambra) and the sadness which results when he realizes that neither art nor love, the two binding forces in life, are capable of restoring or regaining that Paradise. Sensing the imminent approach of death, the poet invokes his unique version of the grim reaper concept—a field on which the grain has been harvested, leaving for the impoverished only seed-kernels and a few random ears of corn. And since poverty is a lack of something, the absence or dearth of what others possess, it is only proper that the "poor in spirit" search there for the most meaningful form of love: self-sacrifice, the promise of resurrection, and reciprocal affection (the implied ties to Christ recall the conclusion of "Frühlingsschrei" where the reference was more obvious). But even for the poor in spirit, access to the kingdom of heaven is possible only by sheer dint of effort: prayer, hard work in a life of loneliness and rejection are the conditions, but the reward is ample. Traversing perhaps the same field laid low by the scythe of the reaper, the poor in spirit come upon the ultimate truth engraved on a cross. In order to underscore the importance of this cryptic but succinctly articulated couplet, the poet sets it apart from the preceding eighteen lines (which consist of six groups of three verses each rhyming $a/a/b$) with the rhyme scheme c/c.[76] A kind of stopping point is reached, an opportunity to rest, in contrast to the remainder of the poem which, especially at its core when love was involved, threatened to run away with the speaker (*hinreißen*).

The significance of this final couplet, which Brentano made the motto of his later life, has been hotly debated by literary critics for over a century.[77] Within the present context, however, an interpretation is possible which can be related back to Brentano's definition of romanticism. Otilie, it will be recalled, achieved a kind of mystical union with a realm beyond the empiric in her own quietly confident fashion. Subsequent poems, however, traced the breakdown of man's intimate relationships, his temporary but tenuous attempts through artistic creativity or secular religiosity to reestablish a center which could "hold," only to see himself thwarted and thrown back upon his own devices, so that Brentano in 1817 could merely plead for consolation from either the Lord or Luise. This final poem, however, taken out of the context of the fairy-tale world, no longer has the hubris of the Beethoven group or the humbleness of the servant's spring cry, but rather a humility characteristic of one who has come full circle in life, who can perceive from a new vantage point the interpenetration of divine transcendence ("star") and mundane transience ("blossom"), of essence ("spirit") and appearance ("garb"), of happiness ("love") and heartbreak ("sorrow"), of "temporality ("time") and timelessness ("eternity"). Much has been made of the concepts enumerated here, but one should perhaps also look more closely at the innocuous paratactic "and" linking all of these pairs, except the one ("Lieb, Leid") which Brentano felt most keenly and which affected him most often.

The virtual "eternal recurrence" of these cryptic verses throughout the late works of the poet may not so much convey the impression that he was expressing firm conviction as it does the suspicion that only by such incantatory, liturgicallike repetition could he ever succeed in convincing himself of their validity. Even though we see through a glass, darkly, we still see; the romantic perspective remains intact, the individual serves as the medium of perception, only we must also be ready to accept the mediation of the medium. Amey's initial reaction to these verses is noteworthy in this frame of reference: "I understood them through and through, and could still not explain them. I understood their essence, and had no other words for them, but themselves" (W, 3:857). Such is the sense and essence of all great poetry, and it is also the hallmark of the great poet.

CHAPTER 3

The Prose Stylist

E VEN though Brentano's reputation today rests primarily on his accomplishments as a lyric poet, there is no doubt that he also contributed significantly to the development of German prose during the nineteenth century. This chapter will examine his major and most lasting contributions to several fictional genres—the novel, novella, and the fairy tale. There is a tantalizing paradox which surfaces in conjunction with Brentano's fictional works as opposed to his forays into the area of religiously edifying literature (a mode which came into vogue during the second quarter of the preceding century). Those works which have aroused the greatest controversy or have been closely scrutinized by critics of literature (the novel *Godwi*, the fairy tales, and short prose *the Chronicle of the Traveling Student* and *The Story of Honest Casper and Fair Annie*) for a century and half are not the writings which have had the greatest impact on the Western world. That place must be assigned to his version of the Emmerick papers,[1] which have always enjoyed a vast reading public of a cosmopolitan, but basically nonliterary stamp. In recent years, however, they have kindled heated debates among clerical and literary scholars alike.[2]

I *The Novelist: Godwi*

An analysis of the full itle of Brentano's only completed novel— *Godwi or The Stone Statue of the Mother: A Novel Run Wild, by Maria* (1801)—yields some interesting preliminary data which is important for an interpretation of the work as a whole. First of all, the name "Godwi" may be, as has been suggested, a corrupt form of the English patronym "Goodwin" or, as Brentano himself indicated to a friend at a much later date in his life: "This wild novel is called Godwi so that the reader may immediately say to himself, 'God, how stupid!' "[3] (the pun in German derives from the similarity in sound when pronouncing the protagonist's name and the phrase "Gott wie"). Symptomatic of the aging writer in this comment is the tendency to deprecate the works of his youth: but even more significant is the fact that plays on words—a practice which the poet indulged in throughout his lifetime and for a variety of reasons, most of which transcend mere verbal virtuosity—form an integral feature of the novel itself. Frequently whole pages or extensive tangential sections seem to have been inserted merely for the sake of such linguistic fireworks.[4]

The second element in the title, the stone statue (or image), is a recurrent topos in romantic writing, from the inception of the movement around 1797 to its waning years in the late 1820s. Essentially, the statue signifies a life grown rigid and cold, an existence from which all the warmth and life's blood have been removed—by death or spiritual petrifaction. That the stone image here is of "the" mother is noteworthy with regard to the book both extrinsically and intrinsically, since Brentano's own mother, the beautiful Maximiliane, exerted even in death a powerful influence on the poet. In the novel itself, every family household portrayed is either motherless or bereft of maternal influence (and, as a corollary to this, the vast majority of father figures in the work are seen in a negative light). The somewhat derogatory appendage "a novel run wild" (or "out of control") seems to imply little adherence—or even a deliberate affront—to the canons of form and structure established for the genre by that work which ostensibly served as the model for most romantic novels to emulate: Goethe's *Wilhelm Meister's Apprenticeship*. Although *Godwi* bears certain superficial resemblances to Goethe's novel, it nevertheless employs techniques and embodies thought processes of a generation which both admired the patriarch of German letters and consciously sought to transcend the acknowledged limitations of his artistry. But Brentano also recognized the aesthetic shortcomings of his own offspring and spoke of it as a "sickly, crippled child" which is generally misunderstood and greatly disdained, but yet fills its creator with paternal pride.[5] Finally, if the authorial designation "Maria" is intended to be a concealing pseudonym, it certainly is transparent. Brentano had not only inaugurated his literary career in the romantic circles of Jena in 1800 with a satiric-parodistic piece (*Gustav Wasa*) under the pen-name "Maria," but also Clemens *Maria* Wenzeslaus Brentano had by 1801 become a force to be reckoned with both in the camp of the romantic contingent as well as in the ranks of the antiromantic faction.

A. *Content of* Godwi

Volume 1 of this two-volume work is in the form of an epistolary novel consisting of twenty-eight undated letters which construct a complex and closely interwoven network of secret affiliations and relationships among the various correspondents and recipients. Godwi, the son of a wealthy English Merchant of the same name (the latter will henceforth be designated Godwi[f]; his son, the hero of the novel, will be referred to as Godwi[s]), writes to his somewhat sober and staid friend, Karl Römer, currently in charge of the business firm of Godwi[f], telling of his encounters with three contrasting women: the mature and passionate Molly (who is later revealed to be Lady Hodefield of England), the naive and sentimental Joduno von Eichenwehen, and the pristine child of nature Otilie Senne.

At the outset of his aimless wanderings, Godwi[s] arrived at the city of B., where he made Molly's acquaintance. Once this torrid romance had run its course, however, Godwi[s] left the lady's villa and moved on to the castle of the country squire of Eichenwehen, whose daughter, the ingenuous Joduno, proved attractive to him as a spiritual contrast to the worldly Molly. Joduno, in turn, corresponds with the aging hermit and harpist, Werdo Senne, and in the latter's daughter, Otilie, she has a true confidante. With Werdo and Otilie lives a mysterious young lad, Eusebio, entrusted to them years before for his upbringing by Lady Hodefield (Molly). Eusebio is actually the son of Francesco Firmenti, an Italian painter, now residing with Godwi[f]. Firmenti had fallen in love with his foster sister, Cecilia, had abducted her from a cloister just before she was to take vows, and married her. However, pangs of conscience and the death of Cecilia drove Francesco temporarily insane, and following his release from a mental institution, he came to Germany and to the employ of Godwi[f], who commissioned him to paint scenes and persons from his (Godwi[f]'s) life. During Francesco's confinement, Molly had gained custody of his infant son and subsequently brought the child to Werdo.

Upon Joduno's urging, Godwi[s] pays a visit to the recluse Werdo Senne at the dilapidated castle ruins of Reinhardstein, and Godwi[s] finds Otilie so charming and captivating, that he decides to remain here for some time. It seems that this simple, natural, and unaffected creature is able to restore peace to his restless soul and thus satisfy— even if only temporarily—his vague and undirected yearnings.

Meanwhile, Karl Römer, having set out on a business venture on behalf of Godwi[f], comes into contact with Molly in B. However, when the latter learns his identity, she abruptly and unceremoniously puts an end to their relationship. It is subsequently revealed in her letter to Werdo (with whom she, as Lady Hodefield, kept in close contact), that Römer is actually her son. To make matters even more complicated, Römer's father is none other than Godwi[f], with whom Molly–Lady Hodefield had had an affair many years ago. Thus Godwi[s] and Römer prove to be half brothers. None of this information is revealed in straightforward narrative or even in the letters which constitute volume 1 of the novel; rather it must be fitted together like the pieces of a jigsaw puzzle scattered willy-nilly before the reader.

Volume 2 introduces the figure of Maria, the fictitious editor of the letters which comprise Volume 1. It seems that Römer was supposed to introduce Maria into the business world, but gave him instead the task of arranging and editing Godwi[s]'s correspondence when he realized that Maria was unsuited for any commercial enterprise. As a reward for the successful execution of this task, Maria was promised the hand of Römer's daughter. Since, however, he fails to perform this literary assignment to Römer's satisfaction, Maria is denied his prize and, consequently, sets out for Godwi[s]'s country estate in order to gather firsthand information and impressions of the hero whose biography he had, up to now, so badly bungled. Living with the protagonist is an old acquaintance of Maria's, the writer-translator Haber, as well as a mischievous and mysterious singer-dancer-actress named Flametta. Godwi[s], who from the outset proves to be more mature and placid than the impetuous youth of volume 1, unravels some of the perplexing entanglements which arose due to the veiled allusions and resultant illusions of the epistolary section.

In a rather bizarre fashion and in a manner calculated to destroy the fictional underpinnings of the narrative in the reader's mind, Godwi[s] comments on several pictorial representations of some major and minor figures in his life as well as in that of his father. These art works had been commissioned by Godwi[f] from Francesco Firmenti. We learn, too, that Godwi[f] had enjoyed a rambunctious youth but, over the years, grew to be a skeptic and a cynical seducer—Lady Hodefield (Molly) numbering among his conquests. He deserted her for further amorous adventures in Germany, not knowing that she was pregnant at the time (the son she bore him is Römer).

Finding a warm reception at the home of the merchant Wellner, Godwi[f] fell in love with the latter's daughter, Marie. In order to win this girl for himself, Godwi^f confiscated the letters from her fiancé, Joseph, who at the time was on a trip around the world. Godwi^f even went so far as to forge a death certificate for Joseph, and with this document he succeeded in deceiving Marie. Since her father had just encountered heavy financial losses, he was anxious to have the well-to-do Godwi^f as a son-in-law, and thus the marriage was arranged. But the unexpected return of Joseph from America destroyed this brief happiness built on deception. At the sight of her erstwhile fiancé standing on the bridge of a ship, Marie dashed from the shore into the waves to greet him. Even though Marie drowned, her infant son, Godwi^s, was saved. These events so unhinged Joseph's mind that he withdrew from society and lived the life of a recluse under the name of Werdo Senne.

At Werdo–Joseph's castle Francesco Firmenti finds his son, Eusebio, with whom he had lost contact after his mental breakdown. A picture of Molly at the home of the Godwis led him to this discovery, since he recognized her as the woman who had taken custody of the child following the death of his wife. Through Francesco, Molly is reunited with Godwi^f and the latter, in the course of time, becomes reconciled with his former rival Joseph–Werdo. Finally Francesco takes Otilie as his wife.

Volume 2 also relates the fate of several other incidental figures— Francesco's brother Antonio and the latter's bitter conflict with their father; Marie's sister Annonciata whose unhappy love affairs and tragic death are not only allegorized in the paintings in the gallery of Godwi^f, but also transcribed in verse and then narrated in prose. We are informed at a disarmingly rapid rate that she subsequently lived an incognito life at the country estate of the Godwis under the name of Kordelia.

There still remain several loose ends of Godwi^s's life to be tied together, but since Maria, due to the rigors to which he had subjected himself, grows ill, Godwi^s must take over the narration of his own life. He tells in minute detail of his amorous encounter while on a Rhine journey with a certain Countess G., an uninhibited, if not wanton, woman, who did not stop short of compelling one of her own daughters, Violette, to peddle herself as a prostitute. The countess, whose provocative motto in life is that "whoever is born for lust and does not indulge in it leads a life of vice," also fell in love with Godwi^s, but he soon tired of her and wandered off to Italy.

Upon his return, Godwi^s discovers that French revolutionary troops have ravaged the Rhine castle, that the countess has died, and that Violette, caught between her inherently pure nature and the unrestricted eroticism to which she had been subjected, still lingers there in a state of despair and confusion. Realizing now that she had competed for his love with her mother, and shocked by her sorry plight, Godwi⁵ has Violette and her half sister, Flametta, taken to his country estate where they remain until death claims the former. Violette's tragic downfall, however, has a kind of purifying effect on Godwi⁵, and in her memory he has a monument erected portraying in allegorical-symbolic form (as both a series of bas-reliefs and as a statue crowning the hexahedron) her life, death, and transfiguration. This monument dealing with the fate of a "respectable prostitute" stands not only in proximity to, but also in correlation with, the statue of Marie holding the infant Godwi⁵, an artifact which had played a seminal role throughout volume 1 of the novel, as indicated by the fact that it gave the subtitle to the work.

There follows a brief epilogue in which Godwi⁵, the protagonist of the book, recounts the final days of the author-editor, Maria, whose illness—culminating in a paralysis of the tongue—grows progressively worse until he eventually succumbs to this mysterious malady. A number of poetic tributes parodying the styles of prominent contemporary authors (Tieck, Schiller, Forster, etc.) provides the final accolade for the now departed Maria. The closing poem in this cycle, "To Clemens Brentano," implores this young writer to take over where Maria left off, to descend Orpheus-like into the depths of the spirit and rescue the poetry of life from the prosaic death which threatens it in contemporary society.

B. *Critical Reception of* Godwi

Ever since the appearance of Alfred Kerr's pioneering study of *Godwi* in 1898,[6] this novel has stood in the limelight of literary criticism, much of the interest perhaps being fostered by the fact that it had been deleted from the 1852 edition of Brentano's *Collected Works* due to the stress on the sensual side of man's nature as well as to the expurgating tactics of the editors (two of whom were members of the author's family).[7] This early investigation emphasized primarily questions of influence: the autobiographical roots and real-life prototypes of the character constellations were traced, Brentano's predecessors and contemporaries in the novel were examined for their use of similar themes and techniques, and lastly *Godwi's* progeny or elective affinities in later nineteenth-century German prose were pinpointed.

Not only is the novice author show to be indebted to contemporary German writers such as Heinse, Goethe, Tieck, and Friedrich Schlegel, but also to a vast panoply of European novelists ranging from Cervantes to Sterne.[8] On the other hand, the novel's often startling pronouncements on sex and the emancipation of the flesh, together with the kind of existential ennui which plagues the hero, are regarded as anticipatory of the thematic substance of later trends, from Young Germany down to literary movements at the turn of the twentieth century. A figure such as the countess, for instance, might be said to embody certain strands mentioned above: to a considerable extent she is modeled on Madame de Gachet, a French emigrée who hovered on the periphery of Brentano's early life yet made a deep impression on him; to some degree she resembles the courtesan Lisette from Friedrich Schlegel's *Lucinde*, while in her opposition to moral sanctions and social mores, she anticipates the attitudes of a figure such as the grisette Marion in Büchner's drama *The Death of Danton* (1835). Danton's existential malaise and his boredom with the routine of living could also be said to recall traits in both Godwis.

A major impetus for a more modern approach to Brentano in general and to *Godwi* in particular was supplied by Paul Böckmann in 1935.[9] In keeping with his thesis that Brentano inherited from Friedrich Schlegel a strong awareness of the sanctity of self, or self-confidence and self-assurance in spite of clashes with prevailing opinions and social tabus, Böckmann postulated that the central concern of the protagonist is "the apprehension of his selfhood" amid the panoply of life's manifold and often conflicting forces. The reader is confronted with a single event or experience via several diverse modes of perspective and perception, each of which can magnify, diminish, or even distort the incident presented, but of necessity contributes a unique refraction or heightened degree of awareness to its overall portrayal. Böckmann touches upon a host of such "conditions of refraction" and illustrates how a change in perspective can radically alter the attitude of the reader. For example, events recorded in emotionally charged letters in part 1 are reported in part 2 in a dry, matter-of-fact tone or, in the case of Annonciata-Kordelia, as a footnote reference. The life story of Violette is depicted in a variety of media—the prose description of her statue together with its allegorical reliefs is followed by a series of sonnets and a concluding canzone which represent poetically the same sequence of events, and finally Violette relates in first-person narrative her own fate.

Böckmann insists, however, that no single mode of "refraction" is absolute in itself, but rather relative to all the others, with the result that we are constantly in the process of apprehending the essence of an incident, an object, or a situation. We know these only as the focal point or point of intersection of a number of avenues of access, each of which imparts a certain coloration to what it presents, in accordance with the nature of its medium or the mental set of the reporting agent. In a sense, the readers beome members of a jury which must hear a number of conflicting or complementary testimonies concerning a particular incident which took place, and then must decide where the ultimate truth of the situation lies. The series of "rotating perspectives" or poly-perspectivism in *Godwi* brings us closer to the essence of things, but no single viewpoint by itself should be considered definitive, but rather in correlation with all others.

Godwi criticism subsequent to Böckmann has refined or elaborated upon his basic premises, but no one has succeeded as yet in refuting them.[10] Whereas two major studies of the work in larger contexts (within the panorama of German romanticism or the Age of Goethe) regard it as either derivative, as a compositum of all the ingredients of the early romantic novel—but in decline—or as the attempt of an inexperienced writer to put into practice Friedrich Schlegel's famous yet potentially dangerous postulate that the arbitrariness of the poet tolerates no law above itself,[11] other specialized analyses view it in a more sympathetic light. Franz Norbert Mennemeier, for instance, finds *Godwi* a book "without a tendency," that is, without the teleological target of the classical novel. In fact, the marked "anticlassical composition" of the work signals a kind of parody of the German novel of development.[12] Time is no longer an unbroken and meaningful continuum, but rather a succession of fleeting and disjointed moments; the device of debunking is applied to even those elements in the work which have a certain mythical quality about them (the figure of the ethereal nature-child Otilie, the ill-fated Kordelia, or a mysterious nocturnal visitor in part 1 who seems to personify the maternal instinct in its purest form but is later unmasked as Molly Hodefield, a woman whose maternal qualities are certainly not exemplary), and they are unceremoniously demythologized, if not demolished. Mennemeier's persuasive conclusion, however, is that the overriding of these techniques and theories aim is to reinforce Schlegel's principle of "becoming" over "being," to convey through many mediated visions and textual "translations," processes of life which are not directly transmissible through either one-dimensional intellectual or purely emotional means. Claude David carries the "anticlassical" hypothesis a step further by regarding the work as an "anti-novel," the aim of which is to annul at one moment the mood which a previous page or passage has evoked.[13] Just as part 2 annuls part 1, so, too, do elements of jocularity level out emotional intensity, and irony and humor deflate serious issues previously raised.

A number of critics refuse to be misled by Brentano's puzzling label "a novel run wild," and they have uncovered hidden principles of cohesion. Benno von Wiese, for instance, contends that the qualification "run wild" or "out of hand" is to be interpreted as self-irony; since the aim of the book is not simply accommodation to the world but rather to portray the author's personality in its manifold and complex manifestations in interaction with the world, the result must, of necessity, be what appears to be a fragmented or splintered configuration.[14] Maria embodies Brentano's self-destructive tendencies, and figures such as Godwi^f and Godwi^s incorporate his traits of cynicism and wanderlust. Since Godwi^s experiences the objective sphere only as a projection of the self, to the exclusion of the social milieu as an extrapersonal dimension, the author presents a number of viable alternatives in the attempt to live life as a totality without any pragmatic purpose: the hedonistic pursuit of the pleasure principle, the quest to find in art and literature an unbroken whole to combat the fragmentation in other spheres, communion with a still uncorrupted realm of nature, the longing for love as a complete, unequivocal commitment—all of which, however, are frustrated and end in failure.

Gerhard Storz rightly disclaims the work as either a *roman à clef*[15] or a loosely thrown together conglomeration of disjointed parts. He devises a neatly worked-out system of coordinates and correspondences for the major and minor figures as well as for the overall structure of the book. The concealing strategies of volume 1 are counterbalanced by the revealing devices of volume 2; mirror-image reflection can be found in the two pieces of statuary—the mother figure Marie at the outset and the unfortunate prostitute Violette at the close. Each individual change of perspective is to be considered a temporary corrective to the previous view, the upshot being an awareness of the inadequacy or tenuous nature of all fixed formulations when judged by the incommensurable fullness of the phenomenon itself or by the standard of an appropriate literary rendition of some envisioned ideal.

Two short studies concentrate on the opening and the closing paragraphs of the novel respectively. The first discovers a number of contradictory or dualistic principles of both content and style in the opening pages of the book and demonstrates that this technique of complementary contradiction permeates the entire work;[16] the second interpretation proceeds from the opposite end of the fictional spectrum, so to speak, and looks at the conclusion of *Godwi* to see whether or not it achieves the aim articulated by early romantics, such as Novalis, of creating a synthesis, a reunification of disparate realms, of aestheticizing reality—the answer being in the negative.[17] Instead of achieving the romantic synthesis, the work embodies the disintegration of the romantic ideal. What appeared to be spontaneous expressions of emotion in part 1 are unmasked as highly stylized, artificially constructed stage props, movable scenery (*Versatzstücke*) which the author, like the scenic designer in the theater, merely assembles and reassembles for maximum effect. The apparently natural landscapes in the environs of Otilie are replaced by an artificial nature in the decor of Godwi's hunting lodge. By consistently employing such "massive destruction of the poetic construction" the novel constantly looks over its own shoulder, so to speak, and documents its own devices—a technique known as romantic irony and a phenomenon which has been examined exhaustively in secondary literature.[18] The death of Maria at the close of the work is the final proof of the demise of the romantic synthesis; the novel has merely affirmed the failure of the envisioned ideal and the inevitability of that failure.

A group of interpretations has concentrated on the manner in which the other artistic media—painting, sculpture, music, and related literary genres (lyric poetry, dramatic dialogue, and even operatic elements)—are incorporated into the framework of prose fiction. The most comprehensive of these treats the novel as a total work of art (in the sense of Wagner's *Gesamtkunstwerk*), as an attempt at an "aesthetic synthesis—to combine the arts for maximum appeal to the senses," with the result that a reciprocal illumination of the various media occurs (a poetic account of a painting, for instance, transforms the spatially coexistent into the temporally sequential).[19] Viewed in this manner, *Godwi* can be acquitted of the charge of "formlessness" usually leveled against it, since much of what was considered external trappings or concessions to contemporary fads is shown to be integral and functional to the overall conception of a work which should not be measured by the canons of the classical novel.

Two arts touched upon in the previous analysis—music and the pictorial media—have subsequently been investigated in greater depth and detail in specialized studies. In the first of these, music and musical imagery are examined in relationship to what is commonly acknowledged to be a prime concern of Godwi's life: love and the realm of the erotic. [20] This dual premise is later expanded to form the triadic constellation of music, love, and death in interrelationship throughout the novel within the larger context of the Orpheus myth, while the novel as a whole becomes the focal point for an examination of a phenomenon labeled the "synesthetic," a conscious reunification of love and art under the aegis of music, as both thematic substance and structural technique of the narrative. [21] The second study turns our attention to the two statues and the paintings in the gallery of Godwi's father as life situations raised to a higher power through art, in order to show how the romantic allegory liberates itself from the limitations of the traditional mode of that genre. [22] Brentano's allegorical presentation not only overcomes the tendency to present a plethora of disparate emblematic attributes in favor of a restricted number of emblems in an organic, dynamically interconnected relationship, but also abandons the static in favor of a form of metamorphosis. This dynamism links the romantic allegory more closely with the symbol and the symbolic (which, as Brentano himself had indicated, should be "a metamorphosis, taking place before our eyes, of matter into an image of its meaning"). A detailed examination of three portraits and the two plastic artworks reveals another unique quality of Brentano's allegory: a state of tension between the generalized, traditionally fixed meanings of the objects depicted and the individualized, fluid contours with which the poet endows his representation. These dual aspects stressing process and perspectivism dovetail well with the characterization of romanticism given by Brentano elsewhere in the novel, the delineation of which then served as the framework for this investigation.

C. *Commentary on* Godwi

Almost from the opening pages of the novel—indeed, already in the foreword to the work proper—there is evidence of romantic poly-perspectivism from the standpoint of both thematic substance and structural technique. For example, Maria announces in his prefatory remarks that over a year has elapsed since he committed this story to paper, and he realizes now, having gained what we today call aesthetic distance from his work through the medium of elapsed time, that it contains "too much of me [Maria] and not enough of itself" (W, 2:15). As a result, he vows to destroy this subjective additive in order to "reach the power of objectivity" (W, 2:15). But to correct all his shortcomings would entail his ascending "that final pinnacle" from which one has a total overview; and whereas this is admittedly a tantalizing prospect, it is one which constantly eludes his grasp (W, 2:15).

Whether or not these remarks are intended as a *captatio benevolentiae*, as a rhetorical formula with which an inept novice begs in advance the indulgence of his reader for some grievous errors of commission or omission, is a moot point. One wonders, for instance, how such infractions were perpetrated in the first place, if Maria ostensibly did nothing but arrange some correspondence. But even in such ordering and editing a nonobjective component manifests itself, for by selecting certain letters for inclusion, deleting others, and establishing a sequence for the undated letters, a subjectively conditioned perspective comes into play. What emerges may conform to the truth of the situation or it may only convey a "reality" of events as viewed through the particularly honed, uniquely tinted "field glass" of the editor. Incidentally, it is somewhat strange that Maria should lament this personal intrusion since, as has been amply demonstrated, the essence of romanticism involves a prismatically refracted image of objectively given elements.

A second key concept is Maria's assertion that he forever approaches but never reaches the lofty vantage point from which an all-encompassing overview would be feasible. Yet when, in volume 2, he is informed how far he actually fell short of this envisioned goal, he has the narrative turn 180 degrees in the opposite direction—to an ironic destruction not only of the superficial, but even of the essential. That which could not be successfully deployed is systematically destroyed. A ruthless dismantling of characters, impressions, and situations results.

The foreword to volume 2 reiterates the accusation of editorial-authorial incompetence leveled at the outset of volume 1, but with even less redeeming rhetoric: "Unfortuntately I infused into these letters too much of my own self" (W, 2:225). The attempt to rectify the error by going directly to the source (Godwi[s]) is doomed to failure almost from the start, since the protagonist defines the very essence of romanticism as a subjectively mediated objectivity and the editor is thus attempting to work against the grain of this concept. That crest from which one could survey the territory in sovereign, objective fashion proves in the last analysis to be not only chimeric but also sirenic, as Maria laments:

and what will my final lot in life be? I have ventured out onto the endless sea in too fragile a boat, and I float along driven by the waves. O you few hearts which cling to me in love, you see me setting sail without mast and rudder, trusting to luck . . . already the winds are rising up from all directions, the waves are agitated, and I, in my small craft, will most likely go under. (*W*, 2:227)

Like Heine's seafarer in the poem "die Lore-Ley"—a conceptualization which, incidentally, Brentano had introduced to the literary world decades earlier in this very novel where the ballad is sung by Violette—Maria keeps his glance fixed on the heights above and forgets the depths below. And it is those dangerous waters of life which ultimately cause his demise, aesthetically as well as physically, while from the cliffs the enticing voice of romanticism still beckons: "Lore Lay, / Lore Lay, / Lore Lay, / Als wären es meiner drei" (*W*, 2:429) ("Lorelei, / Lorelei, / Lorelei, / As were the three my own"—which also could be rendered as: "As if there were three of me.") There is as much truth as poetry in this concluding verse, since Brentano does project a kind of partial portrayal of himself into the three principal male figures in the book: Godwi, Römer, and Maria.

In Godwi's very first letter to Römer, the problem of polyperspectivism surfaces as both theme and technique, the former in Godwi's assertion that he always regards a situation (such as his departure from Molly) with bifocal vision, as a cause for both laughter and tears. In his description of the manner in which he observed his surroundings while riding off in haste, there is an attempt to convert spatial concepts into temporal relationships: "around me the objects flew past like moments" (*W*, 2:24), as if he could recapture concrete reality in time.

Even more indicative of the multifaceted romantic manner of perception is the description of his arrival at the Gothic castle of Eichenwehen. As he is led up several dizzying flights of winding stairs, the external experience becomes metaphorically internalized as the "spiral staircase of my mood," and the latter then wends its way from the intimate boudoir of Godwi's heart, now grown dismal and dark, to the barren chamber of his mind. This condition stems, no doubt, from his prior entanglements with Molly, and the lethargy he now experiences is equated with an empty hall after the masked ball has ended; the final bars of music have faded away, and all that remains is a sense of fatigue and satiety. The transformation of the actual winding staircase into the metaphoric spiral stairs of his mood then evolves into a reminiscence of Molly descending the darkened staircase upon leaving the masked ball, a memory which is abruptly jarred by the chamberlain of Eichenwehen who admonishes Godwi not to tarry too long on this stairwell. The manner in which an entity from the phenomenal world is prismatically and metaphorically filtered through the mind's eye of a receptive subject, then enhanced by the dimension of personal recollection, illustrates already on the opening pages of the novel that quality of the romantic perspective expounded theoretically several hundred pages later. On the other hand, the abrupt return to the "real" staircase at the end of the passage underscores the prerogative of the romantic writer to retract a mood he has created at will (or whim), for one of several reasons: because he, as the creator, has the divine right to do so; because an author is uncomfortably aware of the inadequacy of the verbal idiom to render or sustain the impression beyond a certain point, or, as is often the case with Heine in the terminal stages of romanticism, because of the writer's suspicion of the fraudulent nature of both the poetic construct and the emotional correlative which gave rise to it.

Considering the structural techniques employed to convey a sense of romantic perspectivism, one might also begin with the initial letter in which Godwi presents his account of Molly's final visit to him as he lay sleeping, emphasizing her farewell kiss of which he learned only "after the fact" via his servant. Römer's response to Godwi's ambivalent portrayal of Molly's behavior is couched in predictably unambiguous terms. Condemning rather sharply what he feels to be Molly's feigned virtues (Godwi had used the image of a "masked ball," the "amphitheater of her arms," the "spectacle of her mind") (W, 2:27), Römer finds no laudable attributes in her final visit, but rather compares it with the act of an artist of Mozart's caliber who, at the behest of a boorish patron, demeans himself by performing as an encore a shoddy song on the violin. Römer amplifies his view via another medium—landscape painting—where the diminishing size and decreasing clarity in outline of objects in the distance cause us to see even those at close range as a form of "optical illusion" (literally, "the deceptiveness of perspective") (W, 2:32). This sobering concept is intended to put what Godwi had observed through rose-colored glasses, as it were, into proper perspective. The final stage in this tripartite presentation of the same scene is given by Molly herself when, some fifty pages later in the novel, she outlines for Werdo Senne her version of the nocturnal visit and the parting kiss. Her extensive and sentimentalized disquisition focuses on the common denominator between love and art: both require total commitment, an all-encompassing embrace, in which dividing lines disappear, barriers of demarcation are torn down, and the artist creates without interference from the conscience or from consciousness. At such moments, both the aesthetic and the erotic experience become "total works of art," entities devoid of fragmentation. The vantage point is such that the artist looks over everything without overlooking anything. Consequently, no single aesthetic medium suffices, just as no one phase of love (neither pure sensuality nor unadulterated spirituality) in isolation proves satisfactory. Molly admits that her artistic ideal is that of transition, of interchange, and agility, to such an extent, that the plastic or pictorial media alone would be too restrictive. Indulging in a similar kind of logical acrobatics with regard to time and space as Godwi, she declares that it is "nicht der Blick, . . . der Augenblick des Blicks" W, 2:99) ("not the glance, but the instant of glancing") for which she yearns. The fixed glare would be static, and she, like Godwi, must regard things in a synamic perspective, her point of view is multidimensional.

Throughout the course of Molly's long and involved analogy linking art and love as correlated modes of conception and perception, two diametrically opposed positions emerge. The first is the now familiar romantic viewpoint of poly- or multidimensionality; the second is the philistine point of view or mono-dimensionalism. The former requires a certain psychic predisposition, the injection of ample dosages of fantasy into the bloodstream of everyday reality. Molly cautions, however, against an overdose of this life-sustaining substance: Eusebio, for instance, is unable to discern the simple, clear outlines of existence because he has so entangled them with the "skeins of his fantasy" that the web of his own imagination ensnares him (W, 2:84). Then she goes on to speak of Godwi's "image-laden fantasy" (W, 2:88), a trait which he confirms when relating scenes of his childhood to Otilie: when life became too routine for him, he would look at the world through a piece of glass "in which everything appeared reversed" (W, 2:142). In the same vein, he tells of his preference for wandering through those paths of life in which "beauty plays in the mirror image of my fantasy" (W, 2:40), as opposed to walking the straight and narrow or following the golden middle way. But looking and living are two separate entities, and so when Godwi tries to "re-form" things in accordance with his personal perspective, the results are often disppointing. Thus this fantasy, which he was unable to curb in his youth and which was ineffective in altering the external world, became directed inward and carried him across the darkening seas and uncharted realms of his soul, back to the primordial sphere of the mother. Tempered by time, his fantasy enabled him to heighten (*potenzieren*) reality; he sees pieces in a game of chess not merely as carved figures, but as living personalities engaged in a dramatic, life-and-death struggle; likewise the billiard balls on the velvet table became cosmic constellations moving through the vast expanses of the universe.

What emerges from this analysis of fantasy and multidimensionality of perspective is the following. In the case of Eusebio, the inherent danger of the unchecked imaginative faculty becomes so overwhelming, that the individual loses sight of the catalyst from reality which set it in motion. Whereas young Godwi almost fell prey to the same danger, the mature protagonist overcame the threat and was able to establish an equilibrium in which fantasy and reality were brought into a state of correlation, even though not into a condition of permanent, peaceful coexistence. Opposed to this situation, however, is the limited and limiting perspective of the philistine which marks a strictly one-track mind. Surprisingly, Römer inclines toward this mono-dimensional outlook initially, perhaps as a result of his early orientation in the world of commerce. But just as Godwi develops from the uncontrolled child of fantasy to an adult in whom the realia of life serve as a springboard for flights of imagination, so Römer evolves during the course of the novel into an individual in whom the romantic perspective comes to the fore. This manifests itself in his graphic account of the *bureau d'esprit*, a colorful mosaic in which the members of the Butler family and their friends are viewed in terms of geometric concepts, of zwieback, and a host of other fanciful concoctions.

The figure in the novel, however, who exemplifies philistinism best (and perhaps so one-sidedly, that he functions as a mere caricature) is Joduno von Eichenwehen's brother, Jost. A champion of ancestral honor, of the sublime truth of the natural sciences in an enlightened century, and above all of Kotzebue's sentimental and heartrending family dramas (over Shakespeare's "comedy" *Macbeth*), Jost prefers military march music to the opera, takes metaphors literally, and sprinkles his stilted German with tidbits of fractured French (for instance, he speaks of a "negligence" instead of a "negligée"). In short, Jost stands at the opposite end of the spectrum from Eusebio with regard to depth perception and range of perspective. Whereas the latter envisioned only what his fantasy dictated, the former viewed only what reality predicated. Both fail to see that critical point of intersection where the concrete real is heightened by the infusion of the intangible ideal, a marriage of components in which neither partner forgoes his intrinsic essence completely, but rather through interaction with the other, serves as a powerful potentializing agent while simultaneously attaining his full power potential.

Two incidental figures whose life-style and thought processes embody most consistently and convincingly this romantic perspectivism are Werdo Senne and Otilie. For Werdo, the chasm separating life from death, the living from the dead, has closed, and he no longer draws fine lines of distinction between these domains. Any boundaries, if they exist at all, are fluid. Just as Werdo's silence speaks as eloquently as his song, so too are the incidents in life correlated with death. Being stranded here ("diesseits stranden") is tantamount to having landed there ("jenseits landen"), it is a matter of total perspective rather than isolated perception. Whereas Werdo's music and philosophy strike the reader as minor in mode, those of Otilie are distinctly major in tone. Godwi observes that she is "intimately and deeply tied to all being" (W, 2:142), and, as seen from the analysis of her poem "Speak from the distance," the words she utters tell of a reciprocity between the terrestrial and transcendental worlds.

However, as indicated earlier, these magical moments, when near and far, light and dark, personal and universal are conceived in such correlative harmony, were both rare and transitory. Otilie soon passes from the scene, only to be recalled parenthetically in volume 2 when she and Godwi are asked if they ever intend to marry—a query which elicits from both quarters an emphatic "no." Otilie is subsequently married off to Francesco Firmenti on a kind of ad hoc basis and the couple, together with other members of the cast, is dispatched to Italy for the honeymoon. They fly in migratory bird fashion with Eusebio (anticipating the roles of Homunculus and Euphorion in Goethe's *Faust*, part 2) leading the flock, the bridal couple immediately behind, and Godwi, Joseph-Werdo, and Molly Hodefield bringing up the rear. The coup de grâce is administered to Otilie by Godwi when he, amid the Dionysian wining and wenching of his Rhine journey, vows to forget her together with the other "odd-ball, noble souls, whatever their names might be" (W, 2:390) after the first beaker of wine.

This rapid-fire bit of recapitulation thus disposes of a cluster of characters who, in varying degrees, embodied the romantic perspective. Yet a triumvirate of principals lingers behind to champion this cause against the inroads of philistinism. Römer, having demonstrated his progress beyond the confines of the mono-dimensionalism which once threatened to stifle his better self, reveals that he not only can see behind the facade of factuality and the phenomenal, but also listen with a kind of extrasensory perception. Near the close of volume 1, he reported that a voice emanating from below his window in groaning, broken tones was that of a wretched old woman who was forced to sing religious songs in order to eke out a livelihood. He finds it particularly disarming that an individual, because of poverty, is compelled to perform in such a manner, that the tones which are the result of sighs and lamentation, assume the guise of merry tunes. Yet it is this quality of jubilant melancholy which gives such music its moving quality (W, 2:200). Such an insight could be designated the romantic mode of acoustical or auditory perception, a counterpart to the previously treated visual perspectivism. The genuine romantic apprehends simultaneously the gay melodies and the grim sighs which gave rise to them, he hears as well as sees multidimensionally.

This acoustical frame of reference is later expanded by Maria when, after juxtaposing Godwi's's erotic victories on the Rhine with his own amorous defeats, he recites a long poem entitled "The Merry Minstrels" that treats the same dilemma introduced by Römer: the compulsion to utter joyous sounds through a veil of tears, whereby the happy tones mask the sorrow and suffering for all but the most discriminating listener. Whereas the short, four-line introductory verses of each stanza enumerate the different and difficult circumstances under which the minstrels must perform, the eleven-line refrain—presumably sung in unison and repeated with only slight variations a total of eleven times—reinforces, by virtue of a powerful cumulative effect, the conflict which seethes below the surface of their boisterous music and thus glaringly belies their merriment:

Es brauset und sauset
Das Tambourin,
Es rasseln und prasseln
Die Schellen drin;
Die Becken hell flimmern
Von tönenden Schimmern,
Um Kling und um Klang,
Um Sing und um Sang
Schweifen die Pfeifen, und greifen

Ans Herz,
Mit Freude und mit schmerz.

(W, 2:400)

The tambourine / Is hustling and bustling, / The bells join in / With jingling
and jangling; / The cymbals glimmer brightly / From the shimmering
sounds, / With tinkling and tone, / With singing and song / The pipes ramble
and seize / The heart / With joy and with pain.

In the fragmentary continuation of the novel following the illness
and death of its author (Maria), Godwi, in reporting his adventures at
the castle of the Countess G. and her daughter, Violette, tells how he
reached his decision to leave this environment after wandering off
into the forest and climbing up to a castle high on a nearby hilltop. In
the deserted tower of the castle he finds a field glass which, he asserts
with tongue in cheek, might be of use to those who have not understood the novel but who like precise geographical locations. Ironi
cally, the clearer perspective which he promises others and which he
imagines he has gained from this vantage point is actually denied him.
His resolve to forsake the Countess and leave Violette to her fate, falls
into the thought-pattern of the mono-dimensional man. Like the
pragmatically oriented individual he fails to recognize the depth of
soul hidden beneath Violette's exterior self. Later he atones for this
tragic miscalculation (Brentano had an inherent distrust and aversion
for the "vulture of reflection" gnawing perpetually at the enchained
Prometheus, W, 2:218) by having her fate immortalized in stone
statuary, just as his father had perpetuated the memory of Marie and
the wrongs he (Godwi) had committed against her, by erecting a
marble monument.

Godwi notes cryptically that the path from the statue of his mother
to that of this prostitute only appears to be long; it proves, upon closer
inspection, not to be so, and, furthermore, encompasses the entire
spectrum of his spirit (W, 2:372). This statement contains one of those
striking paradoxes with which romantics loved to alert kindred spirits
and alarm closed minds. Appropriately enough, it is Maria who
articulates the essence of the ties linking such apparently disparate
realms as those of the mother and prostitute. Peering at the
moonlight-bathed monument to Violette from his window, Maria
grows so agitated by its sensual appeal that he hurries down to the
garden in order to have a better view. But the closer he gets, the more

evident it becomes that the original impression of Dionysian rapture has been tempered by one of Apollinian transfiguration:

I felt as though I could see myself in St. Mark's square in Venice at carnival time; all things flowed into one another, and the individual colors which continually appeared among the myriad figures, fused together; shadow and light intermingled in playful movement, and hardly had I followed one figure with my glance, than it turned into a hundred others. Towering above all else, however, like the artificially fashioned streams of a huge fountain, like strangely dancing, heaven-directed flames of a pure, white fire, soared the image of Violette toward heaven, rising above all the sordid entanglements, the apotheosis of a lost child. . . . (W, 2:291–292)

Enhanced by the "field-glass" lens of the plastic arts, Maria's perspective can penetrate beyond the merely sensual to discover dimensions previously concealed from view. In fact, when he later sees the same statuary in the morning sun, he goes so far as to maintain that such "lost" women have become the repository of love in the current age of matrimony, just as in times of barbarism the good in this world invariably took refuge in the realm of the poetic (W, 2:294).

The *sine qua non* of this brand of analogy is the designation of those women, scorned by philistine minds, as the harbingers of untapped human potential, or, to quote Maria's startling statement: "and they still stand there today, as once romantic poetry stood there" (W, 2:294). Rather than merely disparage or disregard those like Violette, the romantic focus is able to detect a dimension which transcends the phenomenal sphere, which takes us to the frontiers of a world in which the commonplace and the uncommon, the well-known and the unknown coexist. If we once inhabited such a realm in the dim, distant past during the childhood stages of mankind, in the so-called golden age, we have, as Brentano and many romantics came to believe, forfeited our access rights to this paradise forever. Brentano, it will be recalled, contrived several surrogates for this loss—the work of art and its fantasy worlds, personal relationships, as well as the interpersonal brotherhood of a religious creed and calling. In spite of the multifaceted perspectivism of his first novel and, concomitant with this, the attempt to articulate the goals of romanticization, the work still must look beyond itself to realize the impossible dream—it must summon Clemens Brentano to perform the Orphean rescue mission. This is a tacit as well as overt admission that *Godwi per se* had failed. But this proved to be the perpetual lot of the romantic: he suspected that his quest was doomed from the outset, yet this could not deter him from setting out to perform it. Did not Maria announce in the preface to this novel: "I have ventured out onto the endless sea in too fragile a boat . . . and I, in my small craft, will most likely go under"?

II   *Shorter Prose Fiction*

The discussion of Brentano's shorter prose fiction will include his forays into such representative forms as the chronicle, novella, and fairy tale, some of which have an immense theoretical literature on which to draw,[23] while others have attracted scant critical attention.[24] Whereas no systematic attempt can be made here to outline the directions which this vast body of theory has taken, pertinent features of the respective genres will be mentioned in conjunction with the role they play in Brentano's work. As has been the case so far, the approach in the commentary section will not be exhaustive, but merely selective, seeking to isolate those features of a romantic perspectivism which have served as the red thread for the analysis as a whole.

A.   The Chronicle of the Traveling Student *(1802–1806) and* Excerpts from the Chronicle of a Traveling Student *(1818)*

The designations "chronicle" and "traveling student" in the title of both the early and late fragments are intended to evoke in the reader's mind a feeling for ages past, especially for the medieval period when the chronicle as a record of events in chronological order and the concept of student-scholars moving on foot from university to university were familiar components of daily life. And in the very first sentence of both versions, a precise date—1358—is cited, lending an air of authenticity to the account (for which Brentano did indeed consult several source works, including chronicles) (W, 2:1189). But one may wonder why Brentano selected this date for a story which focuses sharply on the unflinching piety of the Middle Ages, since it was at the midpoint of the fourteenth century that the solidarity of the church and the faith of the flock were being sorely tested by the "Babylonian Captivity" to which the papal office had been subjected, an ominous prelude to the great schism which came in its wake at the end of the fourteenth century. But the term "traveling" also implies a quest, a pilgrimage perhaps toward some goal, a haven which the student appears to find at the home of a congenial knight in Strassburg

Yet both versions of the tale remain fragmentary, suggesting that the odyssey of the student may have led him to look even beyond the confines of this city for the ultimate path toward salvation. Since the two works break off at different stations on the journey of the protagonist in time as well as into the world, the following summary will present separate accounts of each.

1. Content of The Chronicle of the Traveling Student (1802–1806)

On the morning of his twentieth birthday in the year 1358, a traveling student named Johannes awakens to find himself in an entirely new milieu—the city of Strassburg. The evening before he had been taken into the home of the knight Veltlin von Türlingen, where he is to serve as a scribe. Enjoying the amenities of Veltlin's garden as well as a view of the magnificent Strassburg Cathedral, Johannes relates to his venerable host reminiscences from his childhood in Franconia recorded in a little notebook.

The focal point of his first account is his mother, a poor yet pious woman who earned her daily bread by spinning. While visiting a nearby cloister to sell some of the yarn she had spun, Johannes's mother has a mass read for his father, a knight named Siegmund. Following this pious tribute to Siegmund, Johannes and his mother visit a small ivy-covered forest hut near the Main river where she had grown up and where she now proceeds to tell of her youth. As the daughter of a huntsman and fowler, she was raised in poor circumstances, a hard life made even more difficult by the death of her mother. In spite of her father's admonitions that nothing could come of her love for Siegmund, the young girl continued to traverse the river to his castle as often as possible, and soon friendship blossomed into love. Following the death of her own father, Johannes's mother went to live in the castle of Siegmund's family as the foster child of the porter, Kilian, an acquaintance and one-time rival of her father for her mother's hand. At this point, Johannes's mother tells of a falcon, also called Kilian, bequeathed posthumously by her father to her new foster parent (the porter Kilian); at this juncture she seems to be unable to continue her narrative, in spite of her son's prodding.

Johannes's narration is also interrupted now as Knight Veltlin presents his four daughters, two of whom, Otilia and Gundelindis, are his own children, while the others, Athala and Pelagia, are adopted. After an exchange of views on the nature of prayer and devotional singing, on the transitoriness of earthly existence, on church bells in the cathedral as a source of consolation and edification for both the congregation and the countryside at large, Johannes tells several of the townspeople—knights and craftsmen of Strassburg— how the tones of the bell had led him to Veltlin.

That evening in the garden Knight Veltlin informs Johannes about the contrasting personalities of his four daughters: Otilia, reserved and shy, the bride of heaven, seems destined to become a nun; Gundelindis, worldly-wise and open, is already engaged to a noble-man; Athala, the orphaned child of a locksmith, is a sad and troubled soul, while Pelagia, a child Veltlin found in Jerusalem and had baptized, is the artistic type who plays edifying music on the organ while singing secular and religious songs to the same melodies. Veltlin's comments on her artistic talents induce Johannes to report the fate of a master mirror-maker who gradually forgot the divine source of his talents and fell into a life of worldly arrogance and dissipation until he and the entire city in which he worked were consumed by flames caused by the rays of the sun reflecting in one of his mirrors. This leads to an analysis of art and the need of the artisan to show reverence for the supreme creator and a respect for the spiritual as well as material components of the aesthetic artifact, just as in the nonaesthetic sphere the noumenal and the phenomenal exist in a state of mutual reciprocity. There follows a pious evening song sung by Veltlin himself to the organ music of Pelagia, after which the knight together with his four daughters and Johannes retire to the library. Here, after they have contemplated a book illustration por-traying three maidens at sea in a sinking ship while three other girls hasten to their rescue, Johannes reads aloud to the group the accom-panying parable "Concerning the Tragic Demise of Temporal Love."

This very complex and multilayered narrative structure begins with a moralizing admonition against forfeiting the eternal soul be-cause of preoccupation with the temporal aspects of the flesh. The story proper first tells of three sisters who, standing at the sea shore, hear the enticing tones of a song performed by the mysterious figure known as the Pearl Spirit. Residing on the cliffs overlooking the waters, the Pearl Spirit, through the power of music, lures those who sail by to a whirlpool near the rocky crags. Two of the girls succumb to this force of attraction and set out in a rudderless, sailless ship. On old fisherman informs the third sister that the Pearl Spirit can assume either male or female form, depending on the gender of the victim, and that her siblings can only be saved by the tolling of the chapel bell. But the foolish girls fail to heed even this warning and are drawn down into the whirlpool where they are destined to remain until they can forget themselves, their reckless act, and personal misfortune, and shed a tear of sympathy for the plight of the others down below (since such tears themselves become pearls of salvation).

The fisherman takes the third sister to his hermitage and shows her a book written by his predecessor here, the Handsome Beggar. The book as well as the dwelling place contain much evidence of mother-of-pearl trimmings. The fisherman explains that when the evening star shines above the sea and one sings Ave Maris Stella, the songs of the Pearl Spirit are temporarily silenced and one can peer down into the latter's watery castle and see, among other things, the unfortunate victims of his wiles. Some who fall prey to his charms, however, are kept in a yet more remote place, a chamber reached by passing through the Heart Ventricle of Petrified Remorse to the Bitter Spring, where those who weep eternally must dwell.

And indeed, when the girl and the fisherman that same evening venture into the domain of the Pearl Spirit, they observe in the Heart Ventricle the Handsome Beggar and his beloved both crystallized by her tears; further on, in the confines of the Bitter Spring, they discover her sisters together with a throng of other victims. At this moment, however, another star known as Wermut (vermouth, wormwood, bitterness) hovers above the Bitter Spring and the Pearl Spirit, now freed from his temporary enchantment, can again resume his singing. This induces the fisherman and the girl to return to the hermitage, where she insists on hearing the full story of the Handsome Beggar and the Pearl Spirit.

The latter, we are told, is the embodiment of earthly vanity, secular love and joy, together with their concomitant remorse, a plight which befalls those who forsake the eternal for the temporal. These victims are condemned to weep until the sea grows bitter; but since all remorse has something redeeming about it, they may simply weep until they forget themselves and their own fate, at which point their tears become pearls; and with such pearls it is possible to win their release. The cliffs of Petrified Remorse were formed by a queen who fell prey to vanity and temporality, while the Bitter Spring stems from her daughter, from whose lineage the Pearl Spirit descends. The latter, hermaphroditic in nature, once appeared on earth as the water sprite Melusine.

In order to impress upon the girl's mind the destructive powers of the Pearl Spirit's song, the old fisherman now tells her of the Handsome Beggar, a young artist, the son of a siren and a fisherman, who lived with a hermit on an island and learned to defiantly counter the singing of the Pearl Spirit with his own song, thereby saving the lives of many potential victims. Once, while he was visiting the Heart Ventricle of Petrified Remorse and the Bitter Spring, the Handsome Beggar came across a book which contained fascinating pictures and the chronicle of the Pearl Spirit's family. Unable to read the contents of the book, the Handsome Beggar found a young girl in an island castle who swam across the sea to him and taught him the art of reading—until the Pearl Spirit in the female form of a siren, extinguished the light and the girl perished in the waves. The Handsome Beggar was so despondent that he wept and took his own life—whereupon he and his beloved became enshrined in the Ventricle of Petrified Remorse. This girl was actually the daughter of the fisherman who is now relating this tragic story to the steadfast sister. After hearing this heartrending account, she decides to remain on the island with the fisherman, helping him to caution the frivolous and unwise about the dangers inflicted by the Pearl Spirit. Subsequently she founds a cloister in which she holds sway as the abbess, while the fisherman establishes a monastery. The nuns and monks of the respective orders are those who have been rescued from the whirlpool of the world. A vision of redemption and salvation for those thus evading the seductive enticements of the Pearl Spirit closes the fragment.

The later version entitled *Excerpts from the Chronicle of a Traveling Student* (1818) expands the account of Johannes's first day at Veltlin's by the addition of many edifying asides on piety and the need for humility, as well as some new poetry such as the lyrical lullaby "Oh mother keep thy little child warm." In this new adaptation, Johannes's mother is named Laurenburger Els and his father is identified as the Knight of Laurenburg. The background information on Els's early life with her father is also augmented by many details, including accounts reported by her dying mother. The fragment concludes with the latter's death and burial, followed by the sad return to the family home "in which my mother was no more" (W, 2:635).

2. *Critical Reception of the* Chronicle *Fragments*

Until the decade of the 1970s, studies focusing attention on either fragment of the *Chronicle* had been relatively rare. In 1912 there appeared an article in a rather obscure periodical which traced the sources (both bibliographic and literary) of the best-known versions of the story at that time—the *Excerpts* of 1818.[25] With the publication in 1923 of the full and authentic text of the original *Chronicle* manuscript,[26] one would have expected a flood of analyses or at least comparative studies of the two adaptations, but neither of these was forthcoming until the advent of Elisabeth Stopp's pioneering work in the present decade.

In a postscript to the 1971 edition of the original *Chronicle*, Stopp compares the apparent disorder and disarray of the narrative structures in *Godwi* with those of the chronicle and postulates that the clarity of arrangement and craftsmanship manifest in the latter work may represent a kind of therapeutic exercise on the part of the author.[27] Respect for principles of order and organization permeate not only the thematic substance of the work (the hierarchical authority of the medieval church, social and political institutions), but also its composition (the integration of narrative threads) and symbolism (the recurrent scenic backgrounds and tripartite time divisions). Those figures in the *Chronicle* transgressing the prescribed order by forsaking the eternal for the temporal are destined to endure a tragic fate, but one which arouses both our sympathy and empathy as well as the hope of redemption—an offshoot of Brentano's pedagogical tendencies. Stopp astutely links what she feels to be the central theme of the story—the interrelationship of time and timelessness—with some of its major symbols (the garden, the Strassburg Cathedral, the tolling of the church bell), thereby reinforcing the claim of a meticulous craft of fiction against the charge of careless artistry frequently leveled at Brentano.

In a subsequent extension of her original analysis, Stopp outlines in detail the narrative strategies of the work, their symmetrical design, and their function in underscoring the interdependency of "time and transience." By juxtaposing the early and late adaptations she comes to the valid conclusion that the version of 1818, had it been completed, would have resulted in a radically new work which must be read in the light of the poet's growing skepticism concerning the propriety of the purely aesthetic artifact.[28] Working with "frenzied force" in an effort to salvage something worthwhile from his shattered past, Brentano produced a pious pastiche bearing all the earmarks of external theory grafted onto an alien growth, religious trappings superimposed in such a fashion, that the subtle poetic ambiguity of the original is excised in favor of a sugary contamination, "embarrassing by its lack of artistic reticence and would-be naiveté, repository art rather than the real thing."[29] Brentano's possible awareness of the "literary patchwork" which he, due to "temporary pauline blindness," had produced, may have accounted for his inability to carry the revisions to their logical conclusion. Stopp cautions against the common practice of combining the two fragments when interpreting the *Chronicle*, for this tactic, she argues, results in a wholly new, imaginary work—one which Brentano never intended and could never have conceivably written.

In the wake of Stopp's pioneering studies, a number of critics have continued to uncover patterns of aesthetic structure and symmetry in the original *Chronicle*, these being features which distinguish it from the genuine chronicle since the latter is essentially a chronological, factual report of events.[30] Anton Kathan, for instance, after stressing how the work of art subtly filters the infinite dimensions of existence through the finite, human perspective, contends that this aesthetic mediation enables us to overcome the gloom which we, like the petrified victims of the Pearl Spirit, experience after having given the temporal priority over the eternal in our lives.[31] He draws the provocative conclusion that the original version actually constitutes a "closed fragment," having at its core a process of sin and redemption which, in its eternal recurrence, can be repeated but never completed.

Niklaus Reindl discusses the original *Chronicle* with regard to the role of the Middle Ages in Brentano's œuvre, and he concludes that the historical epoch merely serves as a vague backdrop for the encoded expression of the author's most personal concerns.[32] The historical past, consequently, is dehistoricized in order to poeticize romantically what is really important—the revelation of the mysterious essence of things hidden beneath their surface. Contrary to the uniform narrative style of the genuine chronicle, Brentano's poetic adaptation is said to fuse at least three divergent genres (autobiographical reminiscences, diary accounts of events in the immediate present, and legendary or fairy-tale elements from the mythical past), while source material from three disparate eras is incorporated in anachronistic fashion (the description of the cathedral from the sixteenth century, the falcon episode based on emblematic literature from the baroque epoch, and the discussion on the significance of the tolling of the church bell as a counterpart to Schiller's "Song of the Bell" of 1800). A triadic rhythm likewise pervades Reindl's analysis of the thematic composition where he distinguishes between intrinsic and extrinsic elements as well as features which are unique to Brentano—such as the interweaving of existential and aesthetic concerns.

Whereas Stopp and Reindl both stress tripartite structures in the composition of the original *Chronicle*, other critics have underscored quadripartite strategies employed by the author. In the context of one investigation examining how the mirror image is used in the romantic period to portray certain aspects of the artist's dilemma, Brentano is found to incorporate four levels of artistic potential in the *Chronicle*: Pelagia as the stage of naive, unconscious artistry; Johannes as the embodiment of the pious, reverent artisan; the mirror-master as the personification of the arrogant, destructive appropriation of art for art's sake; and finally, the Handsome Beggar as the figure who passes through all the above levels and ultimately attains redemption through divine grace.[33]

The postulate of a quadruple format reaches its *non plus ultra* in Martin Huber's monograph which investigates both the figural constellations and the compositional principles of the *Chronicle* on the basis of C. G. Jung's theory of the "quaternion" as expounded in the latter's *Mysterium Coniunctionis*.[34] The four daughters of Veltlin are found to be in a quadripartite interrelationship, whereby they complement each other in their physical and spiritual attributes, and constitute, in the total spectrum, the full scope of human potential (they are also linked with the four seasons, the four elements, the four compass points, the four times of day, etc.). By means of a clever bit of logical deduction, the critic is able to show that even the familiar romantic triadic concepts may be unmasked as covert quartets—a view in keeping with the alchemical-theosophical ideas fostered by Brentano and his contemporaries. An alchemical tri-unity, for instance, because of the duality of its central component, may prove to be quadruple in nature. With regard to the *Chronicle*, the cardinal virtues embodied in three of Veltlin's daughters—Otilie as faith (*fides*), Pelagia as hope (*spes*) and Gundelindis as love (*caritas*)— become augmented by a fourth when Athala, in her downcast state, is shown to function as the negative counterpart to Pelagia's *spes* in the form of *de-sper-atio*. Comprehensive analyses of the other figures reveal that Veltlin incorporates the paternal principle, while Johannes's mother represents the maternal sphere in its most perfect form (not only in the composite attributes of the quaternion, but also as the perfect circle, the latter symbolized by her spinning). Johannes passes through a course of personal and artistic development akin to that of Novalis's *Heinrich von Ofterdingen*: anticipation (as the lonely wanderer, the quester, eternal student, etc.) and realization (as the mediator between conflicting forces and as redeemer of mankind).

Huber's analysis of the narrative modes likewise entails four considerations: the fictitious present (a single day in 1358), the recent past (Johannes's arrival in Strassburg), the remote past (tales of Johannes's life with his mother), and a timeless, mythical epoch (the parable of the Pearl Spirit and the Handsome Beggar).

3. *Commentary on the* Chronicle

One might label the romantic point of view in *Godwi* as polyperspectivism or rotating perceptions since no single presentation of a situation at a given moment in time was felt to be absolute or definitive, but rather valid only in relation to all other accounts both preceding and following it. At the same time, a second tendency in the novel seemed to be a condemnation of the narrow-minded range of perception exhibited by the philistine mentality, a mono-perspectivism which failed to probe behind the external phenomena of life to discover extra dimensions of significance lurking beneath the surface. What we encounter in both *Chronicle* fragments is the predilection of the medieval mind for regarding things not as self-contained entities but as signposts pointing toward a deeper, spiritual meaning. There are at least three areas in which this quality of depth perception operates: the realms of nature, art, and morality.

The keynote for a potentially more sophisticated mode of observing nature is sounded early in the story by Johannes when, in looking around Knight Veltlin's garden, he remarks that the flowers have taken on a new aura of significance for him due to his increasingly "pious and reverent" attitude toward God's creations: "so then," he adds, "nothing can remain constant in view of man's disposition [*Gemüt*] which transforms all things according to itself" (*W,* 2:520). In this context such a statement sounds like a religiously tinged variation of Godwi's characterization of romanticism as "the definition of the object by means of the form of the glass." In Johannes's case, his perception of nature has been conditioned by the religiously refracted lenses through which he is learning to regard the world. In a similar vein, natural phenomena also become for him a source of symbolic wealth: "all my gold is the glow of the sun, all my silver the surface of the river, all my lovely carpets and tapestries the green meadows with their flowers" (*W,* 2:524).

If the eye of the beholder, conditioned by his mental set or spiritual predisposition, does indeed determine the meaning which nature holds in store for him, the same may be said for the manner in which he confronts man-made objects and art works: For instance, the Cathedral of Strassburg is not only a monumental stone structure, but also seems to strive for the incomprehensible, standing in its towering majesty like "the key to heaven," a sacred messenger from God giving us an inkling of our future existence on a higher plane (W 2:521).

Not only the visual media, but also the audible forms of artistic expression invite interpretation which goes beyond the mere surface message conveyed. The tolling of the church bells, for example, signifies different things to different people, according to their psychic constitution at the moment of apprehension. It summons some to prayer; for the orphaned it holds the promise of a home, while for those embroiled in family strife, the tones become an instrument of peace. In this divergence of interpretation of the same acoustical stimuli we have an affirmation of Johannes's premise that "man's disposition transforms all things according to itself." The pure sounds are apprehended within the orbit of the religious framework from which they emanate, but what they signify is colored by the individual consciousness of the hearer, so that their ultimate significance entails a fusion of two components: the universal impetus stemming from the church as the mediator of divine will, and the individual stamp which the apprehending subject affixes to that suprapersonal stimulus.

The above concept is illustrated more vividly in the case of the creative artist: negatively with regard to the mirror-master who, in his aesthetic hubris, flagrantly scorns the transcendental dimension behind his art; positively, with reference to Pelagia who treads adroitly on that precarious path between heaven and earth; and ambiguously in the fate of the Handsome Beggar whose demise in the temporal realm after falling prey to the danger of self-idolatry is counterbalanced by the parable's closing tableau of ultimate redemption once the tears of remorse have liberated him and his beloved from the state of petrifaction and lead them toward a utopia of eternal happiness.

Art is defined at one point in the narrative as "God's eternal unceasing evolution" (W, 2:570), a concept which recalls Friedrich Schlegel's pronouncement that romantic poetry was "progressively universal," and as such it must not be permitted to stagnate in purely temporal concerns. But this is not to say that the finite or mundane quality is to be eliminated completely; rather, it must be put into "proper perspective," as it were, with reference to a more sublime correlative, the infinite and transcendental. The quality of a kind of spiritual tight-rope walking or aesthetic acrobatics associated with the artist treading a fine line "between heaven and earth" finds a parallel in the concept of the artifact composed of forces which, seemingly independent, must actually function interdependently.

The adverb "seemingly" in the previous paragraph gives rise to another consideration of the nature of such an aesthetic product. In a passage in which Johannes speaks about the function of art in aiding man to overcome his fears and doubts, he notes: "art sings him a song, so that the felled wood again seems to grow green and the stroke of the falling axe seems to be only the rhythm and tone of refreshing song" (W, 2:570); then, as a codicil, he enumerates the ability of art to overcome the limitations of time and distance, "to make eternal the sacred and venerable aspects of life, giving apparent embodiment to the hidden and deep spirits of the soul" (W, 2:570). Noticeable throughout this ostensibly unequivocal endorsement of artistic activity are the qualifications "seems" and "apparent." Brentano is making us aware that the essence of aesthetic activity involves a certain degree of appearance, an attribute of which the recipient must remain forever cognizant, so that he does not confuse such representation with shallow reality. Whereas the work of art may in the final analysis be rooted in that reality, it does at the same time transcend it.

The section of the *Chronicle* which best illustrates the delicate interplay through the medium of art of the "sacred and venerable aspects of life, giving apparent embodiment to the hidden and deep spirits of the soul" is the scene in which the tones of Pelagia's evening music become fused with the silhouette of the Strassburg Cathedral towering in the background. The tenuous nature of this marriage of acoustical and visual stimuli is indicated by couching the description in the subjunctive mode: "and it was," Johannes comments, "as though the song and the hues in the sky understood one another and were playing with one another" (W, 2:571).

A similar awareness of the transcendent dimensions of morality constitutes the message of the parable of the Pearl Spirit, which contains the injunction: "Thus should the course of our life be begun, with a look back to our home in God . . . " (W, 2:575). Like art, life must constantly renew or reestablish its ties with a force more enduring than the transient human condition. And yet the latter is not to be dismissed or disregarded either, but rather viewed with reference to more permanent correlatives. The parable teaches that the temporal must not constitute the sum total of life, but rather function as one component for which there is a more durable counterbalancing agent, one which throws into clearer perspective by way of contrast the ultimate meaning of our seemingly time-bound existence. When we reach this heightened level of understanding, the pearls formed by the tears of remorse will appear to us as precious commodities not only because they represent terrestrial splendor and fortune, but also transcendent beauty and wealth. In this latter capacity they do not forgo their sensuous appeal, but merely augment it by a dimension of spiritual significance.

B.   The Story of Honest Casper and Fair Annie (1817)

As is the case with many of Brentano's works, some key elements in the story are already contained in the title. In this instance, the fates of the respective individuals become interwoven during the course of the narration, not only by old Anna Margaret, who recounts sequentially the stories of Casper and Annie, but also via the intervention of the anonymous narrator of the novella proper to whom she reports these events, whereupon the former takes measures to join together in death those driven asunder by life. The German adjective used to describe Casper is *brav* and this word could also be translated by "upright," "worthy," "just" or "well-behaved" as well as by "honest." However, the latter term is particularly appropriate since it is etymologically related to "honor," the attribute which becomes a virtual obsession with Casper and leads to his own demise as well as that of his beloved, Annie. With regard to Annie's "fairness of face," one might show that her comeliness together with the rigid code of honor imposed upon her by Casper lead to her undoing. The combined efforts of Casper's grandmother (who is Annie's godmother) and the narrator attain for the unhappy pair an honorable grave, thus giving to Brentano's tale a sense of coherence and consequence rare in his writings.

1.   *Content of* The Story of Honest Casper and Fair Annie

One unusually cool summer's evening at 11:00, the narrator, a writer-poet, discovers an aged peasant woman wrapped in an apron sitting on the steps of a public building and surrounded by an inquisitive crowd which debates her mental stability. After the throng has dispersed and only the narrator, captivated by the firm resolve of this pious soul, remains behind, she recalls that on this same spot seventy years before the officer of the guard tossed her a rose as she sang a song of God's Last Judgment and His ultimate reconciliation with mankind. At this point the members of the guard again pass by, and the officer of the day, visibly shaken by her singing, gives the narrator (whom he knows) a rose and some money for the woman. The latter, in a series of vague allusions, tells of the "departure" of her only grandson, the noncommissioned officer Casper Finkel, and her desire to obtain for him (who during his lifetime sought nothing but honor) an honorable grave, after which she will hasten to join him and all those loved ones who have departed this life—including her godchild, who tomorrow will do the same. The narrator, confused and stunned by these vague references, implores her for clarification, but she continues in her cryptic fashion, relating how Casper, in thought and deed, was possessed by the concept of honor, to which she adds: "Render honor to God alone."

In an apparent shift of focus, she inquires about the narrator's occupation, and he, embarrassed and not wishing to divulge that he is a writer by profession (since there is a certain degree of shame connected with doing business with those spiritual and emotional qualities which heaven grants us) and yet at a loss to supply a term which will not arouse the suspicion of the common people when they hear the word "poet," finds himself in a quandary. Being a poet, he must admit to himself, entails a certain loss of balance, and those who earn their livelihood by the sweat of their brow might say that such an imbalance, like the goose with an overstuffed liver, implies a sickness, even though the liver itself may be healthy. When he, in the face of such pangs of conscience, decides to label himself a "scribe," the aged Anna Margaret is delighted, since she feels he can compose a petition for her to the reigning duke, requesting that the two lovers be allowed to rest beside each other in death and that the bodies of those who took their life out of "desperation" not be brought, as is the custom, to the anatomy class for dissection, but be left intact so that when the Lord summons us for final judgment, the limbs will not be scattered about helter-skelter. Following some passing references to the love of her grandson for her godchild, Annie (whom the "foe" seized with "biting teeth"), she finally begins her account of Casper's career, following which Annie's fate is recorded.

Casper Finkel, a handsome youth, served in France as a cavalryman and noncommissioned officer with honor and distinction, but at one point felt the desire to return home to his family and his fiancée, Annie, in whom he had instilled a strong sense of honor. While he passes the night at a mill, his borrowed horse and his knapsack are stolen by thieves. Casper returns home, reports the theft to the local authorities, and then discovers to his dismay that his father and stepbrother are the culprits. After turning them over to the police, he visits the grave of his late mother and shoots a bullet into his head through the tinsel wreath he had brought as a gift for Annie. In a farewell note he requests an honorable burial for one so dishonored by his kin.

Anna Margaret feels that Casper committed suicide because of the rumors circulating concerning Annie's behavior during his tour of duty in France, a puzzling comment which is only clarified by her account of the sequence of tragic events in the life of her godchild. Already in Annie's youth there were dire signs that happiness was not to be her lot. For instance, when her mother took her to prison to visit the hunter, Jürge, her former lover convicted of murder, and then, on the way home, stopped at the executioner's, the latter's sword in the closet rattled at the approach of the young girl—a sign in folk superstition that such an individual is destined to die by the sword. As Annie witnessed Jürge's execution, his severed head flew toward her and bit firmly into her dress, at which point Anna Margaret took her apron and covered the grim sight.

In spite of such evil omens, Annie's life seemed to prosper, for she was indoctrinated by Casper into a code of behavior in keeping with his standards of honor, and she found employment with a socially prominent family in the city during his service in France. However, the young count succeeded in making her believe that Casper had fallen in battle and, using a magic potion and a written promise of marriage, he seduced her. In despair, Annie subsequently killed the child born out of wedlock by smothering it with the familiar apron and, when arrested, she staunchly refused to name the father in spite of promises of leniency for herself. Consequently, she was sentenced to death for the infanticide and, as Anna Margaret now reveals, the execution is scheduled for this very morning at 4:00. This is the reason for her urgent plea for a petition to the duke in order to secure a respectable grave for both Casper and Annie.

The narrator-scribe determines to hasten to the duke's castle where he has an acquaintance in the guard, Count Großinger, and to submit a written request for pardon. But Anna Margaret objects, saying that justice would be preferable to any such earthly grace or mercy which will be of no avail at the Last Judgment when, as the refrain of her song states, the dead arise and come before God. On his way to the ducal palace, the narrator passes by the home of Großinger from which emanates a song to the accompaniment of a lute telling of love, mercy, and honor, and he interprets this singing together with the veil of roses which he finds on the street as a positive omen for his mission. Somewhat disturbed by a mysterious figure lurking in the shadows, the narrator nevertheless hastens on to the palace and demands that Großinger grant him entrance—which the latter staunchly refuses to do even though he is moved by the narrator's impassioned plea that the honor of two people is at stake.

As the clock strikes 3:30, the narrator resorts to desperate measures and shouts to the duke's window that help is needed to save a "wretched, seduced creature." The duke, intrigued by this nocturnal plea, listens to the history of Casper and Annie, looks sympathetically at the rose-filled veil, and is particularly impressed by the fact that the girl refused to betray the identity of the nobleman who had been her paramour. He then orders Großinger to attach the veil to his sword and to ride with the greatest speed with a reprieve to the place of execution. But Großinger arrives only in time to see the blade of the sword flashing in the sunlight, the din of military maneuvers in the vicinity having drowned out his cries of "Pardon! pardon!"

When Großinger sees the executioner holding out to him the bleeding head of the girl with her lips smiling, he asks for God's mercy for himself and confesses that he was the seducer. The angry crowd beats and kicks him until the duke arrives in his coach accompanied by the caped figure whom the narrator noticed before. The latter, shocked by Großinger's condition, removes the cape and reveals herself to be Großinger's sister. Meanwhile, Anna Margaret, having placed Casper's gold-tinsel wreath on Annie's severed head, covers the bloody area with her apron. The duke, completely broken by this sight, promises the lovers an honorable resting place, promotes Casper to officer status, and orders that his coffin be adorned with Großinger's sword. Annie's body is covered with the veil of mercy. As the lovers are lowered into the grave in the small town in which they lived, Anna Margaret expires in the narrator's arms, and is buried beside them, whereupon the narrator recites her refrain from the song of judgment and resurrection.

Upon his return to the city, the narrator learns of Großinger's suicide and confession about using magic potions to seduce Annie as well as of his written proposal of marriage (which she had burned). The mysterious caped figure who proved to be Großinger's sister, had compromised her honor by having a clandestine affair with the ruler in order to foster her brother's career. The duke now ennobles her as "Voile de Grâce" and they are married. A monument is erected to represent false and true honor, both of which bow before the Cross. Also portrayed in this allegorical sculpture are Justice brandishing a sword and Mercy holding a veil. It is rumored that the people of the land see in Justice features of the duke himself, while Mercy bears a resemblance to his new wife.

2. *Critical Reception of* The Story of Honest Casper and Fair Annie

In contrast to the sparsity of critical studies dealing with the *Chronicle*, the amount of high-quality scholarship devoted to *Honest Casper and Fair Annie* is striking. There have been at least ten specialized interpretations of the story, not to mention numerous treatments of it within the larger context of Brentano's life and works,[35] of monographs on the novella as a genre,[36] or of romanticism in its later, transitional stages.[37] The range of interpretative interest is correspondingly broad, encompassing such diverse topics as: sources of the work; its distinctive modes of narration with regard to style, structure, and perspective; the problems associated with the narrator-poet-scribe; analyses of the ducal monument; and investigations of the manifold forms of "honor" referred to in the tale. The following survey of criticism will present the highlights of these findings and then expand on several categories within the framework of romanticism as previously outlined.

Until 1970 the conjecture that the Casper part of the story was based on an account of military honor told to Brentano by Luise Hensel's mother went uncontested, while Annie's act of maternal infanticide was supposedly modeled on the poem "Weltlich Recht" from the collection *The Youth's Magic Horn*. However, an intensive study of the author's manuscripts and notes led Heinz Rölleke to question the first theory because no verification could be found for it, while the second proved too restrictive.[38] Rölleke traces many folk motifs in the work, deriving from popular songs, customs, oral tradition, and fairy tales, and reaches the conclusion that Brentano incorporated unconscious reminiscences into the prose narration rather than employing conscious montage.

With regard to narrative textures it is generally agreed that an important criterion to be observed is: who is doing the reporting. Whereas the narrator seems straightforward and in full control of his medium when stating what happens, the aged Anna Margaret tends to complicate matters by relating events in an imprecise and often anachronistic fashion, a characteristic of the nonsophisticated storyteller from the folk or peasant class. One must constantly reassess what she has already said in the light of her delayed revelations of identity or her tardy clarifications. Casper's background is presented in a more or less linear fashion with overtones of a moralizing almanac story, but Annie's past seems like a page from a broadside ballad, full of gruesome incidents. [39]

At one time Anna Margaret's status as the purest embodiment of the pious spirit of the people with its fundamentalist confidence in the divine order of things, [40] with an equanimity which stems from the sovereign perspective of one who has experienced many times the best and the worst which life has to offer, was unquestioned; however, this canonical or sacrosanct position has recently been challenged from more than one quarter. [41] The diminution of her role as mediator of the ultimate message has led to a corresponding augmentation of the significance of the narrator-scribe, as well as of the reader in his function as receptive agent (who patches together the real meaning from the diverse strands of information presented). When the narrator simply records Anna Margaret's words, he merits the designation "scribe" which he claims for himself. But when the old woman is no longer present, he becomes the sole mediating agent of the events reported; things are seen and structured from his perspective. Whereas Anna Margaret, in her stoic acceptance of the divine order, [42] tends to devalue life on earth in favor of a resurrection in the hereafter, the narrator, from his vantage point, enables the reader to appreciate the intrinsic worth of finite human effort, as futile or fallible as it may seem when compared with the eternal perfection of the divine. This upgrading in status of the narrator entails a corresponding reassessment of his significance, from the originally disoriented writer ashamed to admit the nature of his craft, to a man who takes charge of the situation and who, but for a set of adverse circumstances, almost wins the day.

If, as a poet, he does suffer from a loss of balance resulting in the "unhealthy" overdevelopment of a single organ (fantasy) to the detriment of the well-being of the entire organism, Anna Margaret might also be accused of a similar one-sidedness since she misses the intrinsic worth of life, seeing it only in terms of God's preordained plan for existence in the beyond. [43] In fact, it is the old woman who remains constant, rigidly unchanged throughout the story, dogmatically unbending in her viewpoint, while the narrator develops from a hesitant, insecure individual into one who proceeds with forthright determination, who no longer shamefacedly indulges in art for art's sake, making aesthetic constructs of human suffering, but who builds the framework for a potentially better future, an accomplishment of

which he can be proud even in failure, since he has done everything
humanly possible to ameliorate the human condition.

The metaphor of the enlarged goose liver as an objective correlative for the hegemony which creative fantasy holds over the poet's life
has provoked considerable scholarly interest, and has recently been
shown to have its roots and off-shoots in other works of Brentano, of
both earlier (1807) and later (1839) vintage, suggesting that the problem haunted him for the greater part of his life.[44] A thought-
provoking paradox has also been raised concerning this image; how is
it possible that in a literary work of consummate artistry, the validity
of the work of art as well as the justification of the artist are called into
question?[45] Perhaps the issue might be resolved in terms of the
central concern of the novella, honor, since the narrator is able to
salvage from his original condemnatory attitude toward the act of
writing as a somewhat less than honorable profession a more con-
ciliatory view insofar as his spoken and written word does succeed in
gaining for Casper and Annie an honorable grave. To a certain extent,
his unflinching resolve to carry his self-imposed mission to its conclusion may have been a motivating force in causing the duke to have the
monument erected—a visual representation of that concept which
ruled and ruined the lives of so many figures in the story.

The ducal monument has also elicited a wide range of diametrically
opposed critical responses: for some it becomes merely a contrived
appendage, a "papier-mâché" touch,[46] an "all-too artificial allegory,"[47] and even a form of irony;[48] for others, it has redeeming,
aesthetically and ethically laudable qualities. For instance, it has
been compared with an operatic reprieve insofar as all the figures and
motifs of the story are united in one place at one time, thereby
transforming the idea of the work into a symbol or function and thus
annulling content, in the Schillerian sense of the term, in favor of
perfect form.[49] This generous assessment has been qualified somewhat since its initial articulation in 1957, but the tendency has persisted to interpret the allegorical statuary as an integral part of the
overall fictional structure. One study regards it in terms of the
"emblem" (a technique widespread in the sixteenth and seventeenth
centuries of linking a certain stereotyped pictorial representation with
verbal axioms in a tripartite system of abstract superscription, scenic
portrayal, and epigrammatic explanatory subscription),[50] while the
preceding stories are considered "exempla" (the "exemplum" being a
classical and medieval form of short, didactic tale exemplifying some
positive or negative aspect of moral behavior)[51] in which the abstract
principle is concretized.[52] From yet another vantage point, the ducal
monument becomes a function of the fairy-tale structure of the story,

the latter being the last of the three orientation possibilities manifest in the work (the first being the peculiar perspective of Anna Margaret, the second that of the narrator-poet).[53] To the extent that poetic justice must prevail in the world of the *Märchen*, this is accomplished by the forms and figures which adorn the pedestal. A rather unique interpretation of the perplexing statuary regards it in terms of that excess or disproportion which destroys the lives of certain characters (Casper's exaggerated concern for his honorable reputation), which tarnishes the image of others (Anna Margaret's preponderantly negative attitude toward human endeavor) or, in the case of the narrator, which threatens the overall health of the organism unless the disease, like an overstuffed goose liver, can be controlled or cured.[54]

From the outset, the various manifestations of "honor" have served as a focal point of critical reaction and have continued to do so down to the present.[55] The range extends from Anna Margaret's *sub specie aeternitatis* attitude of rendering honor to God alone to Casper's inflexible adherence to the commands of military decorum and his social reputation, whereby excess of a virtue becomes a vice. Falling somewhere between these two extremes are such gradations as: compromised virtue leading to loss of honor in the sector of public knowledge (Annie) or private acknowledgment (Großinger and his sister); the psychological basis of the honor syndrome as well as of superstition and fatalism[56] through the power of suggestion; or the genuine perplexity of the narrator who, when confronted by Casper's obsessive quest for an unblemished record, declares: "All kinds of thoughts about honor kept running through my mind. . . . I wish someone could give me a convincing answer."[57] Perhaps it lay within the scope of Brentano's narrative strategy that this scribe, the person in the story who is least certain of what honor is or what his own role in life is to be, becomes the motivating force through which honor is restored within the fictional framework of the tale. Beyond that, he gains a certain modicum of honor for his professional skill in portraying a hierarchical scale of honor values, from the sublimest forms to man's most ridiculous and atrophied formalizations, whereby the ultimate answer concerning the essence of this quality lies not so much in any single manifestation of it, but rather in the total panoply of possibilities.

3. *Commentary on* The Story of Honest Casper and Fair Annie

In one of her frequent digressions during the report of Casper's rise and fall, Anna Margaret answers the query of the perplexed narrator as to what benefit the petition to the duke might bring, with the

seemingly non-sequitur phrase: "Oh, what would there be to life if it
had no end, what would there be to life if it were not eternal!"[58] For
all its apparent irrelevance to the question posed, and taking into
account the caveat that the octogenarian may not always serve as the
unequivocal mouthpiece for ultimate truth as the poet saw it, this
paradox—which in its verbal sophistication seems almost out of
character—could be interpreted as the fulcrum of Brentano's romanticism as it had evolved since the early days of the *Godwi* definition.
At that initial stage, Brentano considered the romantic quality of art
in terms of the the subjective addendum to the objective given, as the
color or shape of the refracting glass through which we gain not a
realistic image but rather a personalized view of the original stimulus.
With the passage of time, however, he came to modify this highly
subjective approach in favor of Novalis's process of romanticization
which called for the integration of a suprapersonal dimension, so that
the finite, the ordinary or the real were infused with the infinite, the
extraordinary, and the ethereal. Three quotations from letters of
1815–1818 addressed to three different acquaintances mark the stages
in Brentano's progression from what one might term his early to his
late mode of romanticism, even though the shifting of attitude was far
more gradual than indicated by the above time-span.

In a markedly confessional letter of 1815 to Wilhelm Grimm, the
Germanist and philologist, he declared:

I have finished my poetic activities, they were too closely connected with the
false path of my nature; I have failed in everything, for one should not adorn
the finite with the finite in order to give it an appearance of the infinite; every
work of art, even the most successful, whose object is not the eternal God and
His workings, seems to me a graven image which one should not fashion, for
fear that it might be worshipped. Because I completely misused myself
through the false aspirations of my mind, and because I feel that I allowed my
development to progress too one-sidedly in the direction of fantasy, I have
now, after a great struggle, and quite in conflict with my nature, turned to an
area in which I am completely forsaken, to mathematical knowledge.[59]

With his typical overstatement of the problem, Brentano categori-
cally rejects the past and vows to move in a diametrically opposite
direction, thereby engaging in another form of "overkill." Disheartened with his previous attempts in which, as he phrases it, he merely
decked out the "finite with the finite" in order to give the appearance
of infinity (much as two mirrors facing each other might seem to
suggest infinite regress through mutual reflection), he now recog-

nizes as valid only the other extreme—a form of artistic expression which incorporates, or better, embodies, the spiritual, the ineffable, the divine. To the Munich physician, Johann Nepomuk Ringeis, he confirms this diagnosis a short time later: "Most vividly I perceive the approach of a turning point in my innermost being because all arts and activities which have their focus consciously in temporal life no longer interest me to a high degree."[60]

Whereas the quotations above speak in terms of temporality, the finite versus the infinite, and decry exclusive concentration on the former, the last comment in a letter to Emilie Linder from 1818 projects the situation into spatial relationships, speaking of a proper domain of art as one which lies somewhere between two realms that transcend human knowledge: "Pray that art might become good, it teaches singing and praising, and lies, like life itself, between heaven and hell, and opens the gates to both; but its animal hide must be tanned in order that it might bear letters and words."[61] Art, so it seems, has the potential to probe unreachable heights and depths, even though it properly occupies an intermediary position between both and is rooted in the real—hence the need to temper, to refine its raw materials (or in terms of the image used here, to tan the animal hide) in such a fashion that the unadulterated bestial component is both modified and yet maintained, since it, too, comprises an essential ingredient in the work.

A similar view was expressed by Brentano in a famous musical image from an unsent letter of 1811, when he recognized the need for a well-tempered medium to replace the previously untuned, uninhibited—and consequently unaesthetic—instrument on which he had formerly performed:

I was a golden harp, drawn with animal strings; all types of weather put me out of tune, and the wind played me, and the sun stretched me. And love played forte so passionately that the strings ripped, ripped in such a stupid way that I can scarcely string a spinning wheel with what remains. . . . Now I have purged the harp in fire and strung it with metal and play it myself. . . .[62]

The paradox of Anna Margaret's declaration that life would be nothing were it not both eternal *and* terminal is to be resolved by acknowledging the validity of both constituents. The fallacious path of human endeavor lies down the blind alley of extremes and the failure to mediate between polarities. Applying this principle to the concept of honor in *Honest Casper and Fair Annie*, one might argue that the exclusively intrinsic approach (socially conditioned) taken by Casper as well as the uniquely extrinsic attitude (theologically oriented) of Anna Margaret represent the two extreme poles between which the true essence of honor emerges in the labyrinthine maze of human existence.

Perhaps this inherently fluid quality of an attribute such as honor accounts for our uneasiness and discomfort at the so neatly worked out symmetry of the monument. To be sure, this allegorical construct seeks to establish ties between the transcendental sphere and the terrestrial realm by portraying "false" and "true" honor bowing before the Cross. But can man's knowledge of the distinction between what constitutes false and true forms ever be that clear and distinct? Is it even proper that such a monument be erected by the duke and his lady, in view of the manner in which they arrived at the "honorable" state of matrimony? Should the figure of Justice resemble the duke even remotely? Does his wife merit her name "Voile de Grâce" or the likeness she bears to Mercy? Whom do the statues of "false" and "true" honor resemble—Casper and Annie or Großinger and Anna Margaret? In the case of each of these individuals, enough arguments could be produced to show that the line of demarcation between true and false becomes blurred and indistinct, so that one can already sense latent objections to such categorizations in the act of making the suggestion. This leads to a disquieting feeling akin to that experienced by readers and critics alike toward the monument, not to mention toward the story as a whole (from which there emerge no unscathed or unblemished heroes).

The conception of honor which the reader derives from the work will therefore be cumulative rather than selective, dynamic rather than static, multifaceted and not pigeon-holed. There is more than a grain of truth in the scribe's exasperated comment when confronted by the many thoughts about honor running through his mind and his wish for a convincing answer. The answer is implicit in his imploration: the stories of honor told to him and by him coalesce in the reader's mind to form a monument more lasting than that erected as a permanent tribute to honor in the tale itself. To pinpoint the essence of this attribute, one might paraphrase Anna Margaret's words concerning life itself: what would the honor of man be worth if it did not come to an end, and what would there be to it, if it were not eternal?

III   *The Fairy Tales*

As indicated in the opening chapter of this study, Brentano's fairy tales can, for the sake of a systematic discussion, be divided into three major categories: the *Fairy Tales of the Rhine* (basically original creations fused with motifs from local legend, and folklore); the minor ("small") Italian fairy tales, and the major ("large") Italian fairy tales (both of the latter groups based on Giambattista Basile's collection *Pentamerone*). In assessing Brentano's contribution to the genre, scholars have generally concentrated on three basic areas: (1) the sources used by the poet and the degree of his indebtedness or independence; (2) the extent of Brentano's success in meeting the quintessential requirements of the hypothetical ideal folk fairy tale (*Volksmärchen*), or conversely, his deviations from such normative restrictions in an effort to create an artistic form of fairy tale (*Kunstmärchen*) with an individual stamp; (3) the comparison of his early and late (much revised) versions of the same tale.[63] However, some attempts have been made (especially in more recent criticism) to examine Brentano's fairy tales from the intrinsic point of view rather than from any extrinsic vantage point,[64] and it is this latter approach which will be applied in the present context, since an exhaustive analysis of all the other problems touched upon in previous scholarship would require a separate monograph.

A. Fairy Tales of the Rhine *(1809–1812)*[65]

The two components which form the title of this collection—fairy tale and Rhine—both had an almost magic ring for the romantic generation in Germany. Virtually every writer of this persuasion contributed in some fashion to shaping the course which the fairy-tale genre—a literary stepchild of the eighteenth century which became the godchild of the early nineteenth—should take, because of the belief that this mode of expression prefigured *in nuce* a pathway to universal redemption, a remedy akin to the romantization or poetization of life which the age was destined to inaugurate. The second element of the title, the Rhine, the father of German rivers and the cradle of German culture and civilization, constitutes an example of modern mythmaking (culminating in Wagner's *Ring* cycle); poets revered this body of water with its castle ruins as the embodiment of Teutonic medieval splendor (Rhine romanticism) or as the source of potential regeneration and growth of the German nation, especially amid the patriotic fervor of the Napoleonic conflict.

1. *Content of the* Fairy Tales of the Rhine

This cycle consists of a frame tale dealing with the fortunes of Miller Radlauf and two subsidiary stories—"Marmot" and "Tailor

Seven with One Blow." In the frame tale Brentano draws upon elements from the Pied Piper of Hamelin, the legends surrounding Bishop Hatto of Mainz, and local sagas of the Bingen Mouse Tower and the Loreley. Miller Radlauf, a young lad living in close communion with the Rhine River, one day observes how the royal barge bearing King Hatto of Mainz, his daughter, Ameleya, and the official heraldic animal, the state cat, meets a ship carrying the queen of Trier, her son, Prince Rattenkahl (the fiancé of Ameleya), together with the mascot of this kingdom, the state rat. When, however, the Mainz cat attacks the rat of Trier, havoc breaks loose and in the ensuing melee, Ameleya falls into the water only to be rescued by Radlauf. In a moment of panic, King Hatto had promised Ameleya's hand in marriage to the one who saved her from drowning, but afterward he reneged on his word. Since Radlauf and Ameleya have fallen in love and want to marry, the Miller becomes embroiled in the cat-rat (mouse) conflict which eventually breaks out between Mainz and Trier.

With the aid of a musical pipe fashioned for him by Father Rhine, Radlauf leads a mouse army against Mainz in order to lay claim to his bride and to the crown of the land. But the treacherous King Hatto dupes the ingenuous Miller and wrests the instrument away from him, only to have a subordinate use it to lure the mice to a watery grave in the Rhine. Meanwhile, Prince Mausohr, brother of Prince Rattenkahl and son of the queen of Trier (both of whom drowned in the Bingen Gap) avenges the insults leveled at his deceased relatives by the children of Mainz (at the instigation of Hatto) by fashioning a magic flute of his own and piping them, like the Rat-Catcher of Hamelin, into the waters of the Rhine to their apparent death. In the interim, King Hatto has fled to a hastily constructed Mouse Tower near Bingen, where he is subsequently trapped and eaten alive by an avenging contingent of mice and rats led by a figure known as Rattenkönig of Trier. (The latter, we learn subsequently, is not only the father of Rattenkahl and Mausohr, but also—prior to his metamorphosis into Rattenkönig—of Radlauf and his brothers, Hans, Georg, and Philipp.)

While these grisly events are taking place, Radlauf, despondent at the loss of Ameleya, undertakes a journey to the Black Forest, the homeland of his ancestors. He does so on the advice of his brother, Hans, who, because of transgressions associated with inquisitiveness and loquaciousness, had been changed into a starling (an avian family which exemplifies similar characteristics). When Radlauf first met

Ameleya, Hans, in compliance with a hereditary prophecy, took his life in order to set in motion the process of redemption for their lineage, and in his last will and testament Hans now advises his brother to complete the redemptive procedure.

In the Black Forest Radlauf learns of the consequences, in successive generations of his family, of an insatiable desire to know what should not be known and also of his mission to bury his accursed ancestors, thereby redeeming the House of Starenberg (*Star*, starling). Returning to Mainz, Radlauf is hailed as the new monarch of the land. All that is missing to make his happiness complete is Ameleya who, together with the other children of Mainz, did not drown in the Rhine, but has been held captive in a crystalline enclosure beneath the waters. Father Rhine is prepared to relinquish his captives, provided that for each child released, a fairy tale be told. The first to comply is Radlauf, who relates the complex story of the Starenberg family in order to secure the release of Ameleya, and then two citizens of Mainz follow suit, at which point the author seems to have grown weary of the enterprise, so that the pending rescue of the majority of the children is never realized.

Radlauf reports how, in the Black Forest, he had encountered a long succession of his male forebears with such picturesque names as Grubenhansel ("Johnny of the Mines"), Kautzenveitel ("Screech-Owl Vitus") and Kohlenjockel ("Coaler Jake"). Their tales, as narrated by their wives, constitute a set of variations on the Melusine theme—the union of an elemental spirit with a human (whereby the former gains an immortal soul), the breach of faith on the part of the husband (who promises not to investigate what his spouse does during her periodic absences), and the punishment meted out because of this infraction. The guilty party must lead a kind of shadow existence of suspended animation until he is freed from this limbo by the self-sacrifice or redemptive act of a later generation, in this case, Hans and Radlauf. In the course of Radlauf's narration of five interrelated case histories, the cosmic-mythological dimensions of the cycle together with the Christian overtones of original sin and its link to forbidden knowledge, emerge quite vividly.[66]

Radlauf's ancestral line began with the marriage of the shepherd, Damon, and the daughter of the moon, Dame Moonlight, a union which proceeded happily until Damon ate the egg of a starling, a bird characterized by curiosity and loquaciousness, thereby incurring the wrath and curse of the queen of the species, Aglaster. Now, as the founder of the House of Starenberg, Damon acquires the attributes of this avian family, especially curiosity, and falls prey to the proddings of Cisio Janus, the embodiment of evil seduction and eternal recurrence, who, in collusion with the simian creature Trismegistus, goads Damon into investigating where Dame Moonlight goes during her periodic disappearances (actually she returns to her cosmic-astrological homeland to play cards with the four elements). As a punishment, Damon must remain buried alive beneath the earth (his beard, having grown into a table, holds him there—echoes of the Barbarossa saga), until he is redeemed by some later member of the family line.

The account of the second generation of the Starenberg house tells of the union of Damon's offspring, Johannes, with Dame Jewel, the daughter of the earth, and of their son Veit, who loves birds and the open air. But once again, due to Trismegistus's machinations, Johannes spies on his wife when she takes her periodic departures, and he is condemned to the limbo of lost memory, to live the life of a subterranean quack named Grubenhansel until the day of redemption arrives. However, when Trismegistus tries through scientific hubris to seduce Veit also, the latter exposes the primate nature of this pseudo-scholar and drives him off. Veit then captures a splendid bird which, in its metamorphosed form, is Dame Phoenix Feather-Glow, who becomes his bride. But jealousy and inquisitiveness aroused by an owl-like creature ultimately goad him into probing her whereabouts in violation of the standard agreement, and by tragic error, he commits her (in her avian form) to the flames—from which, however, she arises rejuvenated. Veit's punishment consists of being decked out in owl feathers, and he is henceforth dubbed Kautzenveitel. The son of Veit and Dame Phoenix, Jacob, lives with a hermit and dabbler in the occult sciences, Berthold Schwarz (the inventor of gunpowder), until Jacob, like his predecessors, violates his oath toward his wife, Dame Phosphorus Fire-Glow, is subjected to a similar punishment, and given the unflattering name of Kohlenjockel.

At this point in his odyssey Radlauf has returned to his mill on the Rhine, only to discover that nothing remains of it but the mill wheel on which sits the water sprite, Lureley, his mother. She tells him of her marriage to the Christel, son of Kohlenjockel and Dame Phosphorus Fire-Glow. The first of their four sons, Georg and Philipp, fell under the spell of a teacher who induced them to observe their mother during her periodic absences from the family, and this act led to their transformation into a little white mouse and a tiny goldfish respectively, while their meddlesome mentor was changed into a stork. But Christel, too, allowed himself to succumb to temptation, and when he probed his wife's whereabouts, he was punished by a loss of memory and given the menial task of grinding grain. Subsequently Lureley left her husband to go to live with Dame Echo at the Lureley Rock on the Rhine, while Christel remained at the mill with Radlauf; Hans, the last of the four sons, was sent as a page to the court of Mainz, but due to excessive talkativeness and curiosity, he was changed into a starling. Eventually Christel forsook Lureley for the queen of Trier, with whom he had two more sons, Rattenkahl and Mausohr. For this act of unfaithfulness, he was transformed by Lureley into Rattenkönig (this term literally means "king of the rats," but it also denotes a tangled maze, a farrago or jumble, concepts derived from its original reference to the sickness which causes the tails of baby rats in a litter to become inextricably ensnarled).

Because Father Rhine is pleased with this well-narrated tale, he releases Ameleya from the confines of her glass prison beneath the waters. In order to secure the freedom of other children, individual citizens of Mainz begin to narrate fairy tales, the first being the fisherwoman Marzibille, who frees her daughter, Ameleychen, with the account of a girl, Marmot, who must suffer at the hands of a wicked stepmother, Wirz and an envious stepsister, Murza, until her inherent nobility comes to light and she is restored to her proper place in society. Finally, Master Meckerling, in order to release his son, Garnwischchen, tells the adventures of "Tailor Seven with One Blow," a bravura piece full of linguistic virtuosity which makes out of metaphors living entities (*Seelenverkäufer*, "kidnappers," become literal "sellers of souls" in an employment agency in which souls are displayed in the window; the *Sündenbock*, "scapegoat," prances about as a lively billy goat) or which derives highly imaginative etymological explanations for geographical entities (the *Ärmelkanal*, the English Channel, is traced back to the wedding of the heraldic French cock and the unicorn of England, at which the bride's huge "sleeves" were torn of during a bit of rowdy byplay). [67]

2. *Critical Reception of the* Fairy Tales *of the Rhine*

Although the fairy tales, ever since their inception[68] and authorized appearance in 1846–1847, have sparked critical debates and disputes,[69] commentators have too often tended to "bite off more than they could chew" insofar as they treated the entire corpus of the tales instead of concentrating on single cycles, or even better, on individual works.[70] Whereas such generalizing does enable the uninitiated reader to gain an overview, it also leads to the obliteration of the peculiarities of the individual story, cycle or cluster of tales. This problem was recognized by modern critics, so that recently attempts have been made to rectify this shortcoming. For instance, one study in the 1970s examines the complex modes of narration in the Rhine tales, from the relatively simple account of Radlauf couched in a quasi-present time frame at the outset to the surrealistic delineation of events in the primordial framework of the mythical family history of the Starenbergs, together with the interplay of the two temporal modes. Such reciprocity of "centrifugal" and "centripetal" forces produces a daring experiment in narrative technique in a genre which is usually not noted for such complex strategies.[71] From this it becomes evident that the *process* of communication can be of even greater magnitude than the content of what has been reported. A particularly successful blend of traditional and innovative methods has recently been attempted in an analysis of the romantic fairy tale in the context of narcissistic self-preoccupation;[72] by taking into account the dialectical nature of what too often have been regarded as mutually exclusive polarities while, at the same time, combining interpretation and explanation in a reciprocally enlightening fashion, such an approach paves the way for a revaluation (if not transvaluation) of some of the standard critical clichés fixing Brentano's place in the fairy-tale tradition.

3. *Commentary on the* Fairy Tales of the Rhine

This cycle, like the *Gockel* story which follows, might be interpreted with reference to a modern concept from the field of photography: viewing through a wide-angle lens for greater depth perception. Not only does Brentano's fairy-tale perspective expand our range of vision horizontally (synchrony), giving us a panoramic view of diverse realms in correlation (hence the wide-angle lens component), but it also extends our appreciation of the temporally vertical (or diachronic) element, thus enabling us to look back in time to the mythical past (consequently the "depth perception" metaphor).

With regard to the first category, one could draw upon the comment of a twentieth-century neo-romanticist, Thomas Mann, who in his novel *Doctor Faustus* (in which, coincidentally, Brentano plays a far from negligible role) makes the observation concerning the structure of musical composition: "Relationship is everything."[73] In the

wide-range view of life presented in the Rhine tales, virtually everything is related as well as relationship, so that in spite of the fragmentary nature of the overall cycle, a feeling of oneness, togetherness,
and even synthesis arises. This cohesion takes place both on obvious
as well as more elusive levels. For instance, a system of correspondences is established between the cosmic, elemental, human,
animal, and even inanimate, realms, Radlauf's lineage is traced back
to the union of a mortal with the daughter of the moon, while
successive generations are linked to the earth, the air, fire, and water
respectively. And yet the Starenberg house is also allied with the
avian sphere of the starlings, literally *ab ovo*, since Damon's eating of
the egg (destined to produce the king of the breed) infused into the
genetic structure and psyche of his progeny the drive to probe
beyond the borders of permissible knowledge. The punishment for
this transgression is only alleviated by Radlauf when he provides a
fitting burial for Hans as well as for each of his forefathers, on whose
grave the epitaph reads: "He no longer desires to know" (*W*, 3:129
and passim). Brentano's hidden symmetry amid this genealogical
conglomeration comes to the fore when one shows graphically how
each progenitor and his mate are provided with a tempter: (1)
Damon—Dame Moonlight—Cisio Janus (Trismegistus); (2)
Grubenhansel—Dame Jewel—Trismegistus; (3) Kautzenveitel—
Dame Phoenix Feather-Glow—the owl; (4) Kohlenjockel—Dame
Phosphorus Fire-Glow—Berthold Schwarz; and (5) Christel—Dame
Lureley—the teacher of Georg and Philipp, the twelve vassals of
Christel. Noteworthy is the fact that no such comparable figure is to
be found in the case of Radlauf and Ameleya, so that one might
assume that the recurrent loss of an idyllic state of happiness due to
the seductive temptation to forbidden knowledge has been superse-
ded by a state of blessed innocence (or perhaps even blissful ignor-
ance, even though Radlauf is aware of the source of his family's
misfortunes). And Ameleya, in contrast to all other female partners in
the family history, is not of superhuman origin; there is no tantalizing
mystery surrounding her life which Radlauf might be induced to
probe and thereby incur the curse which befell his ancestors.

Aside from this seemingly happy resolution of an inherent conflict
which involves cosmic, human, animal, and elemental forces, there
are several other indications in the narrative strategy and in verbal (or
acoustical) tactics which suggest the restoration of an integrated mode
of life. It turns out, for example, that the state cat which instigated the
confusion (thereby also setting in motion the process of redemption

carried out by Radlauf) was the metamorphosed Cisio Janus, the calendarlike figure who originally helped induce Damon to investigate the whereabouts of his wife against her wishes and who embodied in his physical appearance the essence of the punishment meted out to him and his heirs for this infraction—repetition without resolution, eternal recurrence devoid of meaning.

With regard to verbal ties between disparate spheres, one could point to the fact that Rattenkahl, Mausohr, and Rattenkönig have double (in some cases, even triple) frames of reference. On the one level, these are the names of human beings, the two princes and the consort of the queen of Trier respectively. But Brentano plays on the obvious ambivalence inherent in the quasi-rodent allusions, especially in view of the fact that a member of this family serves as the heraldic symbol of Trier (but even here that is a further ambiguity, since Brentano frequently uses the colloquial form for rat *die Ratze* instead of the standard German *die Ratte,* while the term *der Ratz* is not only a dialect form for "rat," but also the designation for a marmot and polecat). With regard to the above-mentioned rodent-triad, we are not dealing with a fairy-tale enchantment (as in the case of the little white mouse or the tiny gold fish), but rather with figures whose behavior patterns and attributes could be interpreted in both human and animal (rodent) terms. In addition, Rattenkahl has a figurative meaning ("bald as a rat") while Rattenkönig, as previously indicated, implies a tangled maze or farrago. Mausohr, on the other hand, links the human frame of reference not only with the animal world, but also with that of plants, since the term signifies a flower of the forget-me-not type.

On the acoustical plane, there is, throughout Brentano's works, a marked tendency to associate with the "ei" (or "ey") sound the element of sorrow, suffering, or anguish (*leiden, scheiden, meiden,* "to suffer," "to part," "to avoid") while the *a* vowel more often denotes states of peace of mind, serenity, or happiness (as in *Paradies*).[74] Naturally, such an assertion is open to debate, and numerous exceptions as well as neutral words with similar tonal constellations could be listed where the theory is invalidated on the basis of semantic considerations. However, the Rhine tales strengthen this conjecture if one considers that the misery of the Starenberg family begins with the eating of an egg (the German word for which consists of the single sound *ei*) in a surrounding which Damon felt to be a haven of peace (a cave which he calls his *Eiland,* the world for island, but also a possible play on "land of the egg"). The name of his bride, *Mondenschein*, like that of the women in the next four generations of Starenbergs, ends with the "ei" sound, and the fates of their respective spouses terminate in a painful state of virtual nonexistence. However, this situation is changed by Radlauf when he marries Ameleya, a girl who shares none of the cosmic or elemental (water, fire, etc.) attributes of her predecessors, but is simply the ingenuous offspring of a malevolent tyrant (on whom the fairy-tale principle of poetic justice is exemplified). If one pursues the hypothesis of sound symbolism suggested above to its logical conclusion, then the vowel constellation in Ameleya's name, "a-ei-a", might be seen in terms of the progression in the story itself; an original paradisaical state (the union of the Starenberg ancestors with a woman of higher than human order) followed by the disruption of that ideal condition due to the intrusion of a desire to know the nature of that suprahuman link which, however, leads to an ultimate restoration of a state of harmony and happiness due to sacrifice on the part of those seeking redemption.

If the above elements of visual superimposition of diverse realms and the manipulation of linguistic components to symbolize the pathway from unity through dichotomy to tri-unity (in a strictly secular sense) could be classified as the fairy-tale mode of viewing through a wide-angle lens, then Brentano's efforts to establish links to the distant past by using similar verbal-visual techniques might be categorized as his unique brand of "depth perception." Centuries fly by in seconds, and we find ourselves in a remote age when earthlings communicated with the fundamental forces in the cosmos. But in spite of the shift in configurations, the unchanging relationship throughout all time is evident insofar as essential conflicts persist and form a pattern of eternal recurrence. And even though this process seems to have terminated through the combined efforts of Hans and Radlauf, we have no assurance that the entire cycle might not again be set in motion once Radlauf and Ameleya embark on a domestic life. There is no placating formula of "and they lived happily ever after" here, since Brentano never completed the work—a fact which, in itself, might be indicative of his uncertainty concerning such a neatly packaged resolution. Radlauf's symbolic name is suggestive of a wheel turning round and round, the principle of circularity in all perpetuity, and this process can never really terminate, but rather continues as long as the River Rhine, like the river of life, flows on. After all, the

German name *Rhein* is not only the homonymic equivalent for the concepts of purity (*rein*) and purification (*Reinigung*), but it also emphasizes the tonal component linked to sorrow and suffering, "ei," as does the abbreviated form of the heroine's name which the poet uses consistently throughout the closing section of the tale: Ameley.

Rational man might argue that what happens here is a wish-dream, perhaps even a pipe-dream. In response to this, however, the romantic may note, with an ironic twinkle in his eye, that the source of such a remark is the type of calculating, dissecting mind represented in the fairy tales by such bogey men as Cisio Janus and Trismegistus, and that for those disposed to believe, no explanation is necessary, while for men of little faith, no explanation is possible.

B. *The Italian Fairy Tales*

Due to the limitation of space, the individual tales comprising the minor and major Italian fairy tale groups will not be treated in detail, but rather in summary fashion. On the other hand, one story, *Gockel and Hinkel* (1815–1816), together with its significant revisions of 1835–1838 under the new title *Gockel, Hinkel and Gackeleia*, and the two additions ("Heartfelt Dedication" and the *Pages from the Diary of the Ancestress*) will be analyzed in the standard detailed format.

The frame for the so-called minor collection of Italian tales is provided by the story of "Dear Little-Heart" (*Liebseelchen*) which tells of a sad princess who can only be induced to laugh when her dancing and decorum instructor, Mademoiselle Pimpernelle, is tripped at the marketplace. This teacher, however, is in reality a witch who condemns Dear Little-Heart to perpetual maidenhood unless she, through much weeping and shedding of tears, can rouse the dead Prince Röhrdopp from his tomb. The sad princess is so moved by the statue of the prince, that she provides an entire bucket of tears, whereupon she collapses with exhaustion. An evil Mooress, Russika, then absconds with the bucket together with the resuscitated prince. However, Dear Little-Heart is so good-natured that she accepts this harsh treatment and gives Russika a parrot, a golden hen, and a magic doll—gifts from women she has helped during her lifetime. Russika places these gifts into the crib of her child—which turns out not to be a living infant, but rather a feather duster wrapped in diapers. The magic doll, which can spin, is compelled to work night and day for Russika, until the figurine grows so rebellious that it threatens to reveal the entire subterfuge to Röhrdopp unless Russika agrees to tell fairy tales to help pass the time spinning. Since Russika herself is not able to do this, she summons ten elderly women who are to narrate their "old wives" tales. Only five stories are completed, and so this grand design, like the fairy tales of the Rhine, remains a torso.

The first of the tales, "Myrthenfräulein" ("Myrtle-Maiden"), tells of a girl who develops from a plant cutting in a porcelain pot to become the bride of Prince Wetschwuth (Wedgewood) in spite of the machinations of her evil rivals. "Witzenspitzel" ("Smart Alec") is an anecdote about a clever lad who outfoxes clumsy giants and jealous courtiers to win the hand of a princess, while "Rosenblättchen" ("Little Rose Petal") tells of another figure evolving from the vegetative sphere of flora (she grows from a flower cutting), who after enduring a Sleeping-Beauty–like enchantment and suffering at the hands of a wicked stepmother, finds happiness due to the intervention of a benevolent witch disguised as a doll. "Hüpfenstich" ("Hopping-Stinger") is a grotesque account of an enchanted flea who becomes such a favorite with King Keep-His-Word, that he is made a baron and, after some tribulations caused by his own hubris and by the meddling of the ever curious Princess Willwischchen (Want-to-Know), is restored to human form and marries the monarch's daughter. Finally, in "Dilldapp" we encounter the happy fool, the ne're-do-well simpleton for whom all things turn out well in spite of his own bunglings. Presumably, had all ten tales been completed, Russika would have been punished for her malicious acts and Dear Little-Heart would have married her prince and lived happily ever after, thus reflecting the common theme of all the subsidiary tales that undeserved suffering will be followed by poetic justice—the rewarding of the good and the punishment of evildoers in a world only temporarily out of joint.

The longer or "major" Italian fairy tales do not have such an all-embracing framework, but consist rather of freely expanded adaptations of works which, in Basile's *Pentamerone*, were much shorter. Whereas the *Fairy Tale of Master Klopfstock* ["Rapping Switch"] *and His Five Sons* comes down to us only in a single version and "Komanditchen" ("Little Limited Liability Company") and "Schnürlieschen" ("Little Lace-Strap-Lise") remained fragments, two others, *Fanferlieschen Schönefüßchen* and *Gockel and Hinkel* underwent major revisions and augmentations in the decade from 1830 to 1840.

The five sons of Schoolmaster Rapping Switch are directed toward their future occupations by their very names, for what they call themselves becomes their "calling." Gripsgraps turns out to be a thief, Pitschpatsch a ship builder, Piffpaff a rifleman, Pinkepank an apothecary, and the youngest, Trilltrall, after studying the language of the birds with an old hermit, devotes himself to art. When they later return home to their father, all have become masters of their trade—except Trilltrall, who, it seems, remains a misfit. Yet it is this singer-poet who wins the hand of Princess Pimperlein, daughter of King Pumpan of Glockotonia, after having rescued her from Knarrasper-Knarratschki, the ominous ruler of the night watchmen. It is not without significance that Brentano accords the highest prize in life to the son whose career most closely resembles his own "calling."[75]

"Komanditchen," as the awkward translation "Little Limited Liability Company" indicates, deals with the world of business ledgers and bookkeeping, a sphere which was anathema to Brentano, so that it is not surprising that this work turns out to be more a satire on the merchant class and the mercantile quest for profit than a fairy tale in the strictest sense of the term.[76] "Schnürlieschen," on the other hand, is a late reworking of *Liebseelchen* which develops the figure of the dancing and decorum teacher, Mademoiselle Cephise la Marquise de Pimpernelle, in such a manner that she appears as a sadist who takes great delight in compelling the princess to wear clothing which is too constricting (hence the name "Little Lace-Strap Lise") and in imposing dogmatically modes of behavior which further impinge upon Dear Little-Heart's freedom.

At first glance, the title of the fairy tale *Fanferlieschen Schönefüßchen* ("Fanferluche-Liese Beautiful Tiny Feet") (*W*, 4:1094) seems inappropriate, since the titular figure functions only in a very peripheral fashion. Instead we hear of the villainous King Jerum ("Dear Me") of the land of Skandalia, the evil successor of the "praiseworthy" King Laudamus. Having fallen under the spell of a malevolent pagan deity, Pumperlirio Holzebock, [77] Jerum has sacrificed a long succession of wives to the wooden idol, and for this and similar transgressions he is banned from the capital Besserdich ("Better-Thyself") to a grim castle Munkelwust. Jerum's most recent spouse, Ursula von Bärwalde, however, is not stabbed to death like her predecessors, but secretly immured in a tower, where she is nourished with food and life's amenities by a throng of friendly birds she once helped. Here she gives birth to a son, Ursulus, who eventually rids the country of the bloodthirsty deity, tempers the mood of his monarch-father by freeing him from the machinations of his new spouse, the malicious Queen Würgipumpa, and reinstates Fanferlieschen to the position of prominence she had occupied under Laudamus. The revised *Fanferlieschen* is two and one-half times the length of the original and indulges in all sorts of verbal pyrotechnics (to which names such as "Skandalia" and "Sandalia" lend themselves) and elaborations on what were previously inconsequential details (Fanferlieschen's educational institution "for man and beast" provokes long digressions on the links between family attributes and heraldic symbols; her life's history as well as that of Laudamus are now reported at great length).[78]

The expansion of *Fanferlieschen* to include background material from the past recalls the aspect of "depth perception" found in the tales of the Rhine. The establishment of close links between ostensibly disparate realms in the universe calls to mind that ability to see relationships between highly diverse entities which was referred to earlier as viewing through a wide-angle lens. Ursula von Bärwalde is not only the name of a human being, but also an allusion to the animal realm in both of its components: the Latin *ursus* ("bear") forms the female name Ursula, and Bärwalde could be translated as Bear Forest (the latter being the name of a territory in Arnim's hereditary estate of Wiepersdorf). In addition, there are also cosmic dimensions involved here, since when Ursula is imprisoned in the tower, she often turns to the constellations of Ursa Major and Ursa Minor for solace. Similar phenomena could be observed in the case of the "minor" Italian tales in which people and plants (Myrtle-Maiden, Little Rose Petal), individuals and insects (Hopping-Stinger), were related in an often confusingly wonderful or wonderfully confusing fashion.

C. Gockel and Hinkel *(1816), and* Gockel, Hinkel and Gackeleia *(1838)*

The first impression one gains from the titles of the original fairy tale as well as its revision is that it deals with barnyard fowl: the German term "Gockel" is a dialect form for rooster, while "Hinkel" can be rendered by "hen." However, it turns out that Gockel is the name of a count (who, nevertheless, comes originally from Hanau—*Hahn*, rooster) married to a woman Hinkel (her native territory is Hennegau—*Henne*, hen, pullet). Yet throughout the work Brentano carefully establishes and sustains a subtly ambivalent relationship between the spheres of humanity and poultry, much to the confusion of the reader and the delight of the author. The matter is further complicated by the fact that barnyard fowl such as Alektryo (Greek "rooster"), the cock owned by Gockel and Hinkel, exhibits human traits (not the least of which is the ability to speak), while Gockel behaves at times in a manner more befitting a cock than a count. Etymological derivations also help to maintain an ambiguous interplay between the domains, since the couple resides in Gockelsruh and Gelnhausen (*gellen*, "to squawk like a chicken"), territories ruled by King Eifrasius ("Egg-Devourer") and Queen Eilegia ("Egg-Layer"), whose son, Prince Kronovus ("Crown-Egg" or "Heir to the Crown") ultimately marries the daughter of Gockel and Hinkel, Gackeleia (*gackeln*," to cackle or cluck like a chicken").

It is of considerable import that the latter name was added to the title of the revised version of the tale (above and beyond the preference of the genre for groups of three), since through the transgression of this child the family both loses and regains its paradisiacal state of blissful existence (again, as in Ameleya, the "a" component in the name, points to a propitious beginning and end, while the intermediary suffering is captured symbolically by the "ei" sound—which, as previously noted, is the word for "egg" in German). She becomes the axis on which the fate of both the human and avian worlds turn, and consequently it is fitting that her name be mentioned in the title. Since the basic plot outlines of the original tale and the later version are essentially the same, the following content summary will be based on the early story, augmented by an account of the important addenda together with the supplementary material in the "Heartfelt Dedication' and the *Pages from the Diary of the Ancestress.*

1. *Content of the* Gockel *Complex*

In the chicken coop of the dilapidated ancestral castle in Gockelsruh near Gelnhausen live Count Gockel, his wife, Hinkel, and their daughter, Gackeleia, together with the hereditary rooster of the family, Alektryo and his mate, Gallina (Latin *gallina* meaning "pullet"). Gockel, once the minister of Pheasantry and Fowl for King Eifrasius, lost his position when he objected to the monarch's construction of a pleasure palace, Eierburg ("Castle of Eggs"), out of hollow egg shells because of the threat posed by this practice to the chicken population. One night, while sleeping in his ancestral home, Gockel is implored by two white mice, Princess Sissi of Mandelbiss and Prince Pfiffi of Speckelfleck, to help them escape from the cat,

Schurimuri, who prowls about in pursuit of them. Gockel fulfills their request by taking them to a safe spot across the river, whereupon they promise to help him in the future.

On his way home, Gockel meets three quasi-philosophers, a triad of Jews skilled in the art of seal engraving, who try, with no success, to purchase the rooster Alektryo from him. It had been prophesied that Alektryo would bring happiness to the family. But when Gallina and her thirty newborn chicks are killed and the blame is placed on Alektryo by Hinkel and Gackeleia (the real culprits are Gackeleia's plaything, the black cat Schurimuri and her kittens), Gockel changes his mind about selling the cock —until the latter suddenly begins to speak and pleads for death by the family sword rather than at the hands of the Jews. Gockel, by a clever ruse, prevents the seal engravers from taking possession of the rooster, and then he overhears them lament that all their efforts have thus been in vain—the attempt of their forefathers to ascertain the secret of the ring by the art of seal engraving, their own machinations at court which led to Gockel's dismissal from ministerial service, their having reduced him to poverty and even their smuggling of Schurimuri into his castle.

Gockel sets a trial to convict the cat for its crime and to punish Hinkel and Gackeleia for their perjury against Alektryo. Avian witnesses such as Mesdames Swallow and Robin Red-Breast testify against Schurimuri, and the latter, together with her entire litter, are condemned to death. Hinkel is punished by having added to her heraldic coat of arms the insignias of *Huhnerbeine* ("chicken bones" or "legs") and the castle of *Katzenellenbogen* ("cats' elbows") on the Rhine, while Gackeleia is forbidden ever again to play with a doll (due to the actions of her most recent "plaything," Schurimuri). Alektryo, despondent over the loss of his entire family, asks to be beheaded, and when Gockel reluctantly complies, there falls from the cock's craw the magic signet ring of Solomon which has the power to grant any wish. By turning the magic ring on his finger, Gockel obtains youth for Hinkel and himself, and a vast amount of wealth, including the restoration of his castle to its previous grandeur.

The citizens of Gelnhausen now eagerly seek to do business with Gockel, and the king, who once sent him off in disgrace, curries his favor with lavish gifts and receives in return some fantastically exotic eggs. But the happiness and prosperity are of only short duration when Gackeleia falls victim to the tempting offer of a dancing figurine from a bearded, elderly man in return for "seeing" the ring. Naturally, this benevolent stranger is a member of the evil triumvirate in disguise, and the ring he returns is a copy, so that Gockel soon afterward loses his wealth and youth, together with any favor at court. When Gockel threatens to whip Gackeleia for her actions, she runs off in pursuit of the dancing figurine (which she insists on calling in sophistic fashion an "artifact", not a doll) and she remains lost from view for a long period of time.

When she returns to her parents, she is no longer a child, but rather a rational, mature young woman. Gackeleia had been aided in her quest for the ring by Sissi, the tiny white mouse, who had been compelled to supply the motor force which animated the dancing figure. Sissi, together with her fiancé, Pfiffi, helped Gackeleia wend the ring away from the wicked engravers, all of whom, in their desire to become sole possessor of the magic object, had been changed into donkies. Once she gained the ring back, Gackeleia wished for measured reason to replace her "dangerous desire for play," and by twisting the ring on her finger, she now restores her parents to their youthful state and the castle returns to its one-time splendor.

Sending off the donkies with bounty for the mouse kingdom in gratitude for its help, Gackeleia then evokes Prince Kronovus as her bridegroom, presenting him with the ring of Solomon. With the aid of this wishing ring, Kronovus then fulfills her last request: all present are to become children again, the entire adventure is to be a fairy tale recounted by Alektryo (who has been revived from the dead) in such a delightful fashion, that the metamorphosed adults clap their hands. [79] As a matter of fact, the hands of the narrator still tingle, he admits, since he was also there—otherwise how would he ever have known the story?

The revised version of the tale retains the basic plot as outlined above intact, but it does augment the text with many extraneous details and expanded descriptions, while incorporating in the concluding section further background material on the ancestors of the Gockel-Hinkel line as well as some private biographical allusions (in the form of veiled references to Emilie Linder and Luise Hensel). The interpolations are of numerous types: there are, for instance, endless verbal acrobatics displaying the poet's linguistic virtuosity (Brentano's predilection for the egg motif extends to the common German suffix "ei," so that, via this pun, virtually any concept in the language can be marshalled for this purpose—with no "eggs-emptions" and many an "eggs-aggeration": *Schmeichel-ei*, "flattery" or *Heuchel-ei*, "hypocrisy," to give just a few "eggs-amples"; finely embroidered accounts of key incidents (Gackeleia's adventures in the mouse kingdom, Sissi's training and tenure as the dancing figurine); minor details ballooned out of proportion (Sissi's numerous dancing costumes are described in ten pages of verse); the insertion of long and involved genealogies (especially of the heraldic rooster); short lyric interludes augmented by many verses; passages of a religiously edifying nature (the mouse cathedral, a picturesque structure built from the bleached skull of a dead horse, becomes the shrine of pious homage to the deity); political commentaries on the contemporary scene (the reforms of Freiherr vom Stein in Prussia); satiric byplay dealing with social organizations (the kittens of Schurimuri—changed to Schurrimurri—now have provocative names such as Gog, Magog, and Demagog, and are linked to the Free Masons); toning down of the earlier anti-Semitism (the philosophers are no longer Jews but merely seal engravers from the East); intensification of the symbolism (especially dealing with flowers, colors, and eggs); parodies of the styles and specific works of well-known writers (Schiller, Matthisson); more frequent intrusions of the narrator and an increase in the number of instances where the story, in good romantic tradition, comments on its own structure or aesthetic quality.

In the process of revising the concluding pages of the original *Gockel*, Brentano did deviate from the earlier format by having Gackeleia conjure up the ancestors of her parents, and in conjunction with her family's progenitor, Countess Amey of Hennegau, he begins to incorporate into the text a haunting couplet "O star and blossom, spirit and garb, / Love, sorrow, and time and eternity!"[80] which runs in refrainlike fashion through the remainder of this adaptation as well as through the entire *Diary of the Ancestress*, thus supplying a leitmotivic link between the two works. Detailed reports are given about the lay orders of mercy for the aid of poor children established in 1317 by Countess Amey (such as Cloister Lilienthal), and these are followed by an account of her inheritance of the land with the evocative name "Vadutz," together with a history of the royal insignia of that fiefdom (the jewels and amarantine buckles or epaulettes). With each object mentioned, Brentano feels compelled to present the background in detail, to trace its roots in secular or biblical history. Finally, when he depicts the wedding of Gackeleia and Kronovus, he introduces the figure of the "powerful, stocky Scotch lady" (*W*, 3:816) (ostensibly modeled on Emilie Linder) seated on the chair of St. Edward and surrounded by a strange retinue of gingerbread figures. Having come to ponder the treasures of Vadutz, she behaves in a decidedly unchildlike manner; but due to the restoration of the childlike state after the turning of the ring, even she shares in the paradisaical blessing of innocence reborn. On the other hand, the beautiful art-figurine which, as Gackeleia insisted, had never been a doll, is transformed into a "proper governess" who supplies the children with cake and cookies—provided they behave correctly. As before, the festivities end with all present clapping their hands, including even the somber little boy (another addition) who throughout all this scene of childlike happiness has experienced visions of the harvest time of life, with the grim reaper striding through the fields and cutting down stalks at the prime of their growth.

The *Pages from the Diary of the Ancestress* embroider the embroidery of the revised *Gockel*, so to speak, by portraying the lineage of Hinkel, Gockel, and Alektryo through a variety of prose media— diary entries on daily life, dream sequences, letters, and religiously tinged observations on events from Good Friday to the summer solstice of the year 1317. There are also accounts of the historical foundation for Amey's claim to the kingdom of Vadutz together with its imperial jewels, her marriage to the original Count Gockel under a linden tree (whereby the name Linder is brought to mind), the events surrounding the magic ring of Solomon, and her establishment of the Order of the Lilies. Several subsidiary figures are introduced here, such as Amey's spiritual mentor, Jacob von Guise; her constant companion, the mentally unsound girl Klareta; the martyrlike figure Verena (who bears a close resemblance to Anna Katharina Emmerick); the lame and half-mad weaver of Vadutz, Jürgo, and that mysterious and pensive little lad who through the diary is said to be "doing his thing" (as an act of penitence and atonement for once having stolen the food of Gallina, he must gather kernels of corn one by one) until, at the harvest of life, he completes his task and finds redemption.

As a kind of counterpart to the "O star and blossom" couplet which, through its poetic linking of disparate realms, suggests an ultimate synthesis of entities which, from the limited human perspective appear as dichotomies, Brentano introduces a quatrain "Fire-red little roses." These verses evoke via the color (red, amaranthine) and fire symbolism (associated with the festival of St. John and the solstice) the concept of ardent passion and underscore the dangers encountered when one surrenders to unrestricted emotion which has not been tempered by some spiritual component.

Finally, the "Heartfelt Dedication" which Brentano, rather cryptically, directs to "Little Grandmother," fuses much of the material in both *Gockels* and the *Diary* with autobiographical data in a highly complex, encoded fashion. For instance, he reveals that Vaduz was actually the name of a private paradise for himself and his sister, a fantasy realm which held them spellbound by its very sound constellation until Brentano was unceremoniously informed that this imaginary never-never land was a real geographical entity, the capital of Liechtenstein. This harsh truth crushed his hopes for a time, and he even sought to deny the validity of the fact until Goethe's mother told him that his Vaduz actually lay in heaven, that no locality on earth could ever satisfy him. Thus he followed her advice and built his reborn hopes on the "winged shoulders of fantasy" (*W*, 3:626) (for which the jewels of Vaduz served as symbols) after fantasy degraded herself by tearing the epaulettes from its own shoulders in full view of the philistine, again leaving him (Brentano) in the lurch until Frau Rath Goethe found a new remedy: the "little clown crawling from an egg" (*W*, 3:627).

Such cryptic allusions make the dedicatory preface extremely difficult reading, especially when they occur in rapid succession, so that one unknown quantity follows another. But such mystifications are not at all fortuitous but deliberate; at this point in his life Brentano was convinced that whatever he wrote would fall on deaf ears since "the children of this age turn their backs on me just as fantasy does" (*W*, 3:629). He concludes by admitting, tongue in cheek, a printing error in the published version of his manuscript: what appears as a "heartfelt dedication" should have read the "heartfelt inclination" (not *Zueignung* but rather *Zuneigung*—a clever manipulation of a single letter evoking a radically altered frame of reference). Cryptically, the obedient grandson alludes to a secret fascination for his "Little Grandmother" who, like Gackeleia's dancing figurine, was no mere "doll" or plaything, but rather a work of art which gave heightened potential to the artist's work.

2.　*Critical Reception of the* Gockel Complex

As is the case with most of the Italian fairy tales, a large bulk of scholarship focusing on *Gockel* has been devoted to source studies, especially the relationship to Basile.[81] Sometimes the results of specific investigations have been surprising, showing a greater dependence on the original than previously suspected.[82] A second area of interest, the comparison of the two versions of the story, has given rise to conjectures as to why the adaptation of 1838 seemed too weighted-down with verbal ballast;[83] whereas earlier critics tended to regard the late *Gockel* as well as the dedication and diary sequel as confused and confusing products of a senile mind,[84] there has been a trend since the mid 1950s to look at all three products of Brentano's last years with a more sympathetic and understanding eye.

This positive approach was inaugurated by Claudia Rychner in 1956 with a very circumspect analysis of the *Diary of the Ancestress* from the standpoint of both form and content.[85] Instead of overlooking or excusing the obvious shortcomings of this work (such as its repetitiveness), Rychner assesses the aesthetic impact on its own merits, as a field of interplay between an ordered mode of expression in measured prose (akin to the chronological framework) and moments of lyrical transport when language and imagery defy any "logical" classification, when words are used not to convey information but merely as tonal building blocks to erect a beautiful acoustical edifice.

What Rychner did for the *Diary*, Wolfgang Frühwald accomplished for the "Heartfelt Dedication" in 1962 with an interpretation which still stands as a masterpiece of literary scholarship as well as a *tour de force* in close textual analysis.[86] Proceeding from the topos of Paradise Lost, Frühwald traces Brentano's efforts to find surrogates for this loss in art (for which the names Vaduz, Thule, Alhambra serve as cyphers) and his use of poetic symbols to evoke a memory of Eden (the jewels and epaulettes of Vaduz). Frühwald proposes the concept of "encoded confession" to categorize this strategy. Such a technique enables the poet simultaneously to conceal from public scrutiny autobiographical information which has shaped his life and yet reveal to initiates of his work what cannot be kept secret. Whereas the fact that "Little Grandmother" turns out to be Marianne Jung, the budding actress with whom Brentano became acquainted in 1799 and who later married a man—Jakob von Willemer—much her senior and already a grandfather (hence the humorous designation for her), is not startlingly new information, but Frühwald's interpretation of such cryptic statements as "I deserve a hobby horse, but no doll" (*W*, 3:627) is quite enlightening: the term *Steckenpferd* as a denotation for a toy is fitting for the childlike atmosphere prevalent here, but the word can also connote "hobby" in the sense of the vocation or avocation of writing poetry. Likewise, the German word *Puppe* not only means "doll" or "plaything," but also "young girl," and this is consistent with the fact that Marianne Jung—von Willemer was indeed not for him, just as a "doll" would not be a suitable plaything for a man. Frühwald's convincing study drives home the point that such adumbrated chains of association, literary cyphers, and disguises enable the poet to express essential truths more accurately by indirection than by falsifying directness, just as the system of arabesques provides a sequence of ornamental border designs surrounding a canvas in the center of which no picture can be painted because the ultimate message defies concrete portrayal.

Several interpretations have concentrated on elucidating significant minor aspects of the *Gockel* complex. The close aesthetic ties between the lithographic illustrations of the 1838 edition and the conception of the author for them, together with the identity of at least one artist who drew them have been recently established.[87] In a similar vein, the relationship of the enigmatic couplet "O star and blossom" to the graphic arts with reference to the emblematic tradition of the seventeenth century and the theories of Runge and the practices of William Blake in the late eighteenth and early nineteenth centuries have been examined in a penetrating analysis of the reciprocal illumination of the media.[88]

Under the ambivalent umbrella-term of "curiosities" (meaning both the "norm" suddenly thrust into an abnormal milieu—a curiosity— as well as the thirst for the new and novel or for knowledge per se—curiosity), an attempt has been made to account for the juxtaposition of heterogeneous elements in the *Gockel* tales and for the penchant to pile minutiae upon minutiae in order to whet the intellectual appetite of the "curious" reader.[89] Finally, one minor study pagewise but a major contribution to our understanding of the *Gockel* complex within the larger context of Brentano's *modus operandi* has investigated the nature of the art figurine.[90] Pointing out such previously overlooked facts as the correlation of Gackeleia's urge to play with the playful drive behind poetic creativity, this subtle interpretation finds hidden symmetries and correspondences (Gackeleia's playful black cats smuggled in by the Jews set in motion an unfortunate sequence of events, but her addiction to the dancing figurine—also introduced by the Jews—with the white mouse as its driving force, leads to a happy resolution) where previously critics had seen only arbitrariness and chaos. Even interpolations—such as the ten pages describing the dancer's costumes—are integrated in a way, which lends credence to the claim that Brentano's humorous fairy tale of the barnyard family may indeed be the story of his own creative life, at the center of which lurks a *homo ludens,* as much the controlling subject as the controlled object of aesthetic play.

3. *Commentary on the* Gockel *Complex*

In many respects the *Gockel* story together with its appendages represents the *non plus ultra* of the fairy-tale perspective as previously developed—viewing through a wide-angle lens with increased depth perception. Without wishing to belabor this point, one might nevertheless maintain that *Gockel* extends our range of vision to such a degree, that we apprehend the world of men and beasts not as separate entities, but as integrated and interrelated. Reciprocal ties and mutual assistance pacts between humanity and poultry (or rodents) become natural facts of life; people behave like barnyard fowl and chickens conduct themselves like human beings, and no grandiose processes of disenchantment in this regard are necessary to make all concerned live happily ever after. In a similar fashion, the factor of depth perception is heightened not only by tracing the roots of families (both human and bestial) back to their origins in the past, but also forward to an idealized present in which the adult can again become the eternal child in all of us. Brentano romantically raises the quest for firmly anchored traditions in the historical dimension to a "higher power," as it were, since, in the dedicatory preface he links the family chronicle of these protagonists to his own beginnings, to the never-never land of Vaduz, its imperial insignia and treasures, as well as to those who helped him cope as both poet and person with their loss.

The Italian fairy tales as a whole and the *Gockel* complex in particular embody another aspect of romanticizing announced in *Godwi* when Maria declared: "The Romantic element is itself a translation." This axiom, together with the subsequent explanation that such a romantic translation "not only depicts its object but also imparts to the depiction a certain coloring," clarifies how Brentano's adaptations from the Italian are unique entities in themselves rather than mere German renditions of Basile. Basile's five-page original *La preta de lo gallo* becomes in Brentano's hands a two-hundred-and-fifty-page extravaganza. The situation is roughly analogous to a musician like Brahms taking a theme from Haydn and creating out of it a tonal and textual artifact far beyond anything the original composer could ever have conceived. Likewise, Brentano not only translates Basile, he consciously transcends him.

One might also cite the Gockel tale and its various ancillary components as illustrative of the techniques of romantic perspectivism outlined previously with reference to the other works discussed in this chapter, so that a brief recapitulation of some of the major findings in this regard would both review material presented earlier and round off the discussion of Brentano's prose. The novel *Godwi* contained *in nuce* the two extreme contrasts in perception: on the one hand, poly-perspectivism, the kaleidoscopic rotation of a maximum number of points of view toward a subject in order to probe all its ramifications; on the other hand, monoperspectivism, the dogmatic, inflexible uni-dimensionality so characteristic of the philistine, which all too often fails to see the metaphorical and metaphysical "forest" (the larger context) for the literal and physical "trees" (the isolated concrete phenomenon). To illustrate the first of these techniques one could point to the various reports by different narrators of family genealogies or the numerous accounts of the origins and history of the Vadutzian jewels (not to mention the finely nuanced shadings of meaning evoked each time the contrastive refrains "O star and blossom" and "Fire-red little roses" are sounded in myriad contexts). Opposed to such an open range of potential significance are the closed minds of the monistically and monetarily oriented citizens of Gelnhausen, merchants who, when they witness the magical restoration of Gockel's castle and the rejuvenation of its inhabitants, are moved only by thoughts of financial gain, failing to appreciate a miracle which transcends belief.

The medieval penchant for discovering an infinite spiritual correlative behind the transient facade of life (*Chronicle*), comes to the fore in the creation of an entire fantasy kingdom and its imperial regalia from the single word "Vadutz," a concept which not even harsh and undeniable geographic reality (Vaduz) can entirely eradicate. The necessity—found in *Kasperl und Annerl*—of mediating between extreme positions and of avoiding dogmatic absolutes even when these seem to be sanctioned by the highest authority, can be demonstrated with reference to the epaulettes of Vadutz which are seen as complementary adornments; an unhealthy spiritual imbalance results if one—especially the left—is favored over the other. Therefore, in full awareness of her own dangerous predilection for amaranthine colors, Amey cautions Gackeleia "never to allow an inclination to something to become too strong, lest it dominate" (*W*, 3:804).

Another phase of the "caveat philistus" has a counterpart in the fairy-tale world. The double-edged sword of language that was used and abused by philistine hands dangles Damocles-like over Gackeleia's head when she insists that the doll is not a doll, but a beautiful *objet d'art*. Both Gackeleia's sophistically liberal and Gockel's sophomorically literal interpretation of these verses must be modified, before potential tragedy is avoided. In addition, the sound symbolism of the constellation "a-ei-a" which came to the fore in the *Tales of The Rhine* could also be applied to Amey and to the little lad, the Büblein, who occupy such a prominent place in the finale of the revised *Gockel* and in the *Diary*. Both names in German end with that tell-tale syllable "ei" which has been shown to imply suffering and sorrow. And, indeed, both are threatened individuals who, nevertheless, find redemption from their sins—whether potential or actual. Amey's susceptibility to mental anxiety and emotional excess is counterbalanced by the warning example of the mentally unsound Klareta (whose name contains a double dose of that sound-cypher indicative of salvation, the *a*) and by the exemplary life of the saintly Verena (resulting in the founding of such orders of *caritas* as the Cloister of Lilienthal). Although the Büblein has sinned and suffers, we are assured that redemption is not far off by the consoling phrase: "Seine Sache hats vollbracht" (W, 3:830) ("he has done his thing"—his act of atonement through penance, collecting kernels of grain one by one). The use of the biblically significant verb *vollbracht* in this context is doubly meaningful, for it not only suggests that the suffering of the little lad for his sins is finally expiated, but it also echoes the words uttered by Christ on the Cross when, in the throes of a death which was to bring the promise of eternal redemption for all mankind, he said: "Es ist vollbracht" ("it is done"). If the analogy seems farfetched, one might recall that even the rooster Alektryo has ties to the biblical cock which would crow three times, signaling Peter's denial of Christ. Such religious touches were not alien to Brentano in 1816, and certainly not in 1838.

CHAPTER 4

The Dramatist

GIVEN Brentano's inherent lyricism and his marked proclivity in narrative contexts to embellish the story with seemingly endless and only tangentially relevant arabesques, it is difficult to image him as a writer for the stage, since the theatrical medium tolerates least the flow of verbiage and requires the most stringent economy of means as well as logicality of construction to sustain audience interest. And it is precisely on these points—tightness and clarity of structure, frugality of expression—that Brentano misses the dramatic mark. And yet, as at least one major study of the poet has demonstrated,[1] he had almost a fixation about the stage during the period prior to his conversion, so that he not only tried his hand at virtually every theatrical genre (satire, comedy, operatic or operetta libretto, tragedy, historico-mythic drama, and allegorical pageant), but also delved into theater criticism with a fair modicum of success. His overall development seems to have been from the early comic medium (with serious overtones) to the tragedy (with comic interludes), following an unproductive interval of almost ten years (1802 to 1811 or 1812), and finally to modes of dramatic spectacle which defy standard classification. But Brentano's career illustrates markedly that being possessed by the drive to achieve certain aesthetic goals and possessing the wherewithal to do so satisfactorily can often work at cross purposes, and one can only regret the hours he wasted on literary endeavors for which he was patently unsuited.

Qualitatively, therefore, Brentano's dramatic output should constitute the shortest chapter in this book, even though quantitatively his completed works for the stage and his many fragments comprise almost as extensive a segment of his total œuvre as do his more successful contributions to other genres. If for no other reason, his stage writings (one has qualms about calling them dramas or plays) deserve attention here for one common attribute, a mode of perspectivism which could give a discussion of these otherwise unruly and amorphous pieces a touch of coherence: the emergence of a better order of things from the shadows of the past or, in some cases, from the shambles of the present. Consequently, each work, in its unique comic, tragic, or dramatic vein, leads us to the frontier of an emerging ethos, we are brought to a vantage point from which we can observe the world through rosier-colored glasses, and it is this element of romanticization which will furnish the common denominator for the following commentaries on individual works.

I   Ponce de Leon (1801)

The original German title of this comedy *Laßt es euch gefallen* (which might be rendered in English as *That's the way it is* or, more liberally as *Take it or leave it*) has a distinctly Shakespearean flavor to it and many of the comic techniques employed by Brentano are reminiscent of Shakespeare's theater. The change in title singles out one figure from the constellations of wooers and lovers as the center of concern. The name Ponce might conjure up for some memories of the Spanish explorer and his chimeric quest for the fountain of youth; but this frame of reference is not exploited in the play. Instead this piece focuses on the problematic figure of a mercurial, indecisive, melancholy, and ofttimes bizarre young man who evolves, in the course of the work, into a more assertive individual, even though the author avoids formulating any clear-cut goals for him except, perhaps, a more secure future.

The fact that Brentano, when preparing a stage version of this comedy for the Burgtheater in Vienna in 1814, could rechristen it *Valeria or Paternal Cunning* and polish it up with a bit of local patriotism (this was during the Napoleonic Wars of Liberation), topical allusions, and other concessions to popular taste (thereby bringing about the destruction—if not desecration—of the romantic charms which had made the early version a delight to read if not to perform on the stage), would seem to suggest that Ponce was not his prime interest after all. Ponce recedes into the background together with the romantic world of 1801, leaving behind a trivial piece not unworthy of the talents of a Kotzebue (whose style and dramatic techniques Brentano had ridiculed mercilessly in his satiric farce, *Gustav Wasa*).[2]

This shifting of title affirms the view of some that the focal point of the play is indeed not character portrayal or comic intrigue, but rather the myriad verbal acrobatics around which entire scenes are often constructed. Heine, for instance, in *The Romantic School*, found the comedy ragged in conception, but he marveled at the manner in which words leap about, dance, whirl, and snort so that above these articulated tones one can detect the inarticulate overtones of Bacchanalian trumpets signaling destruction.[3]

A. *Content of* Ponce de Leon

Act 1 of the comedy opens in Seville where the tailor, Valerio, and his daughter, Valeria, are assisting a handsome, young nobleman, Ponce de Leon, to dress for a masked ball at the home of his friend Aquilar. Whereas Valeria is hopelessly in love with Ponce, the latter can only find time to tease and taunt her. Colonel Sarmiento, the father of another young nobleman, Don Felix, having just returned incognito from military service in the Netherlands (and calling himself Mercado), enlists Valerio's aid in prodding his rather timid son to pursue more aggressively the woman of his choice, Lucilla, whom he has, up to now, merely serenaded from afar. Don Sarmiento learns from Valerio about Ponce and Aquilar, the former a kind of apart and melancholy figure, the latter an avowed hedonist with little real direction in life. In order to observe all three aimless or indecisive men, Sarmiento attends the masked ball disguised as an automaton.

At the gala affair, the robot (alias Sarmiento) convinces Felix to abduct Lucilla and wisk her off to the country estate of the family where his (Felix's) two sisters, Isidora and Melanie, live under the watchful eye of their duenna, Juanna. Ponce's plight is more complicated: he has fallen in love with the image of a girl he formed in his mind based on hearsay, a girl who later proves to be none other than Sarmiento's daughter, Isidora. Now at the dance, Ponce's heart is stirred by the picture of an unknown beauty which he spots on a locket worn by one of the dancers. This type of infatuation seems to confirm the reports of his bizarre mentality.

In act 2 Felix departs for Saragossa in pursuit of Lucilla, and Ponce finds a confidant in the still incognito Sarmiento. The Colonel's overall plan is to assist his son and Ponce in winning their respective ladies, to help Valeria appreciate the love which Porporino, a foundling adopted by Valerio, has for her, to break Aquilar's allegiance to the pleasure principle, and to put his own daughters to the test. Before sending Valerio to his estate as majordomo and Porporino as the family physician, Sarmiento replaces the wary Juanna with a less severe overseer, Donna Isabella, thereby setting in motion the machinery which should guarantee a happy ending for all concerned once the remaining obstacles have been overcome. Ponce, having

been persuaded that the mysterious face on the medallion belongs to
Isidora whom he should woo with all the skills at his command, sets
out with Aquilar for the country estate. Unknown to these adventur-
ers dressed as pilgrims, Valeria has proceeded them there disguised
as a Mooress with the name of Flametta.

The third act is structured around the problems encountered by
the pilgrims in gaining access to the castle and the many intrigues and
near-mishaps which occur as a result of the manifold disguises and
deceptions on all sides. For instance, Ponce is duped into believing
that he has a rival for Isidora's hand, and in a fit of jealousy, he almost
wounds his friend, Aquilar. But the supposed "wounding" of this rival
wooer proves to be a successful ruse through which they are admitted
to the estate.

Act 4 continues the string of misunderstandings which, at times,
flirt with tragedy, but in each instance only skirt the periphery of
serious danger. The two girls, meanwhile, have not remained imper-
vious to the charms of Ponce and Aquilar, and in their mind's eye they
envision what life would be like with Carlos and Juan (the names they
ascribe to the strangers). Through Valeria-Flametta's intercession,
they become even more enamored of the handsome pilgrims. However, the arrival of Felix with his abducted beloved Lucilla (wearing
the clothes of a man) poses complications, since it is feared that they
will be pursued by outraged relatives. But once again, potential
difficulties are averted. Finally, the dénouement of act 5 leads to an
all's well that ends well finale, with five marriages and musical festivities. It is left to the intriguer par excellence, Don Sarmiento—
even now disguised as a gypsy fortune teller—to unravel the tangled
threads of identity and intrigue, so that five marital unions can take
place: Felix-Lucilla, Ponce-Isidora, Aquilar-Melanie, Valeria-
Porporino, and, last but not least, Sarmiento himself with Isabella,
after the wily don reveals that Porporino is actually their son from a
liaison in the remote past.

B. *Critical Reception of* Ponce de Leon

Unlike some of Brentano's other works for the theater which have
suffered—perhaps not undeservedly—critical neglect even in the
twentieth century, *Ponce* has been accorded scholarly attention by
prominent Germanists. Already in 1901 there appeared an exhaustive
study of the play which not only supplied extrinsic background material (sources, stages of development), but also intrinsic data (imagery,

character analysis, types of verbal comedy, style) together with an incisive comparison of the original with the 1814 adaptation outlining how Brentano effectively mangled what the muse of his youth had— even if defectively—conceived.[4] Paul Böckmann, in the process of tracing Brentano's creative roots back to Friedrich Schlegel and Tieck, notes that in *Ponce* the titular hero lacks those very traits of character which a dyed-in-the-wool romantic demanded: self-knowledge and self-confidence.[5] The result is a state of melancholy which, in the course of the play, is transformed into a kind of qualified serenity; one principal means of attaining this condition of reserved or subdued contentment is word play, a mode of human activity which bridges—if only momentarily—the discrepancy between the ideal and the real, the absolute and the relative, making the chasm comically bearable rather than tragically irreconcilable.

After a lacuna of over three decades, two significant contributions to our understanding and appreciation of *Ponce* burst on the scene in a single year: 1968. The first of these is the informative postscript to an edition of the play which makes the dexterity of the German tongue and other verbal factors its prime concern, thus clarifying why it never really had a chance in the Weimar competition for a play of intrigue sponsored by Goethe and Schiller, the contest for which it was originally submitted.[6] Perhaps this linguistic virtuosity accounts for the fiasco of 1814 and for the fact that whereas the public as a whole has never taken the work to its heart, later writers such as Georg Büchner (1813–1837) have been inspired to their own creativity by it.

The second interpretation constitutes a chapter of the book *The Serious Comedy* with the significant heading: "The Play of Masked Figures."[7] The serious aspect in Brentano's comedy stems from the fact that love and human emotions are involved: the comic element is based on the almost labyrinthine network of masks and masquerades with which these people conceal their innermost feelings from others (the play of language) and how, on a deeper level, the very same feelings ultimately conceal themselves from the experiencing subject (playing with language). In view of so much masked play in this play of masks, the critic finds that even the last reprise, with its matching and mating of partners, befits a puppet play rather than a human comedy. The actions of the puppets are seldom comic, because, in the final analysis, this has been a game of charades in which even the marionettes are not able to mask the truth of the human condition. Convincingly, the critic proves that masking is not merely a vehicle to achieve other goals, but rather to show the essence of what the author sought to demonstrate.

C. *Commentary on* Ponce de Leon

The theme of the mask as a concealing device which this comedy introduces on an extensive scale soon established itself as a mainstay of Brentano's work: one need only recall the deliberately or inadvertently hidden identities in *Godwi*, in all of the shorter stories, and especially in the fairy tales. Not only do the figures in *Ponce* mask themselves literally (at the masked ball, for instance, or when Valeria appears as the Mooress), but in some cases, figuratively as well (Ponce and Aquilar pretending to be pilgrims or wounded musicians; Valerio playing the role of a majordomo with Porporino as the doctor) and on occasion, both of the above in combination (the already incognito Sarmiento attends the ball in the costume of an automaton).

Even language has its share in veiling the truth through double entendre and the deliberate equivocation of meaning, both of which become a natural source of laughter via punning and other wordplay. But this comedy of errors is ended arbitrarily by the same *deus ex machina* force which set it in motion: Sarmiento (who, incidentally, appears at the close in the guise of a gypsy woman) unties the knots of identity in the tangled string of relationships as deliberately as he had fastened them at the outset. One is reminded of the somewhat arbitrary and abrupt revelations in volume 2 of *Godwi*. Brentano's thesis seems to be that only when masks of all types are removed can one hope for that coalescing of essence and appearance postulated for the idealized children at the close of the late *Gockel*: "Let us be everything, not just appear as such" (*W*, 3:822).

Until that point in time is attained, our perspectives of ourselves as well as of our relationship to others will remain at best blurred, at worst confused. If, as Kant inferred, our perception of any "thing-in-itself" is determined not necessarily by the latter's true essence but rather by the machinery of our apprehension, how much greater the distortion when the phenomenon to be understood is able to hide its already inaccessible nature behind a deceptive facade. Amid the jubilation of the closing scene, Valerio's emphatic assessment "Laßt es euch gefallen," may not only be an exhortation to accept the arrangements which Sarmiento has made, but also an admonition that such is the fragile stuff that life is made of, so "take it or leave it."

II   The Founding of Prague *(1814)*

Two essential concepts are prefigured by the title of this mythico-historical drama: the first is the idea of "founding" something, of establishing roots in the past for either an individual, a family unit, or, as in this case, an entire ethnic community—the Czech nation. Unsuccessful in anchoring his own existence firmly in the turbulent waters of life, adrift like the "galley slave from the Dead Sea" (a work, incidentally, from approximately the same period), Brentano could project vicariously his wish-dream for a securely based mode of life back in time to the period of prerecorded history, thereby giving a mythical basis for the common wish to become an integral part of a larger organism or social superstructure.

Another phase of this drive to trace the background of family (one thinks in this context of the *Gockel* lineage or of Radlauf) or ethnological ties back to their origins was to undergird this work with a solid basis of fact in the form of a quasi-scholarly apparatus appended to the text. But more than one hundred footnotes on religious ritual, heathen deities, cultic practices, and the like cannot be transmitted to a theater audience; likewise a text of almost three hundred pages presupposes a degree of tolerance which few theatergoers are wont to exhibit. Hence, this work remains a book or "closet" drama, rather than a piece for the living stage.

The second element of significance in the title is Prague, the city which fascinated Brentano during his sojourn in Bohemia. Equally as important as the biographical link, however, is the fact that the playwright accepted the now disputed etymology of the Czech terms "prah, Praha" as meaning threshold.[8] The symbolic and literal potential of this misconception is exploited fully by the poet in the course of the play. The city founded at the conclusion of the drama represents a threshold for the Slavic nation's future growth and development, both as a political entity and a spiritual unity(the pagan rites and heathen practices gradually cede precedence to Christianity). On a different level, this work was meant to be the "threshold" so to speak for a planned trilogy, in the course of which the phases of progress in national cohesiveness and religious faith would be portrayed, a plan, however, which was never to come to fruition.

A. *Content of* The Founding of Prague

The first act of this dramatic poem takes place between midnight and morning of the first day of spring, the threshold of a new season of life. Zwratka, the priestess of Tschart, the primitive Slavic god of darkness, plots how she might win back to her cult the three daughters of Krokus (the legendary ruler of the Slavic people and son of Czech), Libussa, Tetka, and Kascha who have abandoned the older demonic religion for deities of light. In order to reestablish the sisters' ties to the ancient rites, Zwratka will have her apprentices place in the hands of the sleeping girls apples containing the principal symbols of Tschart: a spider, a serpent, and a golden frog. This is also a critical turning point in the fate of the nation, since the people are about to elect a new leader—most likely one of Krokus's daughters, to the chagrin of Zwratka's husband, Lapak, who, as a distant relative of Krokus, aspires to the throne. In addition to these two religious factions, the drama also introduces a third aspect in the figure of the architect from Constantinople, Pachta, and his companion, Trinitas, devout Christians who have come to spread the gospel in these pagan territories.

Three Slavic men, Slawosch, Biwog, and Primislaus—who eventually are to marry Tetka, Kascha, and Libussa respectively—ponder which of the sisters will be chosen leader and how they will cast their respective votes. After their departure, the three maidens appear and relate the history of their family, after which they fall into a deep slumber; as they sleep, Zwratka's apprentices place in each of their hands an apple containing the ancient symbols from the cult of Tschart. The following morning the three men return and announce that the election has given no conclusive results, and so they must resort to a process of divination which will terminate when an eagle comes and circles about the head of one of the maidens. When this actually happens, it is Libussa who is chosen, and without hesitation, she accepts this crown she did not actively seek, forms a body guard, and receives as homage from some Slavic leaders a block of silver from which will be formed the image of a new god, more perfect than those of past or present.

Act 2 witnesses the attack and repulsion of the Avars under Moribud by the Slavic forces led by Wlasta, the daughter of Zwratka and Lapak. In the course of this struggle, Wlasta is wounded and in order to expedite her recovery, Libussa immerses Wlasta's blood-covered bracelet in the waters of a spring and substitutes for it her own armlet which guarantees certain happiness to the wearer. This bracelet had been a gift from her mother, Niva the elf; when the priestess Zwratka demanded a similar token of happiness, Niva had had a copy made from the gold of the Moldau. Soon Zwratka discovered it had no magic properties and gave it to her daughter. Now the true bracelet is on Wlasta's arm and when the copy is then found by some Slavic men, they give it to Primislaus for safekeeping, feeling it is Libussa's. When Wlasta is later informed by her parents about the magical artifact, she laments not having known this before, since she easily could have stolen it from her mistress and assured herself of power and happiness. The roots of a growing conflict between her and Libussa, her childhood friend, become manifest. Another divisive force stems from those male leaders of the Slavs such as Rozhon, who are unhappy with the dominant role played by the women and the decisions handed down by Libussa in certain legal disputes. Even though Biwog takes him to task for such criticism, the people have been agitated by Rozhon's invectives and demand that Libussa take a husband. Libussa is somewhat reluctant, feeling that her female-dominated reign has been successful in the war just concluded, but she agrees to marry that man the gods select for her.

Act 3 reveals that, by making concessions to the male faction, Libussa has stirred the hostility of the women in her entourage, especially of Wlasta, who, wounded by a magic love-arrow, finds herself drawn to Primislaus. At his hut she discovers an armlet hanging on a plough which she believes is Libussa's magic bracelet, and so she exchanges it for the one she is wearing, confident that she is now in possession of magic powers. Meanwhile the assembly of men has met and decided that the time is at hand to curb the impertinence of the women led by Wlasta: Libussa must marry. As evening falls, Libussa goes to her bath, saddened at the growing rift between her and Wlasta and unaware that Rozhon is about to attack her. When the latter enters with his armed troops, she cries out: "My entire kingdom of Bohemia for a sword!" and Primislaus, who happens to be nearby, gives her his, not realizing the full implications of his act. This nocturnal treachery against the ruler further convinces the populace that Libussa must have a husband, and she agrees to submit her fate to the stars—at which point flashing comets in the heavens seem to signal that the time for marriage has indeed arrived.

As the fourth act opens, we find Pachta and Trinitas preparing the mold of metal with which they hope to cast the statue of the new god. Pachta explains to Libussa and her siblings the mysteries of the Trinity, and after they have fallen asleep, Trinitas replaces the symbols of the pagan deity Tschart which they received at the outset with corresponding Christian symbols—a chalice, a lamb and a dove. To Wlasta's chagrin, Libussa selects Primislaus as her future husband and dispatches envoys to bring him to her. Demanding from Zwratka a flask containing a potion of hatred, Wlasta precedes the messengers, but collapses in front of Primislaus's hut in a cateleptic fit, recovering only in time to see the man she wants being led away to her rival.

The final act develops the motif of nascent Christianity as Pachta finds that only the statue of a pelican has been successful, and he interprets the symbolic significance of this outcome in Christian terms. Trinitas, herself ready for martyrdom, decides that Hubaljuta, one of Zwratka's apprentices who has converted to Christianity, is prepared for baptism and takes her to the shore of the Moldau. Here they encounter Zwratka and her maidens eager to perform a heathen rite, and in the ensuing confrontation, Trinitas is pierced by an arrow and Zwratka is also slain. At another location, the marriage ceremony of Libussa and Primislaus is about to take place, but it is interrupted by the arrival of the angry Wlasta and then by Trinitas's funeral procession. Tetka, the most ethereal of the sisters (Kascha tended toward the depths, Libussa mediated between the upper and under-world), prophesies the ultimate victory of Christianity—at which point Hubaljuta, having drunk the blood from Trinitas's poisoned wound, likewise dies a martyr's death. Two Slavic nobles join the throng, bringing with them carpenters who, when asked what they are building, reply: "Prague, the threshold." This concept inspires Libussa to a prophetic vision of coming secular splendor, glory, honor, and happiness, as well as of religious faith and salvation, so that Primislaus and all present can join in the closing chorus: "Prague, Prague, you, the threshold of our salvation and faith."

B   Critical Reception of The Founding of Prague

The critical literature dealing with this work has, since the heyday of positivism at the turn of the century, come full cycle, insofar as the first major study devoted to the play,[9] an important analysis two decades later,[10] and the most recent and penetrating interpretation[11] have all dealt in their own fashion with a similar topic: the comparison of Brentano's approach to Libussa and the Czech past with those of other writers, especially with the *Libussa* of the Austrian dramatist Franz Grillparzer (1791–1872). Whereas the earliest of these investi-gations is panoramic in scope, tracing the Libussa figure through all of German literature, the latter two have restricted their focus to the two poets mentioned.

Over fifty years ago Günther Müller's comparative study charac-terized Brentano as the musically oriented, tonally dominated lyric stylist, incapable of achieving architectural symmetry in spite of his expressed intent to do so, while Grillparzer emerged as the born dramatist, the fundamentally unlyrical talent with a fine sensitivity for human conflicts and the psychological workings of the innermost mind of his figures. Brentano's text is seen as mythological and organic; Grillparzer's context is logical and dramatic. What the last critic in this triumvirate—Oskar Seidlin—does, is to take a single concept from each of the respective works and trace its interweaving on many levels throughout the texts. In the case of Brentano, the premise developed is the positive image of the "threshold," while for Grillparzer the central concept on which the interpretation is structured is that of an endpoint, a termination, so that we perceive in Brentano's case a sense of an imminent new beginning while with Grillparzer the feeling is that the end of an era has been reached: there are no bright prospects on the horizon, no new frontiers lie ahead. What makes Seidlin's approach so convincing is his ability to elicit the threshold quality in a variety of modes: life situations faced by characters in the work, poetic images stressing mediation, temporal scenes of transition (dawn, twilight), so that a remarkable degree of consistency is achieved, a consistency which cannot help but convince.

Between the earliest and the latest commentaries on *Libussa* and the *Founding of Prague* fall two doctoral dissertations which deserve mention since each of them delves into the mythological qualities of Brentano's play. Whereas the first of these develops the view of myth as man's inevitable progression away from the maternal source of life with its security, its cosmic unity, and divinely ordained order,[12] the other underscores myth as organic process, an historical evolution taking place in time and moving inexorably away from that primeval oneness with the origins of life (postulated as ideal by its predecessor) in the context of a pilgrim's regress.[13]

C. *Commentary on* The Founding of Prague

The subtitle of this play reads "an historical, romantic drama" and, whereas many have questioned the historical aspect and others the designation "drama" (feeling that Brentano's alternative characterizations for the work, "poem" or "dramatic poem," are more appropriate), few would debate its romantic qualities. In the announcement of 1813 in the journal *Kronos* Brentano supplied some background information concerning the evolution of his attitude toward the Slavic nations, the Czechs, and especially Prague. Interestingly, the title of this essay uses the description "a romantic play" (the German is actually *Schauspiel*, a word which emphasizes the visual aspect), and in the text Brentano refers to the poet as a seer who infuses "a higher, timeless, eternal poetic truth" (W, 4:528) into events which bland reports in historical documents fail to articulate.

Throughout his somewhat rambling exposition, Brentano underscores the concept of artistic vision, the gift for casting light on the
ultimate significance of events which time has covered with darkness.
He alludes to the diverse sources through which he became acquainted with Bohemia and Prague as a "romantic conglomerate" (W,
4:531), inferring, perhaps, that each of these perspectives on the dim
past functioned like that intermediary force between the "eye" and
what it observed, as an intervening medium which imparted some of
itself to what it transmitted. His account of the moment when he
actually saw Prague rising panoramically before his eyes stresses the
visual and visionary aspects in a manner which calls to mind the
romantic mode of perception as formulated in *Godwi* over a decade
before:

a thick morning mist, its veil torn by the rising sun, revealed gradually to me
the magnificent city towering up in the splendor of the full light, vividly
evoking in my soul the image of Libussa in which she, in her prophetic vision,
sees Prague coming forth from the night of the forests, sees it develop and
perfect itself; interrupting this came the noise of the populace, the chiming of
bells, the singing of the processions, and the harmonious din of warlike
music, all of which awakened in me again the fervent wish, even the calling,
to celebrate in a romantic drama the founding of this city shimmering before
me amid a joyous spring radiance. (W, 4:532–33)

The city on the Moldau, shrouded in fog, gradually revealing its
splendors, gives rise to an internalized or interiorized vision of
Libussa in which she, the mythical prophetess, surveys a Prague not
yet extant, a threshold city opening the way to future prosperity for
her people. But given the incomplete nature of Brentano's "envisioned" trilogy, we, like the protagonist in the play, must content
ourselves with the prospect of what might be, rather than with the
possession of what is—we hover on the same spatiotemporal
threshold as Libussa, knowing that the past is irretrievably lost, yet
hoping that a future of great potential lies ahead, a coming golden age
which the poet, because of insufficient time or talents, due to an
inadequate medium, or to the inherent elusiveness of the concept,
was only able to capture in fragmented form.

Brentano labeled the *Founding of Prague* a "romantic" drama
without any further elaboration of that term in the context of his
vision of the emerging "threshold" city together with his encounter
with its populace. Such a fusion of sights and sounds calls to mind his

review in the *Dramaturgical Observer* of Vienna from the same period (1814) of a performance of Schiller's *Die Braut von Messina* (*The Bride of Messina*). Brentano lauds two contrasting characteristics of this play—its architectural quality and its musicality—and he would like to see it directed by a person "in whom the laws of all arts are combined" (*W,* 2:1081). What could emerge is a kind of *Gesamtkunstwerk* which straddles all the media, but which is at home in none of them entirely. The choruses, for instance, are portrayed in terms of musico-architectural concepts fusing artistic styles of widely divergent eras: "sounding statues, Memnon columns, from the ancient world which ring out when the wonderful dawn (Aurora) of modern, romantic art casts its rays on their forehead and magically rejuvenates them" (*W,* 2:1080). A similar metaphorical frame of reference—architectural design marking the threshold between different aesthetic epochs—recurs when Brentano imagines the principal figures of the *Bride* "standing in a simple temple between the classical and the modern world, on an untouched island of fantasy" (*W,* 2:1082).

If Brentano's own stage works could be described in any sense as architectonic, it would not be in terms of the classic Greek temple but rather in the style of a late baroque church with an overlay of rococo ornamentation. Instead of the clear, monodic sounds of a Memnon column responding tonally to the touch of the sun's rays, the music would be akin to the complex, contrapuntal textures and the intricate linear polyphony of fugal voices echoing throughout the edifice in a bewildering manifold. Several interpreters have actually suggested that works such as the *Founding of Prague* have structural features more akin to operatic than architectural forms.[14] But here, a caveat might be in order: the operatic forms corresponding to Brentano's verbal score would assume the elaborate proportions of a romantic Meyerbeerian "grand opera" rather than the economic structure of a classical Mozartian *Singspiel* or the austerity of Gluck's *dramma per musica.*

CHAPTER 5

Postlude

T HE quasi-musical designations chosen to frame the discussion of Clemens Brentano's life and literary output—"Prelude" and "Postlude"—were not the result of capriciousness or chance, but rather of choice. Aside from the fact that Brentano has been labeled by his contemporaries and by later commentators as the most musical of all romantic (and even of all German) poets,[1] the terms here are intended to suggest the initial statement of the basic themes at the outset of this study and their final recapitulation at the close, so that a sense of continuity and completeness is evoked in the mind of the reader.

The aim of chapter 1 was to summarize the direction which Brentano's career and creativity took within the context of "romanticism" as a literary period concept with distinctive stylistic-thematic components. In order to prevent the discussion from becoming too amorphous, the focus on Brentano's romanticism was kept within the perameters of his own definition of the phenomenon as a mode of observing and recording objective impressions with a concomitant infusion of subjective refraction, a characterization which was then augmented and amplified by quotations from contemporaries such as Novalis and Friedrich Schlegel. The succeeding chapters concentrated on Brentano's lyric poetry, his narrative prose, and stage works respectively, analyzing the writer's major contributions to each genre from a triple perspective: content, critical reception (over the century since the first in-depth but definitely not unbiased biography),[2] and commentary (again within the context of the specifically romantic criteria established by Brentano himself).

The nine lyrics selected for discussion in chapter 2 put into bold relief both the diversity and continuity of Brentano's poetic vision. The first of these (from 1800) and the last (written approximately in 1838) underscore a mode of visual and spiritual receptivity which could detect a mystical bond between the terrestrial and the transcendental, whether this correlation was an immediate "given" or

had to be acquired by dint of sheer effort. Between these two chronological extremes lay a number of lyrics which spoke of alternative or
surrogate modes of discovering links between seemingly diverse
spheres, ties which may exist in erotic relationships of harmonious,
dissonant, or self-destructively ironic proportions, in the aesthetic
and synesthetic realms, or in the religious sphere.

Chapter 3 formulated a variety of alternative modes of romantic
perception through the prose media of the novel, the novella, and the
fairy tale. *Godwi* advocated a poly-perspectivism through which we
may approach—but not necessarily attain—the essence of life's manifold challenges by regarding them from a maximum number of
vantage points. But it also illustrated the deadening effects of a
mono-perspectivism of the philistine stamp, where absolutely no
flexibility or intellectual agility comes into play—the concept of
"play" being significant also in the sense of the romantic writer as
homo ludens. The shorter prose works treated offered a wide spectrum of perception, ranging from the idealized medievalism of the
Chronicle in which man is admonished never to lose sight of the
spiritual dimensions of existence by falling vitim solely to the plea-
sures of the flesh, to *Honest Casper* in which the precariousness of
exclusive adherence either to purely mundane concerns (Casper's
code of honor) or to exclusively ethereal values divorced from human
validity (Anna Margaret's ascribing honor to God alone) is in evidence. Even though the allegorical monument to "honor" at the close
of the work may not satisfy discriminating readers because of its
stilted nature, the human dilemmas portrayed in the course of the
story (especially that of the narrator-scribe) elicit sympathetic reac-
tions from the more discerning audience. Finally, the fairy tales of the
Rhine and the so-called Italian tales (principally *Gockel*) utilized what
was termed a wide-angle lens for greater depth-perception, the range
of vision being extended horizontally (synchronically) to reveal con-
nections between man and beast, between animal and avian worlds,
as well as vertically (diachronically) through time, so that we see
clearly and distinctly the ties of the protagonist to the remote past, to
the celestial sphere, to the four elements, and, in some instances,
even to the vegetative realm.

Similar thematic and stylistic features of romanticism could also be
isolated in Brentano's least successful literary efforts: his works for the
stage treated in chapter 4. A common thematic thread running
through virtually all his theater pieces (as well as through much of his
other writing) is that of concealed identity which is ultimately re-

vealed. In order for this clarification to take place, the participants must acquire a romantic type of apperception: they have to see through the masks people wear as well as the games people play, so that essence and appearance finally coalesce. In *Ponce*, the mask and the masquerade, which seem to provide the means by which life can be endured when unadulterated truth leads to melancholy, ultimately fall with the final curtain, even though the somewhat contrived resolution of the plot does not really constitute a solution to the fundamental problem. *The Founding of Prague* calls for an acuity of vision which can perceive the ultimate unification of a nation or people in times of strife caused either by an external enemy (such as Napoleon) or internal emnity (the primitive struggle between the male and female factions for dominance in the state). The historical-romantic play illustrates how the various factions of a primitive national tribe come to envision the benefits derived from consolidation as opposed to the petty squabbles which divide and debilitate them. This mythically oriented segment of the planned trilogy gives us only a glimpse into that utopian promised land, but we, with the hindsight of history, know that the threshold dream portrayed there is still in the process of becoming, rather than in the state of being.

When Brentano, late in his life, vowed to make himself the faithful scribe of Anna Katharina Emmerick and to record her divinely inspired visions with a minimal amount of intervention from that subjective faculty which earlier had constituted the sum and substance of romanticism, he spoke, it will be recalled, in no uncertain terms, of describing the things of nature "without distorting, fashioning, or transforming them." What is to be avoided in portraying such phenomena are modes of expression "which twist them, turn, color, adorn and overdistill them—something which poetry especially seeks to do." Patently, this was to be his *modus operandi* when recording for posterity Emmerick's accounts of Christ's youth, adult life, and passion as a monumental religious trilogy for an age in which romanticism as well as religion had lost their resonance. Even though Brentano had no qualms about prodding Anna Katharina to continue her reports when she, hampered by exhaustion or ill-health, grew silent (he sometimes sought to "inspire" her by reading from the writings of mystics), he still intended to perform his task like the scribe in *Honest Casper*, with objective accuracy and without embellishments of his own. Scattered comments throughout Brentano's post-1817 correspondence reveal that he now abjured that brand of romanticism which Godwi had espoused at the turn of the century.

Deprecatory epithets such as "zu absonderlich"[3] ("too peculiar") or derogatory comparisons—"his poem sings like a dear spirit, mine like an old, romantic set-designer, artillery gunner, and ballet master"[4] —set the tone. Yet the leopard could not, as the cliché holds, conceal his spots and the circle—or perhaps vicious circle—of Brentano's career closed, in certain key respects, where it had begun.[5] One typical example from the vast Emmerick material might suffice to illustrate this contention.

In spite of his plan to record the stigmatic's visions as a faithful, self-effacing scribe (thus rejecting the romantically tinged "lens" between the thing portrayed and its portrayal), it seems clear from the following description of Salome's infamous dance before Herod that the very vocabulary used here to denounce her performance ("bending," "turning") and, to decry what poeticizing does to all phenomena ("twist them, turn, color, adorn and overdistill them"), has become an integral part of the passage, leading to that unique amalgam of objective datum and subjective addendum which Brentano the "scribe" deliberately sought to avoid:

Salome appeared with some dancers, dressed very daringly and quite transparently. . . . She danced in the middle, the others around her. The dance is not as wild and brisk as our country dances; but it is a constant bending, turning, and twisting of the body, as if they had no bones at all; . . . this particular dance was based on pure lewdness and imitated the most disgraceful passions. Salome outdid all the others, and I saw the devil at her side, as if he were turning and twisting all parts of her body in order to bring forth this abomination.[6]

The most recent comprehensive survey of Brentano has sought to show that "imagination" and "religiosity" functioned, throughout this writer's life, as the two guideposts of his career.[7] If one interprets "religio" in the etymologically unproven but philologically provocative sense of *re-ligare* ("re-unite"), then the applicability of this formula to the romantic perspective of the present study becomes evident. By seeing through, behind, and beyond the phenomenal sphere to its noumenal basis, the romanticist is performing an act of "religature" to the extent of reintegrating what had, over the ages, become disintegrated. But in the process, the romanticist must constantly remain aware of his own doing, ever alert to the function which imagination and fantasy have in the operation, otherwise romanticizing out-of-hand might lead to its own undoing—a condition which, unfortunately, can be amply documented in the case of Clemens Brentano.

This monograph has, admittedly, stressed a single aspect of romanticism in Brentano's best known writings in order to reduce the mass of material to a workable minimum. Much as been glossed over which merits detailed scrutiny: for instance, Brentano's correspondence, his letters not so much as factual, biographical statements as aesthetic artifacts;[8] his accomplishments as a translator, as a literary critic, editor, bibliophile, and even anonymous propagandist for the cause of Catholicism.[9] Most of these topics, although not instrinsically uninteresting, must, like an analysis of the trilogy of Christ's life, await completion of the historical-critical edition, a project which has taken giant strides during the 1970s.[10] Only when the philological groundwork has been laid will the time be at hand for the poetological spadework to begin.

Notes and References

Preface

1. Wolfgang Frühwald, "Stationen der Brentano-Forschung 1924–1972," *Deutsche Vierteljahrsschrift für Literaturwissenschaft und Geistesgeschichte*, 47, Sonderheft Forschungsreferate (1973): 206. Nevertheless, Erika Tunner in her two-volume dissertation *Clemens Brentano (1778–1842): Imagination et sentiment religieux* (Lille: Université de Lille, 1977) has attempted—in over 1,300 pages—to present a comprehensive survey of the poet's life and works, using the polarity of imagination and religious fervor as a framework on which to build her interpretation. For the most up-to-date critique of Tunner's book as well as of most current secondary literature on Brentano since Frühwald, see Bernhard Gajek, "Die Brentano-Literatur 1973–1978: Ein Bericht," *Euphorion* 72 (1978): 439–502.

2. For information concerning which volumes have actually appeared as of this date, see Chapter 1, note 10, and the "Primary Sources" section of the bibliography.

3. Clemens Brentano, *Werke*, ed. Friedhelm Kemp (Munich: Hanser, 1963–1968). Coeditors for volume 1 were Wolfgang Frühwald and Bernhard Gajek. The original *Werke* were later revised and edited by Kemp and Frühwald as *Clemens Brentano: Werke in zwei Bänden*, 2 vols. (Munich: Hanser, 1972). Recently the same two editors produced a *Studienausgabe* in four volumes (Munich: Hanser, 1978).

Chapter One

1. Whereas almost every critical analysis of Brentano's imagery touches upon water metaphors and their relation to mystical and pietistic sources, the only study devoted to this phenomenon is Harry Tucker's article "Water as Symbol and Motif in the Poetry of Clemens Brentano," *Monatshefte* 45 (1953): 320–23.

2. Robert Minder, *Geist und Macht oder Einiges über die Familie Brentano* (Wiesbaden: Steiner, 1972) and Gerhard Schaub, *Le génie enfant: Die Kategorie des Kindlichen bei Clemens Brentano*, Quellen und Forschungen zur Sprach- und Kulturgeschichte der germanischen Völker, 55 (Berlin: Walther de Gruyter, 1973).

3. Werner Hoffmann, *Clemens Brentano: Leben und Werk* (Bern: Francke, 1966), pp. 51 ff.

4. Hoffmann, *Clemens Brentano*, p. 254. See also Rolf Nägele, *Die Muttersymbolik bei Clemens Brentano* (Winterthur: Keller, 1959).

5. Carmen Kahn-Wallerstein, "Clemens Brentanos Verhängnis," *Schweizer Rundschau* 50 (1950–1951): 611–19.

6. *Dichter über ihre Dichtungen: Clemens Brentano*, ed. Werner Vordtriede and Gabriele Bartenschlager (Munich: Heimeran, 1970), p. 257.

7. *Clemens Brentano: Briefe*, ed. Friedrich Seebaß (Nuremberg: Karl, 1951), 1:380. See also the autobiographical "Prologue" to the drama *Die Gründung Prags* in W, 4:547. For some provocative insights on the interrelationship of the siren, the prostitute, and artistic creativity, see Erika Tunner, "Sirene und Dirne. Chiffren der Dichterexistenz und der Poesie in Clemens Brentanos lyrischem Werk," *Recherches germaniques* 9 (1979): 141–59 and Karl Eibl, "Suche nach Wirklichkeit. Zur 'romantischen Ironie' in Clemens Brentanos Dirnengedichten," in *Romantik: Ein literaturwissenschaftliches Studienbuch*, ed. Ernst Ribbat (Königstein: Athenäum, 1979), pp. 98–113. In his article "Zu Brentanos Eheschließung mit Auguste Bußmann," *Jahrbuch des Freien Deutschen Hochstifts* (1978), pp. 291–97, Heinz Rölleke supplies some new information and insights concerning the Brentano-Bußmann marriage.

8. For the most recent discussion of Brentano's musical qualities in his poetry, see John Fetzer, *Romantic Orpheus: Profiles of Clemens Brentano* (Berkeley: University of California Press, 1974), pp. 204–61, and Heinrich Henel, "Clemens Brentanos erstarrte Musik," in *Clemens Brentano: Beiträge des Kolloquiums im Freien Deutschen Hochstift 1978*, ed. Detlev Lüders (Tübingen: Niemeyer, 1980), pp. 74–101.

9. Caroline Schelling, *Briefe aus der Frühromantik*, ed. George Waitz (1871), rev. ed., ed. Erich Schmidt (Leipzig: Insel-Verlag, 1913), 2:541.

10. The bibliography found in W, 1:1261–62 gives an initial overview of secondary literature on the subject, and the following four volumes of the new historical-critical Brentano edition should clarify the issue of authenticity even further: *Clemens Brentano: Sämtliche Werke und Briefe*, vols. 6–8, 9 (pts. 1–3), ed. Heinz Rölleke (Stuttgart: Kohlhammer, 1975–1979). For critical evaluations of this edition, see Bernhard Gajek, "Philologie als Aufklärung: Verfahren und Ergebnisse der historisch-kritischen *Wunderhorn*–Ausgabe," *Schweizer Monatshefte* 58 (1978): 539–42 and Anton Krättli, "Die 'übelangeschriebenen' Lieder: *Des Knaben Wunderhorn*—oder Poesie als Zusammenfall von Natur und Kunst," *Schweizer Monatshefte* 58 (1978): 527–38. Since the Arnim volume in the Twayne World Author Series deals with the *Wunderhorn* in detail, the Brentano monograph will only touch upon it in passing.

11. See, for instance, Heinz Rölleke's article "Die Auseinandersetzung Clemens Brentanos mit Johann Heinrich Voß über *Des Knaben Wunderhorn*: Zwei bisher ungedruckte Aufsätze Brentanos," *Jahrbuch des Freien Deutschen Hochstifts* (1968), pp. 283–328.

12. An excellent introduction to the status of the text of the *Romances* can be found in Wolfgang Frühwald's report on Brentano research "Stationen der Brentano-Forschung: 1924–1972," pp. 187–88 and in W, 1:1193–221.

13. *Dichter* über ihre Dichtungen, p. 165.

14. Eckart Kleßmann, "Romantik und Antisemitismus," *Der Monat* 21, no. 249 (1969): 65–71.

15. The exact spelling of the surname Emmerick is not clear, and some critical sources use the less frequent form Emmerich. A similar problem arises with regard to Brentano's sister, Bettina (sometimes written as Bettine). In the present study, the preferred forms will be Emmerick and Bettina.

16. For a summarizing discussion of this complex relationship, see John Fetzer, "Old and New Directions in Clemens Brentano Research (1931–1968)," *Literaturwissenschaftliches Jahrbuch* 11 (1970): 106–8. New material in this connection which has come to light and which may alter the situation includes the following: Jürg Mathes, "Ein Tagebuch Clemens Brentanos für Luise Hensel," *Jahrbuch des Freien Deutschen Hochstifts* (1971), pp. 198–310, and Hans-Joachim Schoeps, "Clemens Brentano nach Ludwig von Gerlachs Tagebüchern und Briefwechsel," *Jahrbuch des Freien Deutschen Hochstifts* (1970), pp. 281–303.

17. Siegfried Sudhof, "Brentano oder Luise Hensel? Untersuchungen zu einem Gedicht aus dem Jahre 1817," in *Festschrift Gottfried Weber: Zu seinem 70. Geburtstag überreicht von Frankfurter Kollegen und Schülern*, ed. Heinz Otto Burger and Klaus von See (Bad Homburg: Gehlen, 1967), pp. 255–64.

18. Jürg Mathes, "Ein Bericht Clemens Brentanos aus Anlaß der staatlichen Untersuchungen Anna Katharina Emmericks im Jahre 1819," *Jahrbuch des Freien Deutschen Hochstifts* (1972), pp. 228–76. For the most recent account of this question, see Wolfgang Frühwald, *Das Spätwerk Clemens Brentanos (1815–1842): Romantik im Zeitalter der Metternich'schen Restauration*, Hermaea: Germanistische Forschungen, 37 (Tübingen: Max Niemeyer, 1977), pp. 242–49.

19. Bernhard Gajek, ed., *Clemens und Christian Brentanos Bibliotheken: Die Versteigerungskataloge von 1819 und 1853. Mit einem unveröffentlichten Brief Clemens Brentanos*. Beihefte zum *Euphorion*, no. 6 (Heidelberg: Carl Winter, 1974).

20. Frühwald, *Das Spätwerk*, pp. 207–28.

21. Fetzer, "Old and New Directions," *Literaturwissenschaftliches Jahrbuch* 11 (1970): 108–11 and 12 (1971): 177–78; also Frühwald, "Stationen der Brentano-Forschung," pp. 240–49.

22. This thesis, propounded by Joseph Adam in *Clemens Brentanos Emmerick-Erlebnis: Bindung und Abenteuer* (Freiburg im Breisgau: Herder, 1956) has been sustained with modifications in later studies such as Bernhard Gajek, *Homo Poeta: Zur Kontinuität der Problematik bei Clemens Brentano*, Goethezeit, no. 3 (Frankfurt am Main: Athenäum, 1971).

23. Heinrich Heine, *Sämtliche Werke*, ed. Ernst Elster (Leipzig: Bibliographisches Institut, n.d.) 5:308–9.

24. For an account of the aesthetic and religious goals of the Nazarene painters together with their influence on literature, see Gajek, *Homo Poeta*, pp. 227–32.

25. For a concise discussion of Brentano's critical attitude toward autonomous art under the aegis of uninhibited fantasy, see Wolfgang Frühwald's article "Clemens Brentano" in *Deutsche Dichter der Romantik: Ihr Leben und Werk*, ed. Benno von Wiese (Berlin: Erich Schmidt, 1971), pp. 281, 292–94.

26. In the "Nachwort" to his edition *Clemens Brentano: Briefe an Emilie Linder* (Bad Homburg: Gehlen, 1969), pp. 301–17, Frühwald outlines some of Brentano's tactics and then expands on these procedures in *Das Spätwerk*, pp. 331–43.

27. Fetzer, *Romantic Orpheus*, pp. 160–63 and Oskar Seidlin, "Brentanos Jägerlied," *Euphorion* 70 (1976): 117–28.

28. Frühwald, *Das Spätwerk*, pp. 193–203.

29. Wolfgang Frühwald in "Das verlorene Paradies. Zur Deutung von Clemens Brentanos 'Herzlicher Zueignung' des Märchens *Gockel, Hinkel und Gackeleia (1838)*," *Literaturwissenschaftliches Jahrbuch* 3 (1962): 113–92, has unraveled much of the mystery surrounding Brentano's cryptic allusions.

30. Wolfgang Frühwald first coined this term in his article "Brentano und Frankfurt: Zu zeittypischen und zeitkritischen Aspekten im Werke des romantischen Dichters," *Jahrbuch des Freien Deutschen Hochstifts* (1970), pp. 226–43, and then he developed and elaborated this "loss of resonance" concept in his article "Clemens Brentano," in *Das Spätwerk*, and most recently in "Das Wissen und die Poesie: Anmerkungen zu Leben und Wek Clemens Brentanos," in *Clemens Brentano: Beiträge des Kolloquiums*, pp 47–73.

31. *Clemens Brentano: Briefe*, 2:336, 339, 340.

32. To mention only the major works (dealing with the problem of what constitutes romanticism) which have appeared during recent decades, one might cite the following: *Begriffsbestimmung der Romantik*, ed. Helmut Prang, Wege der Forschung, vol. 150 (Darmstadt: Wissenschaftliche Buchgesellschaft, 1968); *The Romantic Period in Germany*, ed. Siegbert Prawer (London: Weidenfeld & Nicolson, 1970); Raymond Immerwahr, *Romantisch: Genese und Tradition einer Denkform*, Republica Literaria, no. 7 (Frankfurt am Main: Athenäum, 1972); "*Romantic' and its Cognates: The European History of a Word*, ed. Hans Eichner (Manchester: Manchester University Press, 1972).

33. Paul Böckmann, "Clemens Brentano," in *Die grossen Deutschen*, ed. Hermann Heimpel, Theodor Heuss, and Benno Reifenberg (Frankfurt am Main: Ullstein, 1956), 2:532–47. Böckmann states on p. 533 that Brentano assumed the "role of mediator between the older and the younger generation . . . so that in him the inner unity and coherence of the Romantic movement is clearly marked."

34. Since this passage on romanticism and several others which follow in the remainder of the chapter are seminal for the entire discussion, they will be quoted in the original German.

35. Translation by Ralph Tymms in his book *German Romantic Literature* (London: Methuen, 1955), p. 226.

36. Tymms, *German Romantic Literature*, p. 226.

37. Novalis, *Schriften. Die Werke Friedrich von Hardenbergs*, ed. Paul Kluckhohn and Richard Samuel (Stuttgart: Kohlhammer, 1960), 2: 545: "Die Welt muß romantisirt werden. . . . Romantisiren ist nichts, als eine qualit [ative] Potenzirung. . . . Indem ich dem Gemeinen einen hohen Sinn, dem Gewöhnlichen ein geheimnißvolles Ansehn, dem Bekannten die Würde des Unbekannten, dem Endlichen einen unendlichen Schein gebe so romantisire ich es."

38. *Kritische Friedrich–Schlegel–Ausgabe*, vol. 2; ed. Hans Eichner (Munich: Schöningh, 1967), pp. 182–83.

39. *Friedrich Schlegel's* Lucinde *and the Fragments*, trans. Peter Firchow (Minneapolis: University of Minnesota Press, 1971), p. 175.

40. *Clemens Brentano: Briefe*, 2:294.

41. *Dichter über ihre Dichtungen*, p. 278.

Chapter Two

1. Walter Müller-Seidel, "Brentanos naive und sentimentalische Poesie," *Jahrbuch der deutschen Schillergesellschaft* 18 (1974): 441–65.

2. Philipp Witkop, *Die deutschen Lyriker von Luther bis Nietzsche*, vol. 2 (Leipzig: Teubner, 1921), p. 34.

3. Most recently, Roberto Fertonani in *Clemens Brentano: Poesie* (Bologna: Guanda, 1977) has translated Brentano's major poems into Italian; this publication is still too new to measure its success among critics.

4. Aside from the collection *An Anthology of German Poetry from Hölderlin to Rilke in English Translation*, ed. Angel Flores (New York: Doubleday, 1960) which contains eleven poems, pp. 91–107, there are available to the English-speaking reader the following texts: *German Verse from the 12th to the 20th Century in English Translation*, trans. J. W. Thomas, University of North Carolina Studies in the Germanic Languages and Literatures, no. 44 (Chapel Hill: The University of North Carolina Press, 1963), pp. 90–94 (five poems with no German text); *Anthology of German Poetry Through the 19th Century*, ed. Alexander Gode and Frederick Ungar (New York: Frederick Ungar, 1964), pp. 190–95 (three poems with German text); *The Penguin Book of German Verse*, ed. Leonard Forster (Baltimore: Penguin, 1969), pp. 305–7 (three poems in prose translation with German texts).

5. *Collected Works*, 1:xvii–xxii and 2:ix–xv.

6. This practice was adopted by Kurt Schubert in *Clemens Brentanos weltliche Lyrik* (Breslau: F. Hirt, 1910) and on a more sophisticated level by Johannes Klein in the Brentano section of his book *Geschichte der deutschen Lyrik von Luther bis zum Ausgang des zweiten Weltkrieges* (Wiesbaden: Steiner, 1960), pp. 434–45.

7. The Flores anthology mentioned above contains a selection almost identical to that found in *Das deutsche Gedicht vom Mittelalter bis zum 20. Jahrhundert*, ed. Edgar Hederer (Hamburg: Fischer-Bücherei, 1957), pp. 199–206. Brentano is represented by the most poems in the collection *Dichtung der Romantik*, vol. 5; *Lyrik*, ed. Karl Balser, Reinhard Buchwald,

and Karl Reinking (Leck/Schleswig: Clausen & Bosse, n.d.). Readily accessible Brentano anthologies include: *Clemens Brentano. Gedichte*, ed. Wolfgang Frühwald (Reinbeck: Rowohlt, 1968) and the editions under the same title edited by Werner Vordtriede (Frankfurt am Main: Insel, 1963) and by Paul Requadt (Stuttgart: Reclam, 1968).

8. In addition to the aforementioned works by Witkop and Klein, one should cite Günther Müller's *Geschichte des deutschen Liedes vom Zeitalter des Barock bis zur Gegenwart* (Munich: Drei Masken Verlag, 1925), pp. 279–93 as well as *Die deutsche Lyrik: Form und Geschichte*, ed. Benno von Wiese, vol. 2 (Düsseldorf: Bagel, 1970), pp. 11–49.

9. Karl Tober, "Das 'romantische' Gedicht? Gedanken zu Clemens Brentanos Lyrik," *Colloquia Germanica* (1968), pp. 137–51; Luciano Zagari, "Deutsche Lyrik der Romantik," pp. 153–60 in Zagari's '*Paradiso' artificiale e 'squardo elegiaco sui flutti.' La lirica religiosa di Brentano e la periodizzazione del Romanticismo*, SStudi di Filologia Tedesca, no. 9 (Rome: Bulzoni, 1971). Especially significant in this regard is Wolfgang Frühwald's "Gedichte in der Isolation: Romantische Lyrik am Übergang von der Autonomie- zur Zweckästhetik," in *Historizität und Sprach- und Literaturwissenschaft*, ed. Walter Müller-Seidel (Munich: Wilhelm Fink, 1974), pp. 295–311.

10. For instance, Günther Müller's article "Brentanos Luisengedichte," *Jahrbuch des Freien Deutschen Hochstifts* (1928), pp. 154–77.

11. Frühwald, "Stationen der Brentano-Forschung," p. 211.

12. The master sleuth in such matters among current Brentano scholars is undoubtedly Heinz Rölleke whose eye for detail has provided him with clues for important discoveries in many areas.

13. Henning Boetius, "Zur Entstehung und Textqualität von Clemens Brentanos *Gesammelten Schriften*," *Jahrbuch des Freien Deutschen Hochstifts* (1967), pp. 406–57.

14. *Chronologie des poésies de Clemens Brentano avec un choix de variantes* (Paris: E. Droz, 1933). See also Henning Boetius, "Entstehung, Überlieferung and Datierung dreier Gedichte Clemens Brentanos," *Jahrbuch des Freien Deutschen Hochstifts* (1970), pp. 258–80.

15. *Die Zeit als Einbildungskraft des Dichters* (1939; reprint ed., Zurich: Atlantis, 1953), pp. 23–105.

16. Hans Jaeger's study *Clemens Brentanos Frühlyrik* (Frankfurt am Main: Diesterweg, 1926) had already pointed in this direction, but its impact was not as widespread as that of Staiger.

17. Walther Killy, *Wandlungen des lyrischen Bildes*, 3d ed. (Göttingen: Vandenhoeck & Ruprecht, 1961), pp. 53–72 and Friedrich Wilhelm Wollenberg, "Brentanos Jugendlyrik: Studien zur Struktur seiner dichterischen Persönlichkeit" (Ph.D. diss., Hamburg, 1964).

18. *Brentanos Poetik* (Munich: Hanser, 1961).

19. For instance, Rosemarie Hunter's article "Clemens Brentanos 'Wenn der lahme Weber träumt' und das Problem der Sprachverfremdung," *Germanisch-Romanische Monatsschrift* 50 (1969): 144–52 and Geri Denbo

Greenway, "Patterns of Rebirth Imagery in the Poetry of Clemens Brentano" (Ph.D. diss., University of Wisconsin, 1970).

20. Frühwald, "Stationen der Brentano-Forschung," p. 231–34 and Heinrich Henel, "Clemens Brentano: Zwei enigmatische Verse," in *Aspekte der Goethezeit: Festschrift für Victor Lange*, ed. Stanley A. Corngold, Michael Curschmann, and Theodore J. Ziolkowski (Göttingen: Vandenhoeck & Ruprecht, 1977), pp. 262–64.

21. Jürgen Behrens, Wolfgang Frühwald, Detlev Lüders, "Zum Stand der Arbeiten an der Frankfurter Brentano-Ausgabe," *Literaturwissenschaftliches Jahrbuch* 10 (1969): 398–426.

22. For some good insights, see Hartwig Schultz, "Vorarbeiten Clemens Brentanos zu einer Sammelausgabe seiner Werke," *Jahrbuch des Freien Deutschen Hochstifts* (1976), pp. 316–51.

23. Gajek, *Homo poeta*, pp. 44–51 draws distinctions between his "total" approach and the selectivity principles of his predecessors.

24. Müller-Seidel, "Brentanos naive und sentimentalische Poesie," after a thought-provoking examination of the critical literature of all three camps, comes to the conclusion that Brentano is best characterized as a "sentimentalischer Dichter des Naiven," "a reflective poet of the naïve" (p. 459). In his recent analysis entitled "Brentanos späte Lyrik: Kontinuität und Stilwandel," in *Clemens Brentano: Beiträge des Kolloquiums* pp. 239–75, Müller-Seidel adroitly synthesizes all three critical stances derived from chronology.

25. These are the chapter headings for the lyric discussion in Guignard's monograph *Un poète romantique allemand. Clemens Brentano* (Paris: Presses Universitaires de France, 1933).

26. *Clemens Brentano: Ein romantisches Dichterleben* (Freiburg im Breisgau: Herder, 1947), table of contents.

27. The principles followed in Frühwald's edition of the *Gedichte* are clarified in his postscript 'Zur Gliederung,' pp. 207–13.

28. As in Zagari's book *'Paradiso' artificiale*.

29. For instance, the title "Wiegenlied eines jammernden Herzens" ("Cradlesong of a Lamenting Heart") was a product of the original editors' imagination, but it has led to many comparisons of this "cradlesong" with others. See note 69.

30. For instance, the poem "Hör', es klagt die Flöte wieder" was originally a dialogue between two figures in *The Merry Minstrels*, but the editors of the *Collected Works* saw fit to eliminate the speaker designations, combine the lines into stanzas, and give the new creation the title "Abendständchen" ("Little Evening Serenade"). Whereas the first alteration has caused much controversy, the second is usually passed over in silence in the critical literature.

31. Frühwald, *Clemens Brentano: Gedichte*, "Zum Text," pp. 201–6.

32. For a brief resumé of the positions of the editors versus their critics, see Wolfgang Frühwald, "Das verlorene Paradies," pp. 145–48.

33. Most of the following are not titles *per se*, but rather the first lines of the poems themselves. Modern anthologies have perpetuated the confusing practice inaugurated by the *Collected Works* of supplying titles for the poems. Aside from the aforementioned "Little Evening Serenade" one finds the following titles, none of which are from Brentano": "Zu Bacharach am Rheine" is "Lore Lay"; "Es sang vor langen Jahren" becomes "The Spinner's (Night) Song"; "Singet leise, leise, leise" has the designation "Cradlesong" while "Was reif in diesen Zeilen steht" is entitled "Prelude."

34. Flores, *An Anthology of German Poetry*, pp. 97–98.

35. Paul Böckmann, "Die romantische Poesie Brentanos und ihre Grundlagen bei Friedrich Schlegel und Tieck. Ein Beitrag zur Entwicklung der Formensprache der deutschen Romantik," *Jahrbuch des Freien Deutschen Hochstifts* (1934–1935), pp. 56–176.

36. Killy, *Wandlungen*, pp. 62–68 discusses this poem in conjunction with his concept of the "Chiffre" or lyric-poetic cypher, a kind of personalized, internalized symbol. The most recent and far-reaching analysis of this poem is Detlev Lüders, "Clemens Brentano: 'Alles ist ewig im Innern verwandt.' Die Dichtung verändert das Weltverständnis," in *Clemens Brentano: Beiträge des Kolloquiums*, pp. 135–62.

37. Frühwald, *Clemens Brentano: Gedichte*, p. 206.

38. Flores, *An Anthology of German Poetry*, pp. 103–6.

39. Robert Minder, "Brentanos Lore Lay," *Insel-Almanach* (1964–1965), p. 24 ponders the tonal qualities of this name.

40. The relationship of Brentano's Lore Lay to his fairy-tale figure Lureley as well as to Heine's later Lore-Ley have been the subject of many comparative investigations. One of the earliest and best of these is Ernst Beutler, "Der König in Thule' und die Dichtungen von der Lorelay,'" *Essays um Goethe*, vol. 2 (Wiesbaden: Dieterich, 1947), pp. 307–69.

41. Some of the confusion concerning the identity of the boatman as well as that of the "I" at the end of the ballad may be attributed to the existence of several versions of the poem and some acts of editorial contamination. See Klaus-Dieter Krabiel, "Die beiden Fassungen von Brentanos 'Lureley,' " *Literaturwissenschaftliches Jahrbuch* 6 (1965): 122–32. New insights into the problem have recently been brought to light by Werner Bellmann, "Brentanos Lore Lay-Ballade und der antike Echo-Mythos," in *Clemens Brentano: Beiträge des Kolloquiums*, pp. 1–9.

42. An extensive analysis of the mirror image in Brentano's entire work is provided by Hans Peter Neureuter, *Das Spiegelmotiv bei Clemens Brentano: Studie zum romantischen Ich-Bewusstsein* (Frankfurt am Main: Athenäum, 1972). The narcissistic qualities of the Lore Lay's dilemma are treated by Heinz Politzer in "Das Schweigen der Sirenen," *Deutsche Vierteljahrsschrift für Literaturwissenschaft und Geistesgeschichte* 41 (1967): 453–57.

43. Minder, "Brentanos Lore Lay," p. 26 and Hermann Pongs, "Die romantische Ballade: Clemens Brentano 'Lore Lay,' " in *Das Bild in der*

Dichtung, vol. 3, *Der symbolische Kosmos der Dichtung* (Marburg: Elwert, 1969), pp. 116–17.

44. Erika Essen, "Clemens Brentano. Lore Lay," *Wege zum Gedicht*, ed. Rupert Hirschenauer and Albrecht Weber, vol. 2 (Munich: Schnell and Steiner, 1964), pp. 245–46.

45. Flores, *An Anthology of German Poetry*, pp. 95–96.

46. It is with specific reference to this poem that Müller-Seidel, in his article "Brentanos naive und sentimentalische Poesie," formulates the thesis that Brentano is not merely the "naive" poet, but rather the highly conscious (i.e. reflective) poet of the naive (p. 459). Müller-Seidel's happy formulation, based on Schiller's famous distinction between poetic types, is not really a new revelation. Ernst Feise, for instance, in "Problems of Lyric Form," *Modern Language Notes* 44 (1934): 293–301, spoke of "a crafty, mathematically rational construction" in the poem which seemed "to issue forth from the unconscious, purposeless depth of the soul" (p. 299). Lida Kirchberger in "Brentano's 'Der Spinnerin Lied': A Fresh Appraisal," *Monatshefte* 67 (1975): p. 418 notes that "the deceptively simple little poem is anything but child's play."

47. One of the first to analyze this structure was Ernst Feise in the article cited in note 46. Since its appearance, Feise's premise has been elaborated or modified by critics, but it still remains basically intact. For another study which has enjoyed success, see Siegbert S. Prawer, "Der Spinnerin Lied," in *German Lyric Poetry. A Critical Analysis of Selected Poems from Klopstock to Rilke* (London: Routledge and Paul, 1952), pp. 121–126.

48. Walter Naumann, "Clemens Brentano 'Der Spinnerin Lied,' " in *Traum und Tradition in der deutschen Lyrik* (Stuttgart: W. Kohlhammer, 1966), pp. 74–76. For a brilliant assessment of the development of the nightingale symbol in Brentano's writing, see Frühwald, *Das Spätwerk*, pp. 228–40.

49. The concept of the girl, deserted by her lover, sitting alone in her room at the spinning wheel is a familiar *topos* in literature.

50. Building on Johannes Pfeiffer's concept of the parallelism between the spinning wheel's circularity and the recurrent pattern of certain word constellations in the poem as interpreted in *Wege zur Dichtung* (Hamburg: Wittig, 1953, p. 48 ff), Richard Alewyn developed these concepts in a short, but seminal article, "Clemens Brentano: 'Der Spinnerin Lied,' " in *Interpretationen*, ed. Jost Schillemeit, vol. 1: *Deutsche Lyrik von Weckherlin bis Benn* (Frankfurt am Main: Fischer Bücherei, 1965), pp. 155–58 (first appeared in *Wirkendes Wort* 11 [1961]: 45–47). Opposed to Alewyn's arguments for circularity are Joachim Klein who, in "Lyrische Fabel und ästhetisches Paradigma: Zu Inhalt und Organisation von C. Brentanos 'Der Spinnerin Lied,' " *Sprachkunst* 5 (1974): 17–26, argues for a linear progression from hopelessness to hope, from longing on earth to longing for the beyond, and Hans-Joachim Schrimpf who in "Nachtrag zu Brentanos 'Der Spinnerin Lied': Text und Kontext," in *Wissen aus Erfahrungen: Werkbegriff*

und Interpretation heute. Festschrift für Herman Meyer, ed. Alexander von Bormann (Tübingen: Niemeyer, 1976), pp. 384–91, indicates "breaks" in the circularity concept. Alewyn's entire approach has been attacked for its imprecise use of terminology by Peter Finke in "Kritische Überlegungen zu einer Interpretation Richard Alewyns," in *Interpretationsanalysen: Argumentationsstrukturen in literaturwissenschaftlichen Interpretationen,* ed. Walther Kindt and Siegfried J. Schmidt (Munich: Fink, 1976), pp. 16–39.

51. Frühwald, "Das verlorene Paradies," discusses the problem of art serving as a substitute for Paradise Lost.

52. Flores, *An Anthology of German Poetry,* p. 95.

53. Albrecht Schöne, "Clemens Brentano: 'Abendständchen,' " in *Die Deutsche Lyrik,* ed. Benno von Wiese, vol. 2 (Düsseldorf: Bagel, 1970), pp. 11–18, argues persuasively for removing the lines from the original context and interpreting the piece as a pure lyric poem with no extra-lyric ties.

54. The technique of projecting one's own situation in life into that of a poetic figure (such as the merry minstrels, the spinstress, etc.) has elements of "role playing" and the German term for such poems is "Rollengedicht." For a discussion of this technique see Oskar Seidlin's interpretation "Brentanos Jägerlied," *Euphorion* 70 (1976): 117–28.

55. Flores, *An Anthology of German Verse,* pp. 96–97. The sense of the second stanza, (not translated in this anthology) might be rendered as follows:

For there slumber in the Rhine
The charming little children now,
Ameleya alone holds watch,
Weeping in the moonlight.

56. Beutler, " 'Der König in Thule' und die Dichtungen von der Lorelay," p. 356.

57. Bernhard Blume, in " 'Murmeln, flüstern, rieseln:' Zur Entstehung von Clemens Brentanos 'Wiegenlied,' " *Modern Language Notes* 75 (1960): 596–602, proves that the famous verb constellation is not original with Brentano.

58. My translation is based on the authenticated manuscript version of the poem as found in the Freies Deutsches Hochstift in Frankfurt am Main. It differs in several respects from the prose rendition given in *The Penguin Book of German Verse,* ed. Leonard Forster (Baltimore: Penguin Books, 1974), p. 306. The latter translation, taken from an adaptation of the poem discovered among Beethoven's posthumous papers, reads as follows: "God, Thy heaven has me by the hair, Thy earth drags me into hell; Lord, where shall I keep my heart so that I can keep safe Thy threshold? Thus I implore Thee through the night, in which my laments stream like fountains of fire which surround me with flaming seas; but in the midst of it I have found foothold, I stand forth like mysterious giants, Memnon's statue, the first suns of morning shoot their questioning rays at my forehead, and the dream which midnight spun I now rehearse to greet the day."

59. Gerhard Friesen, "Clemens Brentano's 'Nachklänge Beethovenscher Musik,'" in *Traditions and Transitions. Studies in Honor of Harold Jantz*, ed. Liselotte E. Kurth, William H. McClain, and Holger Homann (Munich: Delp, 1972), pp. 194–209.

60. A comprehensive interpretation of three of the Beethoven poems considered as a trilogy is found in August Langen, "Clemens Brentano: 'Nachklänge Beethovenscher Musik,'" in *Die deutsche Lyrik*, ed. Benno von Wiese, vol. 2 (Düsseldorf: Bagel, 1970), pp. 19–38.

61. Flores, *An Anthology of German Verse*, pp. 99–101.

62. The element of the "cry" or "scream" and its modern manifestations in literature since Expressionism is stressed in a joint article by Curt Hohoff and Anneliese de Haas, "Clemens Brentano: Frühlingsschrei eines Knechtes aus der Tiefe," in *Wege zum Gedicht*, ed. Rupert Hirschenauer and Albrecht Weber (Munich: Schnell and Steiner, 1956), pp. 199–207.

63. Harry Tucker, Jr., "Clemens Brentano: The Imagery of Despair and Salvation," *Modern Language Quarterly* 14 (1953): 284–97.

64. *Collected Works*, 2:199–200. Since the English translation is based on this version of the poem, it will be used as the basis for the interpretation, even though the editors of the *Werke* have reservations about its authenticity (W,1:1132–33) and give still another adaptation (W, 1:363–64).

65. Flores, *An Anthology of German Poetry*, pp. 93–94.

66. Hans Rupprich, *Brentano, Luise Hensel und Ludwig von Gerlach* (Vienna: Österreichischer Bundesverlag für Unterricht, Wissenschaft und Kunst, 1927), p. 60 ff.

67. Frühwald, "Das verlorene Paradies," p. 164.

68. *Collected Works*, 8:224.

69. Ever since Enzensberger's interpretation of this poem in *Brentanos Poetik*, pp. 23–39, it has aroused much commentary and controversy. See especially: Siegfried Sudhof, "Brentanos Gedicht 'O schweig nur Herz! . . .' Zur Tradition sprachlicher Formen und poetischer Bilder," *Zeitschrift für deutsche Philologie*, 92 (1973): 211–31; Heinrich Henel, "Brentanos 'O schweig nur, Herz.' Das Gedicht und seine Interpretation," *Jahrbuch des Freien Deutschen Hochstifts* (1977), pp. 309–49 and, in the same volume, Hartwig Schultz, "Brentanos 'Wiegenlied eines jammernden Herzens. Zum' Verständnis des Titels," pp. 350–63.

70. Surprisingly, this poem does not appear prominently in Günther Müller's article "Brentanos Luisengedichte," *Jahrbuch des Freien Deutschen Hochstifts* (1928), pp. 154–77 and Geri D. Greenway in "'Schweig Herz! Kein Schrei!' by Clemens Brentano," *Monatshefte* 66 (1974): 166–72 only seems to expand on Enzensberger's findings.

71. Günther Müller, "Clemens Brentano," *Schweizerische Rundschau* 29 (1928): 684–700 makes the quest for permanence ("Bestand") the theme of his article.

72. Staiger, in *Die Zeit als Einbildungskraft*, makes "die reißende Zeit" the central concern of his Brentano interpretation.

73. Flores, *An Anthology of German Poetry*, p. 91.

74. For the most up-to-date and comprehensive treatment of this subject in Brentano's life and works, see Gerhard Schaub, *Le génie enfant*.

75. For a broad, although somewhat unclear, survey of the problem see Klaus Wille, *Die Signatur der Melancholie im Werk Clemens Brentanos*, Europäische Hochschulschriften, Deutsche Literatur und Germanistik, vol. 36 (Bern: Herbert Lang, 1970).

76. Maria Schmidt-Ihms, "Anmerkungen zu Brentanos 'Eingang: Was reif in diesen Zeilen steht,'" *Acta Germanica*, 3 (1968): 153–65.

77. By far the best analysis of this complicated question is Elisabeth Stopp, "Brentano's 'O Stern und Blume': Its Poetic and Emblematic Context," *Modern Language Review* 67 (1972): 95–117.

Chapter Three

1. Werner Vordtriede, "Clemens Brentanos Anteil an der Kultstätte in Ephesus," *Deutsche Vierteljahrsschrift für Literaturwissenschaft und Geistesgeschichte* 34 (1960): 384–401.

2. In addition to the controversial Emmerick material mentioned in Chapter 1, notes 18, 20–22, one must also include the very useful summary of research in Oskar Katann's report "Die Glaubwürdigkeit von Clemens Brentanos Emmerick-Berichten: Zum gegenwärtigen Stand der Quellen und Forschung," *Literaturwissenschaftliches Jahrbuch* 7 (1966): 145–94.

3. *Dichter über ihre Dichtungen*, p. 93.

4. For instance, at one point Godwi trips over the leg of a table ("Der Tisch hat Beine") which leads to a play on the name of the German painter Johann Tischbein (*W*, 2:19). Later examples include comparisons of individuals with geometric figures (triangles) and a long excursion into the senseless crusade of quasi-philosophers of the Fichtean school.

5. *Dichter über ihre Dichtungen*, p. 92.

6. *Godwi: Ein Kapitel deutscher Romantik* (Berlin: Georg Bondi, 1898).

7. Henning Boetius, "Zur Entstehung und Textqualität von Clemens Brentanos *Gesammelten Schriften*," pp. 406–57 and Frühwald, "Stationen der Brentano-Forschung," pp. 259–61.

8. Kerr, *Godwi*, pp. 66–79. Greatly indebted to Kerr's approach (especially with regard to biographical-fictional correspondences) is Horst Dieter Hayer, *Brentanos 'Godwi:' Ein Beispiel des frühromantischen Subjektivismus*, Europäische Hochschulschriften. Deutsche Literatur und Germanistik, vol, 188 (Bern: Lang, 1977).

9. "Die romantische Poesie Brentanos und ihre Grundlagen bei Friedrich Schlegel und Tieck," pp. 56–176.

10. Frühwald, "Stationen der Brentano-Forschung," pp. 260–61. In the best tradition of Böckmann is Susanne Mittag, *Clemens Brentano. "Eine Autobiographie in der Form,"* Frankfurter Beiträge zur Germanistik, vol. 17 (Heidelberg: Winter, 1978).

11. Hermánn August Korff, *Geist der Goethezeit*, vol. 2 (1940; reprint ed., Leipzig: Koehler & Amelung, 1966), pp. 196–204 treats the book under the category "Erotic Unruliness" with subsections on the "Romantic Castle of Venus" and "Romantic Prostitutes;" Hans Heinrich Borcherdt in *Der Roman der Goethezeit* (Urach: Port Verlag, 1949), pp. 435–53 regards it as the early romantic novel in decline.

12. Franz N. Mennemeier, "Rückblick auf Brentanos *Godwi:* Ein Roman 'ohne Tendenz,'" *Wirkendes Wort* 16 (1966): 24–33.

13. Claude David, "Clemens Brentano," in *Die deutsche Romantik: Poetik, Formen und Motive*, ed. Hans Steffen (Göttingen: Vandenhoeck & Ruprecht, 1967), pp. 159–79.

14. Benno von Wiese, "Brentanos *Godwi*," in *Von Lessing bis Grabbe: Studien zur deutschen Klassik und Romantik* (Düsseldorf: Bagel, 1968), pp. 191–247.

15. Gerhard Storz, "Beobachtungen an Brentanos *Godwi*," in *Festschrift für Friedrich Beißner*, ed. Ulrich Gaier and Werner Volke (Bebenhausen: Lothar Rotsch, 1974), pp. 436–46.

16. Christa Hunscha, "Stilzwang und Wirklichkeit: Zu Brentanos *Godwi*," in *Romananfänge: Versuch zu einer Poetik des Romans*, ed. Norbert Miller (Berlin: Literarisches Kolloquium, 1965), pp. 135–48.

17. Marianne Schuller, "Clemens Brentano," in *Romanschlüsse in der Romantik: Zum frühromantischen Problem von Universalität und Fragment* (Munich: Fink, 1974), pp. 111–57.

18. The most comprehensive analysis of this phenomenon to date has been Ingrid Strohschneider-Kohrs' book *Die romantische Ironie in Theorie und Gestaltung* (Tübingen: Max Niemeyer, 1960), an abbreviated form of which appeared in *Die deutsche Romantik*, ed. Hans Steffen, pp. 75–97 under the title "Zur Poetik der deutschen Romantik II: Die romantische Ironie." More recently and on a broader basis, Ernst Behler in his book *Klassische Ironie, romantische Ironie, tragische Ironie: Zum Ursprung dieser Begriffe*, Libelli, vol. 328 (Darmstadt: Wissenschaftliche Buchgesellschaft, 1972), treated the problem within the framework of a larger context.

19. Eugene Reed, "The Union of the Arts in Brentano's *Godwi*," *Germanic Review* 29 (1954): 102–18.

20. John Fetzer, "Clemens Brentano's *Godwi*: Variations on the Melos-Eros Theme," *Germanic Review* 42 (1967): 108–23.

21. Fetzer, *Romantic Orpheus*, pp. 114–21, 189–95.

22. Horst Meixner, "Denkstein und Bildersaal in Clemens Brentanos *Godwi*: Ein Beitrag zur romantischen Allegorie," *Jahrbuch der deutschen Schillergesellschaft* 11 (1967): 435–68.

23. Almost every major study of the German novella, for instance, includes a discussion of Brentano's *The Story of Honest Casper and Fair Annie*. For a handy overview of the shorter narratives, see Gerhard Kluge, "Clemens Brentanos Erzählungen aus den Jahren 1810–1818. Beobachtungen zu ihrer Struktur und Thematik," in *Clemens Brentano: Beiträge des Kolloquiums*, pp. 102–34.

24. Whereas the *Chronicle* fragments have been studied peripherally with reference to the literary chronicle as a genre by Rupprecht Leppla in his monograph *Wilhelm Meinhold und die chronikalische Erzählung*, Germanische Studien, no. 54 (Berlin: Emil Ebering, 1928), Brentano's other shorter prose fiction has been for the most part neglected. One incisive study of *BOGS*, however, should be mentioned at this point since its implications go far beyond the single work in question: Elisabeth Stopp, "Die Kunstform der Tollheit. Zu Clemens Brentanos und Joseph Görres' 'BOGS der Uhrmacher,' " in *Clemens Brentano: Beiträge des Kolloquiums*, pp. 359–76.

25. Alfred Walheim, "Brentanos *Chronika eines fahrenden Schülers*," *Zeitschrift für Österreichische Gymnasien* 63 (1912): 289–315.

26. The 1802–1806 version or "original" *Chronicle* was first published by Wilhelm Kreiten, S.J. in *Stimmen aus Maria-Laach* 19 (1880) and 20 (1881) using a not too reliable copy of the author's manuscript. Then Joseph Lefftz published a more authentic version *Clemens Brentano. Die Chronika des fahrenden Schülers. Urfassung* (Leipzig: Wolkenwanderer-Verlag, 1923) based on the author's own manuscript found in the Alsatian Trappist monastery of Oelenberg.

27. Elisabeth Stopp, ed., *Clemens Brentano. Die Chronika des fahrenden Schülers* (Stuttgart: Reclam, 1971), pp. 112–36. Stopp's premise is expanded by Ingrid Mittenzwei in her article "Kunst als Thema des frühen Brentano," in *Clemens Brentano: Beiträge des Kolloquiums*, pp. 192–215.

28. Elisabeth Stopp, "Brentano's *Chronika* and its Revision," in *Sprache und Bekenntnis: Sonderband des Literaturwissenschaftlichen Jahrbuchs, Hermann Kunisch zum 70. Geburtstag*, ed. Wolfgang Frühwald and Günter Niggl (Berlin: Duncker & Humblot, 1971), pp. 161–84.

29. Stopp, "Brentano's *Chronika* . . . Revision," p. 175.

30. Leppla, *Wilhelm Meinhold und die chronikalische Erzählung*, pp. 55–63.

31. Anton Kathan, "Die *Chronika des fahrenden Schülers*: Zum Erzählproblem bei Brentano, "*Literaturwissenschaftliches Jahrbuch* 13 (1972): 181–215.

32. Nikolaus Reindl, *Die poetische Funktion des Mittelalters in der Dichtung Clemens Brentanos*, Innsbrucker Beiträge zur Kulturwissenschaft, Germanistische Reihe, vol. 6 (Innsbruck: H. Kowarsch, 1976).

33. Ernst Fedor Hoffmann, "Spiegelbild und Schatten: Zur Behandlung ähnlicher Motive bei Brentano, Hoffmann und Chamisso," in *Lebendige Form: Interpretationen zur deutschen Literatur. Festschrift für Heinrich E. K. Henel*, ed. Jeffrey L. Sammons and Ernst Schürer (Munich: Fink, 1970), pp. 167–88.

34. Michael Huber, *Clemens Brentano: Die Chronika des fahrenden Schülers. Eine Analyse der Figurenkonstellation und der kompositorischen Prinzipien der Urfassung*, Gegenwart der Dichtung, Neue Folge, vol. 2 (Bern: Francke, 1976).

35. Guignard, *Clemens Brentano*, pp. 392–97 and Hoffmann, *Clemens Brentano*, pp. 293–95.

36. For instance, Johannes Klein, *Geschichte der deutschen Novelle*

(Wiesbaden: Franz Steiner, 1960), pp. 149–51 or Bernhard von Arx, *Novellistisches Dasein* (Zurich: Artemis, 1953), pp. 114–28.

37. Josef Kunz, *Die deutsche Novelle zwischen Klassik und Romantik* (Berlin: E. Schmidt, 1966), p. 76.

38. Heinz Rölleke, "Quellen zu Brentanos *Geschichte vom braven Kasperl und dem schönen Annerl*," *Jahrbuch des Freien Deutschen Hochstifts* (1970), pp. 244–57.

39. Richard Alewyn, "Brentanos *Geschichte vom braven Kasperl und dem schönen Annerl*," in *Interpretationen: Deutsche Erzählungen von Wieland bis Kafka*, ed. Jost Schillemeit (Frankfurt am Main: Fischer Bücherei, 1966), p. 104.

40. Peter Paul Schwarz, "Brentanos *Geschichte vom braven Kasperl und dem schönen Annerl* im Zusammenhang seiner religiösen Wendung," *Aurora* 32 (1972): 72.

41. Herbert Lehnert, "Die Gnade sprach von Liebe. Eine Struktur-Interpretation der *Geschichte vom braven Kasperl und dem schönen Annerl* von Clemens Brentano," in *Geschichte, Deutung, Kritik. Literaturwissenschaftliche Beiträge, dargebracht zum 65. Geburtstag Werner Kohlschmidts*, ed. Maria Bindschedler and Paul Zimsli (Bern: Francke, 1969), pp. 199–223 and Gerhard Kluge, "Vom Perspektivismus des Erzählens. Eine Studie über Clemens Brentanos *Geschichte vom braven Kasperl und dem schönen Annerl*," *Jahrbuch des Freien Deutschen Hochstifts* (1971), pp. 143–97. In his edition of the story in the series "Literatur-Kommentare," vol. 14 (Munich: Hanser, 1979), Kluge not only supplies comprehensive background material on the novella, but also gives an exhaustive analysis of the genre issue, the romantic and realistic features of the work, the role of the monument, irony, etc., while, in the process, bringing the latest results of critical research into clear focus. See also in this regard Martin Swales, "Narrative Sleight-of-Hand: Some Notes on Two German Romantic Tales," *New German Studies* 6 (1978): 1–13 and Donald MacRae, "A New Look at the Old Woman in Brentano's *Kasperl und Annerl*," in *Literatur als Dialog. Festschrift zum 50. Geburtstag von Karl Tober*, ed. Reingard Nethersole (Johannesburg: Ravan, 1979), pp. 283–93.

42. Ralph Tymms's reference to her "half-witted stoicism" in his *German Romantic Literature*, p. 241 is too strong.

43. Kluge, "Vom Perspektivismus des Erzählens," p. 149 and passim.

44. Heinz Rölleke, "Die gemästete Gänseleber. Zu einer Metapher in Clemens Brentanos *Geschichte vom braven Kasperl und dem schönen Annerl*," *Jahrbuch des Freien Deutschen Hochstifts* (1974), pp. 312–22.

45. Wolfgang Frühwald, "Clemens Brentano," in *Deutsche Dichter der Romantik*, p. 294.

46. Walter Silz, "Brentano, *Geschichte vom braven Kasperl und dem schönen Annerl*," in *Realism and Reality* (Chapel Hill: University of North Carolina Press, 1954), p. 23.

47. Benno von Wiese, "Clemens Brentano: *Geschichte vom braven Kasperl und dem schönen Annerl*," in *Die deutsche Novelle von Goethe bis Kafka: Interpretationen*, vol. 1 (Düsseldorf: A. Bagel, 1956), p. 75.

48. Ernst Feise, "Clemens Brentanos *Geschichte vom braven Kasperl und* [sic] *schönen Annerl*. Eine Formanalyse," in *Corona, Studies in Celebration of the Eightieth Birthday of Samuel Singer*, ed. Arno Schirokauer and Wolfgang Paulsen (Durham: Duke University Press, 1941), p. 209.

49. Alewyn, "Brentanos *Geschichte*," pp. 147–48.

50. Gero von Wilpert, *Sachwörterbuch der Literatur* (Stuttgart: Kröner, 1969), "Emblem," pp. 203–4.

51. Ibid., "Exempel," pp. 240–41.

52. Helmut Rehder, "Von Ehre, Gnade und Gerechtigkeit. Gedanken zu Brentanos *Geschichte vom braven Kasper* [sic] *und dem schönen Annerl*," in *Stoffe, Formen, Strukturen. Studien zur deutschen Literatur*, ed. Albert Fuchs and Helmut Motekat (Munich: Hueber, 1962), p. 317.

53. Lehnert, "Die Gnade sprach von Liebe," p. 203 and passim.

54. Kluge, "Vom Perspektivismus des Erzählens," pp. 174–76.

55. Klaus Heinisch, "Clemens Brentano: *Geschichte vom braven Kasperl und dem schönen Annerl*," in *Deutsche Romantik. Interpretationen* (Paderborn: Schöningh, 1966), pp. 64–75. An interesting approach is taken by Michel Kauffmann in his article "Die Geschichte vom braven Kasperl und vom [sic] schönen Annerl de Clemens Brentano," *Romantisme* 20 (1978): 69–78.

56. Peter Horwath, "Über den Fatalismus in Clemens Brentanos *Geschichte vom braven Kasperl und dem schönen Annerl*. Zur Psychologie der Novelle," *German Quarterly* 44 (1971): 24–34.

57. "The Story of Honest Casper and Fair Annie," trans. Helene Scher in *Four Romantic Tales from Nineteenth Century German* (New York: Ungar, 1975), p. 29.

58. Ibid., p. 34.

59. *Dichter über ihre Dichtungen*, pp. 265–66.

60. Ibid., p. 266.

61. Ibid., p. 270.

62. Fetzer, *Romantic Orpheus*, p. 70.

63. For a complete analysis of the critical literature on the fairy tales, see Fetzer, "Old and New Directions," pp. 166–77, Frühwald, "Stationen," pp. 250–53, and most recently, Bernhard Gajek, "Die Brentano-Literatur 1973–78," pp. 485–89.

64. As, for instance, in Max Diez's article "Metapher und Märchengestalt," *PMLA* 48 (1933): 1209–16.

65. The dating of Brentano's various fairy tales is, with a few exceptions, imprecise and speculative. The dating scheme used in this study is based on Ilse Mahl's *Der Prosastil in den Märchen Clemens Brentanos*, Germanistische Studien, no. 110 (Berlin: Lessing-Druckerei, 1931), pp. 121–22, with pertinent modifications based on later research.

66. Oskar Seidlin, "Brentanos Melusine," *Euphorion* 72 (1978): 369–99.

67. For an excellent discussion of the role which heraldry and heraldic symbolism play in the fairy tales, see Oskar Seidlin, "Brentanos Heraldik," in *Clemens Brentano: Beiträge des Kolloquiums*, pp. 349–58.

68. The controversy centers around the Grimm brothers' championing of "folk fairy tale" and the Arnim-Brentano advocacy of the "art fairy tale." A most concise and clear account of the running feud between the two factions can be found in Hans Schumacher, *Narziß an der Quelle. Das romantische Kunstmärchen: Geschichte und Interpretation* (Wiesbaden: Athenaion, 1977), pp. 73–81.

69. Joseph von Eichendorff wrote a perceptive commentary entitled, "Brentano und seine Märchen," in 1847 and this work is reprinted in *Aurora* 24 (1963): 14–20.

70. Aside from numerous typewritten and printed dissertations, one should mention Hermann Cardauns' *Die Märchen Clemens Brentano's* (Cologne: Bachem, 1895) and Karl Glöckner's *Brentano als Märchenerzähler*, Deutsche Arbeiten der Universität Köln, no. 13 (Jena: Diederich, 1938).

71. Karsten H. Nielsen, "Vermittlung und Rahmetechnik. Eine kritische Untersuchung der 'Rheinmärchen' Brentanos." *Orbis Litterarum* 37 (1972): 77–101.

72. Schumacher, *Narziß an der Quelle*, pp. 81–95.

73. Thomas Mann, *Doctor Faustus. The Life of the German Composer Adrian Leverkühn As Told by a Friend*, trans. H. T. Lowe-Porter (New York: Random House, 1948), p. 47. See also in this regard my article "Clemens Brentano's Muse and Adrian Leverkühn's Music: Selective Affinities in Thomas Mann's *Doctor Faustus*," *Essays in Literature* 7, Nr. 1 (Spring, 1980): 115–31.

74. Fetzer, *Romantic Orpheus*, pp. 236–46.

75. Recently this fairy tale has become the focal point of critical interest, as evidenced by Heinz Rölleke's article "Brentanos 'Märchen von dem Schulmeister Klopfstock' als literarhistorische Allegorie," *Jahrbuch des Freien Deutschen Hochstifts* (1977), pp. 292–308. Jack Zipes, in his study "The Revolutionary Rise of the Romantic Fairy Tale in Germany," *Studies in Romanticism* 16 (1977): 409–50, singles out this particular story in the pages devoted to Brentano (pp. 442–44).

76. Fritz Redlich, "Eine Parodie der deutschen Kaufmannschaft von 1800: Clemens Brentanos Märchen-Fragment 'Komanditchen,'" *Archiv für Kulturgeschichte* 50 (1968): 97–116.

77. In "Pumpelirio Holzebock in Brentanos *Märchen von Fanferlieschen Schönefüßchen*," *Zeitschrift für deutsche Philologie* 97 (1978): 161–76, Jürg Mathes divulges some of the previously unknown sources for the name and form of the idol and posits the theory that there is a concealed, autobiographical incest theme in the work.

78. Oskar Seidlin's analysis "Brentanos Spätfassung seines Märchens vom

Fanferlieschen Schönefüßchen," in his *Klassische und moderne Klassiker* (Göttingen: Vandenhoeck and Ruprecht, 1972), pp. 38–60 is not only a masterpiece of critical acumen regarding this particular work, but also incisive with regard to the poet in general.

79. For the most recent interpretation of narrative strategies employed in this tale, see Lawrence O. Frye, "The Art of Narrating a Rooster Hero in Brentano's *Das Märchen von Gockel und Hinkel*," *Euphorion* 72 (1978): 400–420.

80. The text in German reads: "O Stern und Blume, Geist und Kleid,/ Lieb, Leid und Zeit und Ewigkeit!"(*W*, 857 and passim). For a brief discussion of this couplet in its many contexts, see Fetzer, *Romantic Orpheus*, pp. 172–74.

81. Otto Bleich, "Entstehung und Quellen der Märchen Clemens Brentanos," *Archiv für das Studium der neueren Sprachen und Litteraturen* 96 (1896): 43–96.

82. Margarete Wagner, "Clemens Brentano und Giovanni Battista Basile," in *Essays on German Language and Literature in Honor of Theodore B. Hewett*, ed. Alan Pfeffer, University of Buffalo Series, vol. 20 (Buffalo: University of Buffalo, 1952), pp. 57–70.

83. Karl Glöckner, *Brentano als Märchenerzähler*, pp. 32–51.

84. Hermann Cardauns, *Die Märchen Clemens Brentano's* pp. 15–56.

85. *Der alte Brentano: Eine Interpretation der 'Blätter aus dem Tagebuch der Ahnfrau'* (Winterthur: Keller, 1956).

86. "Das verlorene Paradies," pp. 113–92.

87. Christa Holst and Siegfried Sudhof, "Die Lithographien zur ersten Ausgabe von Brentanos Märchen *Gockel, Hinkel und Gackeleia* (1838)," *Literaturwissenschaftliches Jahrbuch* 6 (1965): 140–54 and Bernhard Gajek, "Brentanos Verhältnis zur bildenden Kunst," in *Bildende Kunst und Literatur: Beiträge zum Problem ihrer Wechselbeziehungen im 19. Jahrhundert*, ed. Wolfdietrich Rasch (Frankfurt am Main: Klostermann, 1970), pp. 35–56. The above articles have been brought up-to-date by Siegfried Sudhof, "Karl Philipp Fohrs Zeichnung zu Brentanos *Gockelmärchen*," *Euphorion* 72 (1978): 513–17 and Peter-Klaus Schuster, "Bildzitate bei Brentano," in *Clemens Brentano: Beitrage des Kolloquiums*, pp. 334–48.

88. Elisabeth Stopp, "Brentano's 'O Stern und Blume': Its Poetic and Emblematic Context," *Modern Language Review* 67 (1972): 95–117.

89. Dietrich Pregel, "Das Kuriose in den Märchen Clemens Brentanos," *Wirkendes Wort* 10 (1960): 286–97.

90. Oskar Seidlin, "Wirklich nur eine schöne Kunstfigur? Zu Brentanos Gockel-Märchen," in *Texte und Kontexte: Studien zur deutschen und vergleichenden Literaturwissenschaft*, Festschrift für Norbert Fuerst zum 65. Geburtstag, ed. Manfred Durzak, Eberhard Reichmann, and Ulrich Weisstein (Bern: Francke, 1973), pp. 235–48.

Chapter Four

1. René Guignard, *Clemens Brentano*, pp. 511–12.

2. The full significance of this very early work has only been recognized in the last decade, initially by Marianne Thalmann in *Provokation und Demonstration in der Komödie der Romantik* (Berlin: Erich Schmidt, 1974), pp. 70–77 and then by Hartwig Schultz in his study "Brentanos *Gustav Wasa* und seine versteckte Schöpfungsgeschichte der romantischen Poesie," in *Clemens Brentano: Beiträge des Kolloquiums*, pp. 295–330.

3. Heinrich Heine, *Die romantische Schule* in *Heine: Sämtliche Werke*, vol. 5, ed. Ernst Elster (Leipzig and Vienna: Bibliographisches Institut, n.d.), pp. 308–9.

4. Gustav Roethe, *Brentanos 'Ponce de Leon,' eine Säcularstudie*, Abhandlungen der königlichen Gesellschaft der Wissenschaften zu Göttingen. Philologisch-historische Klasse, vol. 5, no. 1 (Berlin: Weidmannsche Buchhandlung, 1901).

5. Böckmann, "Die romantische Poesie Brentanos," pp. 154–63.

6. Siegfried Sudhof, "Nachwort" to *Ponce de Leon* (Stuttgart: Reclam, 1968), pp. 163–75. See also Walter Hinck, "Triumph der Improvisation. Zu Brentanos *Ponce de Leon*," in *Ein Theatermann: Theorie und Praxis. Festschrift zum 70. Geburtstag von Rolf Badenhausen*, ed. Ingrid Nohl (Munich: Waidhas & Steinberger, 1977), pp. 121–26.

7. Helmut Arntzen, "Das Spiel der Maskierten: Brentanos *Ponce de Leon*," in *Die ernste Komödie* (Munich: Nymphenburger Verlagsbuchhandlung, 1968), pp. 156–68.

8. Otto Brechler, "Einleitung" to *Die Gründung Prags* in *Clemens Brentano: Sämtliche Werke*, lvi. Oskar Seidlin's article "Prag: deutschromantisch und habsburgisch-wienerisch" in *Von erwachendem Bewußtsein und vom Sündenfall* (Stuttgart: Klett, 1979), p. 96, clarifies some of the confusion surrounding the derivation as well as fruitful development of the error. The opening pages of Fetzer, *Romantic Orpheus*, use Brentano's *Founding* to illustrate one of the basic premises of the book: the threshold condition.

9. Emanuel Grigorovitza, *Libussa in der deutschen Literatur* (Berlin: A. Duncker, 1901), pp. 27–73, 78–86.

10. Günther Müller, "Die Libussa-Dichtungen Brentanos und Grillparzers," *Euphorion* 24 (1923): 617–28.

11. Seidlin, *Von erwachendem Bewußtsein und vom Sündenfall*, pp. 93–119.

12. Hans Taeschler, *Clemens Brentano: 'Die Gründung Prags.' Ein historischromantisches Schauspiel* (Zurich: Juris-Verlag, 1960).

13. Renate Matthaei, "Das Mythische in Clemens Brentanos *Die Gründung Prags* und den *Romanzen vom Rosenkranz*" (Ph.D. diss., Cologne, 1961).

14. Günther Müller, "Die Libussa-Dichtungen," p. 624, suggests the characterization "a symphonic work of poetry" while Robert Ulshöfer in *Die Theorie des Dramas in der deutschen Romantik* (Berlin: Junker & Dünnhaupt, 1935), p. 155, speaks of a "symphony of cosmic experience."

Chapter Five

1. The question concerning the exact nature of Brentano's literary musicality is discussed in my *Romantic Orpheus*, pp. 178–261.
2. P. Johannes Baptista Diel, S.J., and Wilhelm Kreiten, S.J., *Clemens Brentano: Ein Lebensbild nach gedruckten und ungedruckten Quellen*, 2 vols. (Freiburg im Breisgau: Herder, 1877–1878).
3. Previously unpublished letter of 10 February 1830 to Hermann Dietz, in Gajek, *Homo poeta*, p. 484.
4. Previously unpublished letter of 10 March 1830 to Hermann Dietz in Gajek, *Homo poeta*, p. 489.
5. Frühwald, *Das Spätwerk*, pp. 51–67 and passim, discusses the concept of circularity in Brentano's final years.
6. From Brentano's *Das Leben unseres Herrn und Heilandes Jesu Christi. Nach den Gesichten der gottseligen Anna Katharina Emmerich aufgeschrieben*, 3 vols. (Regensburg: Friedrich Pustet, 1858–1860), 2:269–70, as quoted in Joseph Adam, *Clemens Brentanos Emmerick-Erlebnis* (Freiburg im Breisgau: Herder, 1956), p. 290.
7. Tunner, *Clemens Brentano (1778–1842): Imagination et sentiment religieux*.
8. Two publications in the last years have taken steps in this direction: Heinz-Joachim Fortmüller, *Clemens Brentano als Briefschreiber*, Europäische Hochschulschriften, Deutsche Literatur und Germanistik, vol. 143 (Frankfurt am Main: Peter Lang, 1977) and Hans-Georg Dewitz, "'. . . traue den süßen Tönen des Sirenenliedes nicht . . . .' Zur Rolle von Brentanos Briefen in der Forschung," in *Clemens Brentano: Beiträge des Kolloquiums*, pp. 10–24.
9. In this regard, see Dieter Dennerele, *Kunst als Kommunikationsprozeß: Zur Kunsttheorie Clemens Brentanos. Dargestellt an Hand seines außerdichterischen Werkes (Briefe, Theaterrezensionen, Schriften zur Bildenden Kunst)*, Regensburger Beiträge zur deutschen Sprach- und Literaturwissenschaft, vol. 9 (Bern: H. Lang, 1976).
10. As of this writing, only *Das bittere Leiden unseres Herrn Jesus Christi* has appeared as vol. 26 (ed. Bernhard Gajek) of the critical edition (Stuttgart: Kohlhammer, 1979).

Selected Bibliography

PRIMARY SOURCES

1. Editions of Works

Clemens Brentano: Sämtliche Werke und Briefe. Edited by Jürgen Behrens, Wolfgang Frühwald, and Detlev Lüders. Stuttgart: Kohlhammer, 1975–. Of the volumes which have appeared thus far in this comprehen sive and definitive edition, only the sixteenth (containing *Godwi*, 1978, edited by Werner Bellmann) is of significance for this study. The editing and the annotation are exemplary.

Gesammelte Schriften. 9 vols. Edited by Christian Brentano, Emilie Bren tano, and Joseph Merkel. Frankfurt am Main: J. D. Sauerländer's Verlag, 1852–1855. Still useful for Brentano's lyrics and his corre spondence.

Werke. 4 vols. Vol 1 edited by Friedhelm Kemp, Wolfgang Frühwald and Bernhard Gajek; vols. 2–4 edited by Friedhelm Kemp. Munich: Hanser, 1963–1968. Compact, handy anthology of the major works with detailed and informative footnotes.

2. Major Editions of Letters

FRÜHWALD, WOLFGANG, ed. *Clemens Brentano: Briefe an Emilie Linder.* Bad Homburg: Gehlen, 1969. Valuable correspondence once thought lost. Recently augmented by Konrad Feilchenfeldt and Wolfgang Frühwald, "Clemens Brentano: Briefe und Gedichte an Emilie Linder," *Jahrbuch des Freien Deutschen Hochstifts* (1976), pp. 216–315.

SEEBAß, FRIEDRICH, ed. *Clemens Brentano: Briefe.* 2 vols. Nuremberg: Karl, 1951. Well-indexed selection of letters which incorporates many from volumes 8 and 9 of the *Gesammelte Schriften* and supplements these by recent twentieth-century discoveries.

VORDTRIEDE, WERNER, and BARTENSCHLAGER, GABRIELE, eds. *Dichter über ihre Dichtungen: Clemens Brentano.* Munich: Heimeran, 1970. A handy reference guide to key quotations about the works. Revised version by the same editors appeared as *Clemens Brentano: Der Dichter über sein Werk* (Munich: Deutscher Taschenbuch Verlag, 1978).

SECONDARY SOURCES

1. Analyses of Brentano Scholarship and Criticism

FETZER, JOHN. "Old and New Directions in Clemens Brentano Research (1931–1968)." *Literaturwissenschaftliches Jahrbuch* 11 (1970): 87–119; 12 (1971): 113–203; 12 (1972): 217–232 (under the title: "Recent Trends in Clemens Brentano Research: 1968–1970"). Augmented since 1970 by annual reports in the "Romantic Movement Bibliography," *English Language Notes* 9 (1971): 124–25; 10 (1972): 138–42; 11 (1973): 115–20; 12 (1974); 129–33; 13 (1975): 135–39; 14 (1976): 115–116; 15 (1977): 152–54. Analyses and assessments of secondary literature.

FRÜHWALD, WOLFGANG. "Stationen der Brentano-Forschung: 1924–1972." *Deutsche Vierteljahrsschrift für Literaturwissenschaft und Geistesgeschichte* 47, Sonderheft Forschungsreferate (1973): 182–269. A valuable complement to Fetzer, "Old and New Directions," from the German perspective.

GAJEK, BERNHARD. "Die Brentano-Literatur 1973–1978." *Euphorion* 72 (1978): 439–502. Penetrating assessment of both primary and secondary sources.

2. Biographical Studies and Sketches

BÖCKMANN, PAUL. "Clemens Brentano 1778–1842." In *Die großen Deutschen*. Vol. 2. Frankfurt am Main: Ullstein, 1956. Pp. 532–47. Excellent general orientation.

DAVID, CLAUDE. "Clemens Brentano." In *Die deutsche Romantik: Poetik, Formen und Motive*, edited by Hans Steffan, pp. 159–79. Göttingen: Vandenhoeck & Ruprecht, 1967. Makes the highly controversial assertion that Brentano is a poet "for the happy few."

FEILCHENFELDT, KONRAD, editor and compiler. *Brentano Chronik. Daten zu Leben und Werk*. Munich: Hanser, 1978. Very up-to-date and comprehensive listing of the major chronological events in Brentano's career (complements the chronology found in *W*: 1268–77).

FRÜHWALD, WOLFGANG. "Clemens Brentano." In *Deutsche Dichter der Romantik: Ihr Leben und Werk*, edited by Benno von Wiese, pp. 280–309. Berlin: Erich Schmidt, 1971. Best and most incisive short account of the life and works available.

GUIGNARD, RENÉ. *Un poète romantique allemand: Clemens Brentano*. Paris: Presses Universitaires de France, 1933. A still valuable comprehensive study of the poet in the best positivist tradition.

HILTON, IAN. "Clemens Brentano." In *German Men of Letters*, edited by Alex Nathan, 5:51–74. London: O. Wolff, 1969. Highly readable, even though truncated, sketch.

HOFFMANN, WERNER. *Clemens Brentano: Leben und Werk*. Bern: Francke, 1966. Somewhat old-fashioned in approach, linking biography and work too closely.

PFEIFFER-BELLI, WOLFGANG. *Clemens Brentano: Ein romantisches*

Dichterleben. Freiburg im Breisgau: Herder, 1947. Concise monograph incorporating for the first time unpublished documents.

TYMMS, RALPH. "Clemens Brentano." In *German Romantic Literature.* London: Methuen, 1955. Pp. 207–64. In spite of antiromantic bias, often cuts through many vaguries to the heart of the matter. Best brief summary of life and works in English.

3. In-Depth Studies of Specific Works and Problems

ALEWYN, RICHARD. "Brentanos *Geschichte vom braven Kasperl und dem schönen Annerl.*" In *Deutsche Erzählungen von Wieland bis Kafka,* edited by Jost Schillemeit, pp. 101–50. Frankfurt am Main: Fischer, 1966. Volume 4 of *Interpretationen.* Set the tone for most later studies of the novella.

ARNTZEN, HELMUT. "Das Spiel der Maskierten: Brentanos *Ponce de Leon.*" In *Die ernste Komödie.* Munich: Nymphenburger Verlagsbuchhandlung, 1968, Pp. 156–68. Subtle analysis of a central motif in this work as well as in the poet's entire œuvre (masks and masquerades).

BÖCKMANN, PAUL. "Die romantische Poesie Brentanos und ihre Grundlagen bei Friedrich Schlegel und Tieck. Ein Beitrag zur Entwicklung der Formensprache der deutschen Romantik." *Jahrbuch des Freien Deutschen Hochstifts* (1934–1935), pp. 56–176. Highly informative study of the concept of "perspectivism" in *Godwi* and of Brentano's modifications of Schlegel's theories and Tieck's techniques.

ENZENSBERGER, HANS MAGNUS. *Brentanos Poetik.* Munich: Hanser, 1961. Introduces the controversial term of "distortion" (*Entstellung*) as an essential ingredient of the poet's late lyrics.

FETZER, JOHN. *Romantic Orpheus: Profiles of Clemens Brentano.* Berkeley: University of California Press, 1974. Study of the pros and cons of musicality in Brentano's life and works.

FRÜHWALD, WOLFGANG. *Das Spätwerk Clemens Brentanos (1815–1842: Romantik im Zeitalter der Metternich'schen Restauration.* Hermaea: Germanistische Forschungen, 37. Tübingen: Max Niemeyer, 1977. Meticulous analysis of the Emmerick papers and an account of the poet's contribution to "late" Romanticism.

———. "Das verlorene Paradies. Zur Deutung von Clemens Brentanos 'Herzlicher Zueignung' des Märchens *Gockel, Hinkel und Gackeleia* (1838)."*Literaturwissenschaftliches Jahrbuch* 3 (1962): 113–92. Seminal study paving the way for much recent scholarship. Indispensable hints to "decode" the late poet's cryptic allusions.

KILLY, WALTHER. "Clemens Brentano." In *Wandlungen des lyrischen Bildes.* 3d ed. Göttingen: Vandenhoeck & Ruprecht, 1961. Pp. 53–72. Develops the concept of "Chiffre" ("cypher") in Brentano's lyrics, pointing the way to modern trends.

LÜDERS, DETLEV, editor. *Clemens Brentano. Beiträge des Kolloquiums im Freien Deutschen Hochstift 1978.* Freies Deutsches Hochstift: Reihe der Schriften, vol. 24. Tübingen: Niemeyer, 1980. Contributions by Brentano scholars from the Western world to the conference marking the 200th anniversary of the poet's birth. New light is shed on many a topic previously felt to be shrouded in perpetual darkness.

MÜLLER-SEIDEL, WALTER. "Brentanos naive und sentimentalische Poesie." *Jahrbuch der deutschen Schillergesellschaft* 18 (1974): 441–65. Unexpected but enlightening application of Schiller's two categories to an un-Schillerian poet.

RYCHNER, CLAUDIA. *Der alte Brentano: Eine Interpretation der "Blätter aus dem Tagebuch der Ahnfrau."* Winterthur: Keller, 1956. Opens previously locked doors to this difficult work.

SCHAUB, GERHARD. *Le génie enfant: Die Kategorie des Kindlichen bei Clemens Brentano.* Quellen und Forschungen zur Sprach- und Kulturgeschichte der germanischen Völker, 55. Berlin: Walther de Gruyter, 1973. The best and most comprehensive study of the topic of Brentano's "childlikeness" and "childishness."

SEIDLIN, OSKAR. "Brentanos Spätfassung seines Märchens vom Fanferlieschen Schönefüßchen." In *Klassische und moderne Klassiker.* Göttingen: Vandenhoeck & Ruprecht, 1972. Pp. 38–59. One of the most persuasive analyses based on close reading of the text.

———. "Prag: deutsch-romantisch und Habsburg-Wienerisch." In *Austriaca: Beiträge zur österreichischen Literatur. Festschrift für Heinz Politzer*, edited by Winfried Kudszus and Hinrich Seeba, pp. 201–29. Tübingen: Niemeyer, 1975. Contrastive study of two plays having similar subject matter; consistently and convincingly sound.

———. "Wirklich nur eine schöne Kunstfigur? Zu Brentanos Gockel-Märchen." In *Texte und Kontexte: Studien zur deutschen und vergleichenden Literaturwissenschaft*, Festschrift für Norbert Fuerst zum 65. Geburtstag, edited by Manfred Durzak, Eberhard Reichmann, and Ulrich Weisstein, pp. 235–48. Bern: Francke, 1973. A penetrating solution to a long puzzling concept. The two last essays can now be found in Seidlin's book *Von erwachendem Bewußtsein und vom Sündenfall. Brentano, Schiller, Kleist, Goethe* (Stuttgart: Klett, 1979).

SILZ, WALTER. "Brentano, *Geschichte vom braven Kasperl und dem schönen Annerl.*" In *Realism and Reality.* Chapel Hill: University of North Carolina Press, 1954. Pp. 17–28. A commonsense approach linking this work to the novella genre.

STAIGER, EMIL. *Die Zeit als Einbildungskraft des Dichters.* 1939. Reprint. Zurich: Atlantis, 1953. Insights into Brentano's mode of experiencing time as a succession of fleeting, isolated moments.

STOPP, ELISABETH. "Brentano's *Chronika* and its Revision." In *Sprache und Bekenntnis: Sonderband des Literaturwissenschaftlichen Jahrbuchs, Hermann Kunisch zum 70. Geburtstag*, edited by Wolfgang Frühwald and Günter Niggl, pp. 161–84. Berlin: Duncker & Humblot, 1971. The briefest and best of the recent *Chronicle* interpretations.

————."Brentano's 'O Stern und Blume': Its Poetic and Emblematic Context." *Modern Language Review* 67 (1972): 95–117. Very revealing application of techniques of the pictorial arts to literary contexts.

————. "Nachwort." In *Clemens Brentano: Die Chronika des fahrenden Schülers.* Stuttgart: Reclam, 1971. Pp. 112–36. A highly convincing structural analysis.

TUNNER, ERIKA. *Clemens Brentano (1778–1842): Imagination et sentiment religieux.* 2 vols. Lille: University of Lille, 1977. Newest and best of the large-scale interpretations.

WIESE, BENNO VON. "Brentanos Godwi." In *Von Lessing bis Grabbe: Studien zur deutschen Klassik und Romantik.* Düsseldorf: Bagel, 1968. Pp. 191–247. Good summary of previous research plus new insights.

————. "Clemens Brentano: *Geschichte vom braven Kasperl und dem schönen Annerl.*" In *Die deutsche Novelle von Goethe bis Kafka: Interpretationen.* Vol. 1. Düsseldorf: A. Bagel, 1956. Pp. 64–78. Solid erudition together with helpful background material on romanticism.

Index

Page references to entries in the *Notes and Reference* section as well as to those in the *Selected Bibliography* are included only when these entries contain pertinent information or evaluative judgments.

Adam, Joseph, 151n22
aesthetic distance, 75
Alewyn, Richard, 157n50, 171
Alhambra, 63, 126
allegory, 75, 102, 106
Alsace, 25
anti-novel, 72
Anti-Semitism, 20, 21, 123
Apollinian, 84
Arc of the Covénant, 59
Arnim, Ludwig Achim von, 19, 20, *21*, 22, 28, 34, 40, 119
Arntzen, Helmut, 135; *The Serious Comedy*, 135
Aurora, 55, 143

Babylonian Captivity (of the Papacy), 85
Bärwalde, 118–19
Barbarossa, Friedrich, 110
Basile, Giambattista, 27, 107, 117, 125, 128; *Lo cunto de li cunti* or *Pentamerone*, 27, 107, 117; *La preta de lo gallo*, 128
Bavaria, 19, 23, 26
Beethoven, Ludwig van, 54–55, 58, 59, 64, 158n58
Behler, Ernst, 161n18
Bellmann, Werner, 156n41
Berlin, 19, 20, 22–23
Berlin, University of, 20
Berlin Evening News, 20
Beutler, Ernst, 156n40
Bingen Mouse Tower, 108
Black Forest, 108–109

Blake, William, 127
Blume, Bernhard, 158n57
Böckmann, Paul, 71–72, 135, 152n3, 170, 171
Böhmer, Johann F., 27
Bohemia, 21, 137, 139, 142
Bonn, University of, 17
Brahms, Johannes, 128
Brede, Auguste, 18, 21
Brentano, Bettina (von Arnim), 21, 28–29, 151n15; *Clemens Brentano's Spring Wreath*, 29; *Goethe's Correspondence with a Child*, 28–29
Brentano, Christian, 21
Brentano, Clemens: birth and youth, 15–16; collaboration with other artists, 19–20, 34; correspondence, 26, 146, 148; divorce, 18; friendships, 18–19, 22, 28; illness and death, 28–29; library holdings, 24, 148; love affairs, 16, *17–18*, 20, 21, *23–24*, *26–27*, 28, 61–62, 63, 75; marriage, 18; religiosity, 23, 24, 27, 28, 61; schooling, 16, 17

WORKS: EDITIONS
Collected Works, 26, 37, 39–40, 61, 70, 169
Complete Works and Letters (historical-critical edition), 8, 38–39, 53, 148, 169
Works (Werke), 8, 53, 169

WORKS: DRAMATIC, *21–22*, *131–43*, 145–46
Aloys and Imelde, 21
Dramaturgical Observer, The, 22, 131, 142–43
Founding of Prague, The, 21, 136–43, 146
Gustav Wasa, 18, 66, 133

174